Governance and the European Social Dimension

Providing a comprehensive and authoritative analyses of the impact of the Eurozone crisis on the European social dimension since 2010 – understood as the European Union's (EU) competence in employment and social policy – this book focusses on developments in five policy areas (employment, poverty and social exclusion, pensions, wages and healthcare), all of which form part of the EU's economic reform strategy, Europe 2020. It combines original empirical material and uses a unique theoretical approach to analyse the issue of EU governance and reveals that 'progress' under Europe 2020 has its consequences; notably a strengthened Brussels-led neoliberal prescription for EU social and employment policy problems. By drawing insights from political sociology and the strategic-relational approach to actors/institutions, this book will be of interest to students and scholars interested in EU politics, EU governance, political sociology, public policy and European integration.

Paul Copeland is Senior Lecturer of Public Policy at the School of Politics and International Relations, Queen Mary University of London, UK.

Routledge Studies on Government and the European Union
Edited by Andy Smith, University of Bordeaux, France

For more information about this series, please visit: https://www.routledge.com

Governance and the European Social Dimension

Politics, Power and the Social Deficit in a Post-2010 EU

Paul Copeland

Routledge
Taylor & Francis Group

LONDON AND NEW YORK

First published 2020 by Routledge

2 Park Square, Milton Park, Abingdon, Oxon OX14 4RN
605 Third Avenue, New York, NY 10017

Routledge is an imprint of the Taylor & Francis Group, an informa business

First issued in paperback 2021

Publisher's Note

The publisher has gone to great lengths to ensure the quality of this reprint but points out that some imperfections in the original copies may be apparent.

British Library Cataloguing-in-Publication Data
A catalogue record for this book is available from the British Library

Library of Congress Cataloging-in-Publication Data
Names: Copeland, Paul, 1981– author.
Title: Governance and the European social dimension : politics, power and the social deficit in a post-2010 EU / Paul Copeland.
Description: Abingdon, Oxon ; New York, NY : Routledge, 2020. | Series: Routledge studies on government and the European Union | Includes bibliographical references and index.
Identifiers: LCCN 2019020378 | ISBN 9781138545885 (hardback) | ISBN 9781351001762 (ebook)
Subjects: LCSH: European Union countries—Politics and government—21st century. | European Union countries—Economic policy—21st century. | European Union countries—Social policy—21st century. | European Union countries—Economic conditions—21st century. | European Union countries—Social conditions—21st century.
Classification: LCC JN30 .C655 2020 | DDC 337.1/42—dc23
LC record available at https://lccn.loc.gov/2019020378

ISBN: 978-1-138-54588-5 (hbk)
ISBN: 978-1-03-217644-4 (pbk)
DOI: 10.4324/9781351001762

Typeset in Times New Roman
by codeMantra

This book is dedicated to Dr Joanne Milner (1960–2018). You lost your life too soon, but your selflessness will always be an inspiration.

Contents

Figures

Tables and Boxes

Tables

Boxes

Acknowledgements

I wrote this book in what has been the worst couple of years of my life. Events beyond my control made life unbelievably difficult, and there were times when I thought the book would never get finished. Fortunately my partner, Andrew Clark, and our wonderful 'Betty dog' were with me every step of the way. They never stopped loving me, even during days/weeks/ months when I was grumpy and irritable. Thank you. I love you.

To all the other wonderful souls who helped me along the way, I am especially grateful. I want to give a special mention to Kyle Galler. Thank you for all of your help and support; you always go beyond the call of duty. I'm wishing you the best of luck for the future, however that plays out in these crazy times. I'd like to thank Oliver Daddow for reading a draft of the book. Many thanks to Elisa Roller who allowed me to crash at hers during my fieldwork – I love it when we play house. Finally, many thanks to Mary Daly. Some of the work in this book builds on our collaborative projects. Where this is the case, I have made reference to our joint publications. I feel very lucky to have been working with you and look forward to our future projects. As always, any errors within the book remain my responsibility.

Abbreviations

AMR	Alert Mechanism Report
ALMPs	Active Labour Market Policies
AGS	Annual Growth Survey
BEPG	Broad Economic Policy Guidelines
CSRs	Country Specific Recommendations
DG ECFIN	Directorate for Economic and Financial Affairs
DG EMPL	Directorate General for Employment, Social Affairs and Inclusion
DG ENTR	Directorate General for Enterprise and Industry
ECI	European Citizen's Initiative
EMCO	Employment Committee
EPG	Employment Policy Guidelines
EPSCO	Employment, Social Policy, Health and Consumer Affairs Council
EEC	European Economic Community
EES	European Employment Strategy
EFSM	European Financial Stabilisation Mechanism
EFSF	European Financial Stability Facility
ESM	European Stability Mechanism
ETUC	European Trade Union Confederation
EU	European Union
EIP	Excessive Imbalances Procedure
GDP	Gross Domestic Product
IMF	International Monetary Fund
IR	International Relations
MIP	Macroeconomic Imbalances Procedure
MEP	Member of the European Parliament
NRP	National Reform Programme
OMC	Open Method Of Coordination
OECD	Organisation for Economic Cooperation and Development
QMV	Qualified Majority Voting
PASOK	Panhellenic Socialist Movement
RQMV	Reverse Qualified Majority Vote

SGEI	Services of General Economic Interest
SEA	Single European Act
SEM	Single European Market
SMEs	Small - and Medium-Sized Enterprises
SDC	Social Dialogue Committee
SGP	Stability and Growth Pact
TEU	Treaty on European Union
TFEU	Treaty on the Functioning of the European Union
UNICE	Union of Industries of the European Communities
UK	United Kingdom

Introduction

Over the last decade, the process of European integration and thereby the European Union (EU), has suffered from a series of intractable crises, such as the banking crisis, the Eurozone crisis, an economic crisis, the refugee crisis, and of course, the United Kingdom's (UK) 2016 decision to leave the EU, now commonly referred to as Brexit. This book focusses on the economic and social dimensions of these crises which began in 2008 as a banking crisis, but then in 2010 spilled over into a crisis threatening the stability and existence of the Eurozone. The banking crisis, whereby American and European banks had overexposed themselves to the vulnerabilities of the housing market and granted mortgages to individuals who would struggle to repay their debts, was the trigger for the events that were to follow. Once the bubble burst, the economic uncertainty of the crisis saw confidence in the European economy evaporate and a severe economic recession followed. The deterioration of confidence in the economy meant that lenders, all too happy to lend in the decade prior to the crisis, suddenly became more cautious. Private investors decided amongst themselves that a group of Eurozone countries – Greece, Ireland, Italy, Portugal and Spain – who were given the derogatory acronym 'PIIGS', were economically unsound. Purchasing these bonds, which governments use to plug holes in their spending and to refinance existing debt, was a risky endeavour and their price, or the cost paid by governments, increased. And so began the Eurozone crisis in which, over several years, the PIIGS were required to get their national finances in order. EU-driven austerity, in which financial support from Northern Members to alleviate the situation was conditional on recipients cutting public spending to slash national debt and borrowing, became a dogmatic mantra for the EU. The economic consequences of this decision were catastrophic. Youth unemployment (individuals between the ages of 15–24) in 2013 reached nearly 60 per cent in Greece, 55 per cent in Spain and just over 40 per cent in Italy. It is little wonder that people speak of a 'lost generation' stemming from the crisis.

For EU leaders, the banking crisis and subsequent Eurozone crises were a series of exogenous shocks that served to correct not the fundamentals of the governance of the Eurozone, but rather the behaviour of some Member States. The decade prior to the crisis laid claim that some EU governments had not followed the rules of the Stability and Growth Pact (SGP), the latter being the governance mechanism to ensure that Eurozone Members kept their national spending within certain parameters. Importantly, the first countries to break the rules of the SGP were Germany and France in 2003, not those Member States who were hardest hit by the financial crisis (Portugal, Italy and Greece). However, the crisis was not simply a result of some Member States not following the rules, as demonstrated by the cases of Ireland and Spain, which were regarded as Eurozone success stories in the decade before the crisis. These two Eurozone countries had allowed asset bubbles, particularly in the housing market, to develop and burst with catastrophic consequences for the banking system. The government-backed bank bailouts and resultant spikes to government borrowing and debt saw the EU respond with the same austere medicine as it did to Portugal, Italy and Greece, despite the very different economic circumstances behind their situations.

At the heart of the Eurozone crisis is a single currency that is not, in economic speak, an optimal currency area. The Eurozone cobbles together a group of countries with very different varieties of capitalism or economic models and subjects them to the same interest rate, exchange rate, and rules about government borrowing and debt. Relatively speaking, prior to the crisis, the domestic demand-driven economies of the South (including Ireland) were subject to an interest rate that was too low and an exchange rate that was too high. The result was that such countries borrowed, either publicly or privately, to fund growth with a resultant loss of competitiveness vis-à-vis other countries. Meanwhile, the interest rate was suitable for Northern export-driven economies, but the exchange rate was arguably too low and made their exports much cheaper for purchase by non-Eurozone members. Private financial markets were happy to lend to public or private individuals within the Eurozone for two reasons. First, there was a naive belief that the economic good times would continue indefinitely and that under the guidance of a neoliberal ideology, the EU, and thereby the Eurozone, had overcome the 'boom and bust' economic growth cycle. Second, despite the 'no bailout clause' within the EU Treaty, financial markets believed that other Eurozone members would come to the aid of a Member State that was in financial trouble.

EU-driven austerity was, therefore, an attempt to resolve the imbalances of the Eurozone by subjecting Member States to a form of shock therapy, like that experienced in parts of Eastern Europe following the collapse of state socialism and the transition to capitalist democracy. During the good times, the PIIGS had not followed the rules, nor had they sufficiently reformed their economies, meaning they now needed to do so. EU shock therapy, with its savage cuts to public spending, was also accompanied by the need for Member States to liberalise labour markets, reduce welfare dependency, and to reduce or eliminate regulatory rigidities that were regarded as being barriers to competition and economic growth. In the eyes of Brussels and Northern Member States, the economic and social pain that followed was unfortunate, but it was their fault. Unless such countries wished to crash out of the Eurozone all together, which would have been an apocalyptic alternative, they had to accept these conditions to get financial support from the North. This was a choice between the lesser of two evils, but nothing was said about the fact that Southern Eurozone debt was predominantly held by Northern Eurozone Members. Nothing was also said that the success of Northern exporting economies was a complicated story. While these countries are hugely successful economies, their global competitive advantages had been helped by a euro that was undervalued for their economies and gave them a much greater competitive advantage than they would have ordinarily had outside of the Eurozone. Southern Member States were being told that they needed to become Northern Member States despite the success of the north being in part, as a result of the dynamics of a currency union that would not exist if all Member States had Northern economies.

The rolling-out of shock therapy corresponded with the EU's launching of its ten-year economic and social reform programme, known as Europe 2020. Strategies such as Europe 2020 and its predecessor, the Lisbon Strategy, are known as governance architectures and represent strategic and long-term political initiatives of international organisations on cross-cutting policy issues locked into commitments about targets and processes (Borrás and Radaelli 2011). Such architectures are conceived as comprising ideational and organisation components. The ideational component is defined as a set of fundamental ideational repertoires, expressed in notions such as 'governance', 'competitiveness', 'sustainability', 'knowledge-based society', the 'market' and a discourse that uses the ideational repertoires in order to discipline, organise and legitimise the hierarchical relationships between the goals and the policy instruments. Taken together, ideas and discourses give shape to the overall attempt to socialise actors into a specific frame of reference that is supposed to make sense of a complex world of cross-cutting policy problems. The organisational component comprises formal and informal organisational arrangements (politico-organisational machinery) where the ideational repertoires and discourses are defined and patterned through complex political processes of a multi-level nature and the selection of policy instruments and their procedural requirements. In short, initiatives such as Europe 2020 blend policy commitments with specific governance arrangements that aim to guide EU policy over the long term.

Europe 2020 is guided by a series of headline targets and thematic priorities related to employment policy, poverty reduction, research and development and climate change aimed at raising Europe's competitiveness (European Commission 2010a, 2010b). But in response to the crisis, the strategy proposed a step change in economic policy co-ordination through reinforced mechanisms of budgetary discipline and fiscal consolidation (cf. Armstrong 2012). To bring this about Europe 2020 enshrined a new preventive system of ex ante surveillance, the centrepiece of which was a new annual 'European Semester' – an annual governance cycle. During the first stage of the cycle, the European Commission outlines the EU's economic priorities in the Annual Growth Survey (AGS). In this context, governments submit medium-term budgetary and economic strategies for peer review prior to parliamentary approval. This is achieved through the simultaneous but legally separate reporting and evaluation of Europe 2020 with the EU's fiscal framework, the SGP. The aim of this governance reform was to improve the synergies and linkages between the different policy areas within the political economy of European integration. Second, the ability of the EU to offer tailored policy advice through Country Specific Recommendations (CSRs) to guide national reforms were widened to include both macro- and micro-economic issues. The EU's response to the Eurozone crisis was therefore an economic and social reform package that was intended to resolve both the short-term causes and consequences crisis, improve the long-term position of the EU's competitiveness, and to prevent a future similar crisis – all of which was to be monitored and enforced by the European Semester. Europe 2020 is an ambitious programme of reform but given the scale and complexity of the crisis, it is doubly ambitious.

This research critically analyses developments in the European social dimension in the context of Europe 2020 and the European Semester. It argues that since 2010, the European social dimension has become increasingly incorporated into the logic of a market-driven process of European integration. That is, in the policy areas of employment, education and training, pensions, wages, healthcare, poverty and social exclusion, the EU's solution to policy problems overwhelming prioritise extending and deepening processes of commodification and thereby the market mechanism. Despite considerable political agency exercised by EU social actors between 2011 and 2018 within the European Semester, the European social dimension can only be taken forward if it broadly conforms with the neo-liberal macroeconomics of the Semester and European integration. In this context, the European social dimension is not a counter-weight to the Single European Market and Economic and Monetary Union; rather, it is an extension of these two projects that aims to reconfigure the final vestiges of the Keynesian welfare state across Europe and to cement a neoliberal welfare state on the Continent.

The first chapter analyses the historical development of the European social dimension. It does so by focussing on the five distinct periods of its formation, namely the Single European Act (SEA), the Treaty of Maastricht, Amsterdam Treaty negotiations, the Lisbon Strategy and Europe 2020. It argues that the EU's competence in the field of employment and social policy represents a patchwork of policy issues governed by a variety of governance tools of both hard and soft law, with the latter being more common. As soft law is flexible, it constantly evolves to the political dynamics of the EU and the European social dimension is continuously influx. Prior to the

Eurozone crisis, the political debate within the EU was shifting and the left had fractured. On the one hand, some actors on the left have remained committed to post-war Keynesian social democracy. Meanwhile, those on the centre-left have embraced neoliberalism, albeit one in which the edges of the market are softened. The main tussle between the centre-left and the centre-right within the European social dimension is focussed on the *extent* of neoliberalism and not between genuine competing visions of a European social dimension. If we are to understand a post-2010 European social dimension, it is essential that the contours of political contestation are understood, as well as the policy matrix within which they operate.

The second chapter outlines the theoretical lens through which the empirical research was operationalised. Most existing approaches to study the European social dimension situate themselves in the governance literature. Broadly, governance sees policy as being developed, agreed upon and implemented by a broad range of state and non-state actors, thereby gaining the consensus and expertise necessary to identify complex policy problems and their solutions in contemporary capitalism. The governance approach has made a significant contribution to the analysis of European integration and the European social dimension, and the approach has the added benefit of being sufficiently broad to incorporate the range of ontological and epistemological positions found within the social sciences. The chapter and the approach adopted in this research situate itself within the governance approach. However, a key weakness of the EU governance debate is the tendency to view policy areas in isolation from each other and to side-step issues of power and politics. As a result, such research generally supports the status quo and has a tendency towards apolitical findings. To overcome these weaknesses, I develop a governance framework through which to analyse developments within the European social dimension. I refer to this approach as 'governance in advanced European integration', which refers to the period of European integration since the signing of the SEA (1986). From 1986 onwards, European integration as a peace-building project for the European Continent was replaced by the need for the European project to transmit and manage neoliberalism. Governance in advanced European integration conceives governance as featuring power relations and power asymmetries that produce and reproduce hierarchy, priority and privilege. The political hierarchy that exists during the advanced stages of European integration can be divided into grand-order issues and secondary-order issues. Grand-order issues are those that determine the macro economy and are strongly associated with the business and financial community, while secondary-order issues concern policy areas such as employment, poverty and social exclusion, education and training, healthcare – in other words, policy areas of the European social dimension. Whether secondary-order issues conform to grand-order issues depends on a variety of factors and is context-specific, but in general, they relate to the extent to which policy interdependence is exercised, and thereby the degree to which secondary-order actors have autonomy to make decisions. The following three chapters within the research analyse developments within the secondary-order issues of European integration – the European social dimension – since 2010.

The analysis within the empirical chapters is based on the primary working documents produced by the EU and the Member States, as well as interest groups within the EU's political space. The analysis is complemented by 40 interviews that were conducted between 2015 and 2018. During this period, some interviewees were interviewed twice in the context of how they thought Europe 2020, the European Semester and the European social dimension had changed or not. Semi-structured interviews enable the analysis to 'explore people's experiences, practices, values and attitudes in depth' (Devine 2002: 207). They contextualise primary documentation by providing participants with the opportunity to offer reasons and motivations as to why particular courses of action and decisions are taken. The combination of primary documentation and interview material provides a more holistic account of developments than the utilisation of one method alone. Furthermore, the interviews enable the gathering and analysis of primary documentation that is not in the public domain. Such confidential information includes inter-institutional files between the European Commission, the European Council and the European Parliament. Key actors from all of the main institutions and different political backgrounds were targeted for interview. Targeted interviewees were then asked to identify other key actors within the case studies and this generated a snowballing sample of representatives. To further minimise bias, the interview material was cross-referenced with other interviewees (Copeland 2014: 4–5).

The third chapter analyses the structural conditions of the EU's post-2010 economic governance and the European social dimension. The first part of the chapter analyses the causes of the Eurozone crisis and the EU's initial attempts to resolve the crisis. The second section of the chapter focusses on the formation of Europe 2020, as well as the aims and objectives of the reform strategy. The governance arrangements introduced to govern EU fiscal policy and Europe 2020, as well as to improve the policy interdependencies between the various policy areas, are interrogated in the third section. The final section of the chapter outlines the political hierarchy of the post-2010 governance arrangements, and thereby the structural conditions within which social actors are required to operate and achieve their aims. The chapter argues that post-2010 EU economic governance further strengthens the privileged position of financial actors within the EU, understood to be those individuals in DG Economic and Financial Affairs (DG ECFIN), the Economic and Financial Affairs Council, and national finance ministries. Europe 2020 and the European Semester appear to give little room for market-correcting policies in the second-order issues. That is, in the European social dimension the evidence suggests a tendency towards policy reform that reduces policy problems to being resolved by introducing ever greater market principles to the labour market. Progress around the employment and social policy components of Europe 2020, therefore, faces considerable obstacles in moving the European social dimension forward in a progressive sense.

The fourth chapter analyses the politics and policy outputs of the European Semester between 2011 and 2018. It develops a unique coding framework that categorises the CSRs along a five-point continuum ranging from decommodification to commodification. Since the mid-1990s, the conventional concept of decommodification has struggled to find relevance during the reform of the welfare state and the introduction of active labour market policies (ALMPs) across the European Continent. However, as this chapter will argue, the concept remains relevant to understanding the post-Keynesian welfare state, but it requires being placed on a continuum alongside the concept of commodification. Commodification and decommodification are therefore situated at the opposite ends of the continuum, but as the categorisation of employment and social policy is not zero-sum, policy can be positioned at various points along the continuum, as it will most likely feature elements of both concepts, albeit to varying degrees. The analysis within this chapter reveals that between 2011 and 2018, the clear majority of the CSRs can be categorised as either commodifying or partially commodifying. This finding demonstrates that within the European Semester, reforms for the European social dimension ultimately aim to create pure, efficient labour markets that treat human beings as though they are pure commodities, such as goods and services that find their price by the laws of supply and demand. The chapter is divided into five sections. The first section outlines current approaches to analysing and coding the European Semester. The second and third sections explore the relationship between commodification and decommodification and outline the continuum used within the analysis. The fourth section presents the main findings from the analysis, while the final section presents the small number of CSRs in the field of health. These are analysed separately owing to the commodification/decommodification continuum not being directly applicable to the area of healthcare. The purpose of this separate analysis is to complete the picture regarding developments in the European social dimension.

The fifth chapter accounts for the policy outcomes of the coded CSRs between 2011 and 2018. EU activity within the European social dimension tends towards deepening market forces for labour across the Member States and extending neoliberal economic integration to European welfare states. However, there are some recommendations that are either decommodifying or partially decommodifying, but they remain small in comparison to the overall thrust of the European Semester. The challenge is, then, to be able to account for such developments in the context of the structural and agential factors that interact within the process of European integration and, specifically, the European Semester – in other words, how social actors navigate and negotiate the hierarchy of the European Semester to achieve their outcomes, the strategies they pursue and the compromises they make along the way. The analysis within this chapter reveals that as a consequence of the political agency of both the Barroso and Juncker Commissions, the European social dimension has experienced increased political activity and attention within the European Semester, but it has been unable to fundamentally challenge the prevailing political hierarchy, as established during the forging of Europe 2020 and the European Semester and arguably, the process of European integration at large. This chapter is divided into three substantive sections. The first section focusses on the policy areas of pension reform and wages and how they were captured by the EU's financial actors within the European Semester. The second section analyses the political strategies of the Barroso Commission, while the third section analyses the political strategies of the Juncker Commission. The conclusion serves to highlight the significance of the findings in the context of the political struggles of European integration.

The final chapter analyses the consequences of the findings in the context of EU democracy and EU legitimacy. The chapter argues that ideological contestation within the EU's political space post-2010 has narrowed to a simple choice between more or less neoliberalism, and that genuine alternatives to the current trajectory of integration for the EU and its European social dimension are on the margins of the political debate. As a result, the EU suffers from what I refer to as a 'social deficit' in terms of the interests it represents and the policies it pursues. After outlining the limits of current literature on EU democracy and legitimacy in the first section of the chapter, the second section analyses the first dimension of the social deficit, namely the hollowing out of democracy by technocratic governance in the European Semester. The third section of the chapter analyses the second dimension of the social deficit, namely that the EU is not producing the kind of policies its citizens want, that is, the overwhelming emphasis on commodification as a driver of European integration and the European social dimension produces political backlash and undermines support for the EU. The chapter serves to highlight the severity of the problems faced by the EU and the need for it to change the course of European integration beyond tokenistic policy reforms with catchy headlines that continue to commodify individuals.

The concluding chapter reflects on the findings of the research for the significance of the broader process of European integration.

1   The political economy of the European social dimension

Introduction

The 1990s and early 2000s witnessed references both within academic literature and EU policy documents to the concept of a European social model
(Council of the European Union 2000a; Ebbinghaus 1999; Grahl and
Teague 1997). The origins of the concept can be traced to a European Commission White Paper published in 1994, while several academic publications that mentioned the concept appeared during the late 1990s. However,
early academic references to a European social model did not claim that
one existed; rather, they were explorations of the barriers and political divisions surrounding the formation of a genuine European social model. For
Scharpf (2002: 645), the barriers stemmed from the nature of the process of
European integration, which created a constitutional asymmetry between
policies promoting market efficiencies and policies promoting social protection and equality. National welfare states are legally and economically
constrained by European rules of economic integration, liberalisation and
competition law, whereas efforts to adopt European social policies are politically impeded by the diversity of national welfare states. The key challenge for the EU was for it to find a solution to this conundrum and to
construct a genuine European social model or welfare state as a counterbalance to the process of market-driven integration. By 2005, Jepsen and
Serrano Pascual could identify no less than four different definitions of
a European social model, thereby indicating that in short space of time,
the debate had moved on from identifying the barriers of integration for a
European social model, to whether it was possible to speak of a European
social model as a *fait accompli*. For Jepsen and Serrano Pascual (2005), the
first approach to identifying a European social model rests on a definition
that includes common institutions across the EU Member States, as well
as specific values and forms of regulation that focus on the capacity for
political regulation of the market economy. The second approach identifies
a European social model as an ideal model with policy combinations from
different welfare states. In this approach, the UK, Sweden and Germany
are put forward as paradigm examples. Specific policies from the different

models is then identified as showing the best way forward to construct a transnational European social model. Third, there are those who see a European social model as a European project under which the European welfare states are committed to a certain basic level of welfare provision that distinguishes them from liberal models, such as the USA. Finally, Jepsen and Serrano Pascual (2005) add their definition, in which they argue that the concept of a European social model is utilised within European discourse as an instrument for optimising the adjustment of social protection systems to market forces.

The academic debate surrounding a European social model mirrored some of the confusion that was coming from the EU institutions. During the Lisbon decade (2000–2010), the European Commission was reluctant to provide an official definition of the European social model, yet it continuously referred to it in official documents. Furthermore, the Commission often referred to the European social model, as well as the existence of various European social models. Referring to a European social model is to highlight the EU's competence in the area of employment and social policy, as well as the similarities and convergence within the Member States under the banner of EU governance, while to make reference to the European social models is to highlight the different welfare states within the EU and to suggest that they remain distinct from each other (Copeland 2014a: 22). The debate regarding the European social model was to resolve itself, albeit in the most unfortunate way, because of the 2007/2008 financial crisis. The collapse of the US housing bubble and exposure of many European banks to the US sub-prime mortgage market gradually spilled over into a financial crisis and fully fledged Eurozone crisis. In 2007, EU-27 debt and deficit levels amounted to 59 per cent and 0.9 per cent, respectively (Degryse 2012: 69–70). While these were comfortably within the margins determined by the Maastricht Criteria and the SGP for the whole of the Eurozone, there were significant differences in these levels between the members. Crucially, the no-bail-out clause of the Treaty, i.e., that Eurozone members were to stay within the rules of the SGP, as other Eurozone members would not come to their aid should they get into financial difficulty, meant that each Eurozone member issued its own bond to cover short-term lending and to refinance existing obligations. The interest rates of these bonds, therefore, varied from country to country, while they shared a common currency. Following successive bank bailouts and EU-guided stimulus packages to prevent a recession, the financial sustainability of some Eurozone Members – Cyprus, Greece, Ireland, Italy, Portugal and Spain – was called into question (Dyson and Quaglia 2012: 197). Rather than enacting significant reforms to the governance of the Eurozone with the sharing of debt and/or the issuing of Eurobonds, the EU's response to the crisis was to push forward with austerity-driven reforms in the form of significant cuts to public spending (Ladi and Tsarouhas 2014). This ideological response to the crisis resulted in drastic cuts to public spending which increased unemployment and reduced welfare-spending. The concept of a European social model, whether it be as an aspiration or a reality, was over. Europe, as a neoliberal market-making project was firmly identified as the EU's main priority.

From 2010 onwards, references to a European social model, therefore, became increasingly rare, and both the EU institutions and the academic literature preferred to use the term 'European social dimension' (Copeland 2014a; Costamagna 2013). The concept of a European social dimension serves to highlight the political dynamics of the policy field and the patchwork of competences the EU holds, as well as the various governance tools used. In this frame of thinking, the European social dimension is comprised of a mixture of both hard and soft law, with the latter being more common. As soft law is flexible, it constantly evolves to the political dynamics of the EU, thereby sometimes creating confusion and uncertainty. The result is that the function and purpose of the European social dimension are open to interpretation, reinterpretation, ideological change, political manipulation and an increase or decrease in the EU's list of priorities. All of this depends on the political configurations of the EU at any one time. The purpose of this chapter is to analyse the historical development of the European social dimension to understand the many twists and turns it has taken. It argues that the EU's social dimension is an ideological patchwork of policies and governance mechanisms, but the nature of political contestation has changed. Prior to the Eurozone crisis, the political debate within the EU was shifting, and the left within the EU's political space had officially fractured. On the one hand, some actors on the left have remained committed to post-war Keynesianism and social democracy. Meanwhile, those on the centre-left have embraced neoliberalism, albeit one in which the edges of the market are softened. The main tussle between the centre-left and the centre-right within the European social dimension is therefore focussed on the extent of neoliberalism and not between genuine competing visions of a European social dimension. The first section focusses on the market-making origins of both European integration and the European social dimension, and emphasises the complexities of the policy field. The remaining sections divide the historical development of the policy field into five distinct periods: the SEA, the Treaty of Maastricht, Amsterdam Treaty negotiations, the Lisbon Strategy and Europe 2020. The conclusion reflects on the European social dimension on the eve of the Eurozone crisis.

The market-making origins of the European social dimension

At the Treaty of Rome, it was decided that employment and social policy, also referred to as the welfare state, was to predominantly remain an intergovernmental area in which close cooperation between the Member States combined with 'the functioning of the Common Market' would favour the harmonisation of social systems. Twelve of the 248 articles in the founding Treaty were therefore devoted to employment and social policy with the justification for their inclusion grounded in the overriding principle that a distortion of the rules of competition was to be avoided at all costs (Hantrais 2007: 2–3). To this end, two policy areas were identified as requiring harmonisation-equal pay and common social security measures for migrant workers. The former issue was driven by French interests regarding unfair competition that could be derived by paying women less than men within European Economic Community (EEC). In social security and free movement, all discrimination based on nationality was prohibited with regard to 'employment, remuneration and other conditions of work and employment', while the Commission was given the specific task of implementing common measures to coordinate the social security of migrant workers. In other policy areas, such as training, employment, labour law and working conditions, and social security and collective bargaining, the Commission was given the responsibility of promoting close cooperation between Member States in matters. The Commission was permitted the task of 'making studies, delivering opinions and arranging consultations both on problems arising' (Treaty of Rome 1957, Article 118). Finally, the Treaty of Rome also included Articles (123–128) concerning the European Social Fund (one of the few EU redistributive EU policies) – a redistributive policy instrument designed to make employment and re-employment of workers easier and to encourage geographical and occupational mobility by providing assistance with the cost of vocational retraining and resettlement allowances (Hantrais 2007: 3).

It should therefore be noted that the fundamental legal principle of integrating within the European social dimension has always concerned the promotion of market competition between the Member States. As noted by Leibfried (2010: 265), the social dimension is often advocated as a corrective to market-building, but in practice, it seems to have been part of it, as free movement and increasing competition have prompted court cases and thus expanded the bite of European law on national social provisions. In other words, the primacy of the market takes precedent when decisions are made in EU employment and social policy. It is important to always remember this point in that at the apex of the EU's political hierarchy is the aim of making markets. Hence, up until the 1980s, the UK's Labour Party was divided on the issue of UK membership of the EEC with party members arguing that European integration was too focussed on pursuing market competition, which would prevent the full implementation of socialism. It was only under the leadership of John Smith in the early 1990s that the party shifted to the political centre on this point. Importantly, it was the position of the UK Labour Party that changed, not the process of European integration. In terms of the political economy of European integration, not only is it underpinned by a market-making agenda, but it is the principle to which all other policies are, not necessarily determined, but moving towards.

Fritz Scharpf (1999) has argued that the institutional architecture of the EU in combination with the political, economic and institutional heterogeneity of the Member States creates a structural asymmetry between the policies of liberalisation and those of social regulation. Central to this observation is Scharpf's distinction between negative and positive integration. Negative integration describes the elimination of tariffs, barriers to trade, and distortions to free competition such as state aid – it is almost always market-creating. It is driven by the European Court of Justice (ECJ) based on the four freedoms (goods, services, capital, people), as well as decisions taken by the European Commission in competition law. By contrast, positive integration is understood as the exercise of economic and regulative competences at the supranational level and can either be market-making or market-correcting. Positive integration is a political decision-making mode that requires a broad consensus among national governments and the European Parliament (Scharpf 1999: 50–51). Given that such a broad consensus is difficult to obtain under Qualified Majority Voting (QMV), especially in a diverse union of Member States with different production regimes, political compromises often only represent the 'lowest common denominator' (Höpner 2013: 75–76; Scharpf 2006b: 851; Seikel 2016: 1402). In short, market-correcting EU employment and social policy is unlikely to emerge from Brussels, and when it is proposed, it will most likely be watered down to become more market-making.

However, the political wrestling and division around the European social dimension have resulted in an ideological patchwork of policy outcomes. Not all employment and social policy within the European social dimension is market-making; some of it can be market-correcting, while some EU policy features both market-making and market-correcting objectives. The Working Time Directive serves as an example of a market-correcting EU policy. Agreed upon in 1993, the legal provision of the Directive is Article 153, which covers health and safety at work. The overarching aim of the Directive is to ensure that the well-being of workers is not jeopardised by working excessively long hours. Amongst other provisions within the Directive, workers are permitted to work no more than an average of 48 hours per week calculated over a reference period of four months, although this can be extended to up to 12 months via collective agreement. By contrast, EU regulation on the Coordination of Social Security Systems (2004) is designed to ensure that migrant workers within the EU are entitled to the same welfare benefits and rights as workers born within the Member State they have relocated to. It also serves to ensure that pension entitlement is coordinated for workers who have been employed throughout their working life in two or more EU Member States. Whilst it is essential that individuals are protected when they moving to work in another EU Member State, the overarching aim of the regulation is to ensure that the EU's labour market functions correctly. In this regard, the legal framework within this field is much more about making markets than it is about correcting them.

The complexities of the European social dimension are furthered in that it utilises a patchwork of governance tools that aim to harmonise, coordinate, guide and influence the policies of its Member State, albeit to varying degrees. Historically, over the last three decades, EU agreements using the legal instrument of traditional directives, which have a harmonising effect, have been in decline in the European social dimension (ter Haar and Copeland 2010). EU leaders have preferred to opt for more flexible modes of governance, such as the Open Method of Coordination (OMC), which sets EU benchmarks in policy areas and encourages the Member States to make progress by periodic peer review, regular reporting and the issuing of CSRs by the EU institutions for areas of policy weakness. An important difference between such an innovative method of soft law and EU hard law is that unlike the latter, in the former the ECJ does not have the jurisdiction to ensure Member States engage and comply with the OMC. The extent to which such an approach to governance has real bite remains an open question (Copeland and ter Haar 2013; Idema and Kelemen 2007; Zeitlin et al. 2005). Earlier iterations of the OMC, such as those found within the European Employment Strategy (EES) and the Lisbon Strategy, appear to be much weaker in terms of their impact on the Member States than the more recent version found within Europe 2020 and its governance mechanism of the European Semester. In short, while the market-making origins of the European social dimension can be more easily traced, the construction of the policy field lends itself to a more complex series of political events.

The Single European Act and the emergence of the European social dimension

By the early 1970s, the Council of Ministers had signalled its intention to move forward on the issue of creating a social action programme. A 1974 Council Resolution concerning the social action programme stated that economic expansion within the EEC should also result in an improvement in the quality of life. The programme set out to achieve action in three areas of employment policy: the attainment of full and better employment; the improvement of living and working conditions; and the increased involvement of management and labour in economic and social decisions, and of workers in the life of undertakings (Hantrais 2007: 4–5). Importantly, these objectives chimed with the broader macroeconomic policy of Keynesian economic theory, which had dominated post-war capitalism until the collapse of the Bretton Woods System of stable exchange rates. The latter collapsed in 1971, with Keynesian economics being slowly replaced with neoliberalism throughout the 1980s. The post-war adoption of Keynesianism across North America and Western Europe put capital and labour on a more equal footing than the relationship that has subsequently developed under neoliberalism (Strange 1998: 188). Neoliberalism gives a primacy to capital and attempts to reduce the power of labour to exert its influence over the economy. The objectives of the 1974 Council Resolution were therefore aligned with the macroeconomic objectives of the Member States at the time, even if they were slowly becoming outdated. However, despite the correlation between the Resolution and the preferences of the Member States, the latter continued to prefer a coordinating role for the EEC, rather than a pooling of sovereignty. In accordance with the Treaty, the Resolution aimed to promote further cooperation, rather than serving to deepen integration in the field. The Social Action Programme set the scene for the development of the European social dimension over the next decade. The 1970s saw a spate of action in the areas of education and training, health and safety at work, workers' and women's rights and poverty, leading to the establishment of several European networks and observatories to stimulate action and monitor progress in the field (Hantrais 2007: 4–5). Action in the field during the 1970s is therefore responsible for creating the foundations of the European political space for a broad set of social and employment actors, which has proved itself to be an important driver behind the European social dimension in subsequent decades.

The signing of the SEA in 1986 represents a significant turning point in the process of European integration, as it aimed to both deepen and widen the integration of the EEC (Armstrong and Bulmer 1998; Nugent 1999). It also represents a regional attempt to both define and consolidate the post-Keynesian capitalist order of neoliberalism. Pressure was also building for a more regulatory role for the EEC in the field of employment and social policy. The origins of this pressure can be traced back to France and the 1981 election of the Socialist President, François Mitterrand, who put the issue on the EU's agenda during France's Presidency of the Council in 1984. Mitterrand's idea of a social space (espace social) was taken up by Jacques Delors when he became President of the European Commission in 1985. EU employment and social policy were promoted as a means of strengthening economic cohesion, to be developed on the same bases as economic, monetary and industrial policy. For Delors, it was a natural complement to the internal market and a means of resolving the stalemate around legislative agreements. Progress within the social space was to be achieved by bringing the social partners together at the European level and allowing them to forge agreements around the harmonisation of employment and social policy. It was hoped that such an approach to the European social dimension would allow integration to progress and not succumb to the negotiation deadlock in the Council that had hitherto been the case (Copeland 2014a: 11–12). Delors and his team organised the 'Val Duchesse' discussions between the social partners in 1985 (named for the château in which the meeting took place). The discussions themselves soon broke down as the Union of Industries of the European Communities (UNICE)[1] failed to agree upon the scale and scope of any resultant agreements with the European Trade Union Confederation (ETUC) (Hantrais 2007: 6). UNICE wanted a guarantee that the Commission would not use the joint opinions as a basis for legislation – precisely what the Commission had aimed for. In response to the political stalemate, Delors and his Commission changed tactic and strengthened the capacity of the ETUC. The aim of this approach was to force UNICE back to the negotiating table over concerns of the strengthened capacity of the ETUC. Directorate General V (DGV), the predecessor to Directorate General Employment, Social Affairs and Inclusion, began to finance the internal activities of the ETUC. This allowed the ETUC to pay for new personnel and to build a larger, more autonomous headquarters (Martin and Ross 1999). The Commission also nourished privileged networks of communication between itself and the ETUC (ibid). The relationship encouraged the internal restructuring of the Confederation in that it became an organisation consisting of cross-national sectoral bodies rather than just national confederations.

Despite these efforts by the signing of the SEA there had been very little progress towards the construction of the European social dimension. As part of the Treaty changes, significant reforms were introduced to speed up and facilitate the decision-making process in the field. Article 118 was supplemented to stress the importance of the working environment and the health and safety of workers. QMV was extended to the area of health and safety and the introduction of the cooperation procedure strengthened the role of the European Parliament and enabled the EU institutions to tackle an issue that had previously been difficult to reach agreements under unanimity voting. The consequence of the reform was to both deepen and widen EU policy in the field of health and safety at work. Note that the concern here is with employment, rather than the broader welfare of EU citizens; the EU's desire to move forward in the field was as much driven by the desire to create a level playing field for competition within the Single European Market as it was driven by a desire to protect workers from potentially hazardous working conditions. Despite progress in health and safety, the broader field of the European social dimension remained untouched, albeit President Delors continued to push the 'social space', which was gaining broad support across some of the Member States.

By 1989, the efforts of President Delors began to pay off. Except for the UK, the governments of the Member States adopted the Community Charter of Fundamental Social Rights of Workers, heralded as the social dimension of the Single European Market (Council of the European Union 1989). The objective was to create a level playing field in the area of employment and social policy. Under the Charter, the Community is obliged to provide for the fundamental social rights of workers under the following headings: freedom of movement, employment and remuneration, improvement of living and working conditions, social protection, freedom of association and collective bargaining, vocational training, equal treatment for men and women, information and consultation and participation for workers, health protection and safety at the workplace, protection of children and adolescents, elderly persons and disabled persons. To implement the Charter, the Commission drew up an Action Programme containing 47 proposals for initiatives of various types, both binding and non-binding. The main success was the adoption of directives concerning health and safety of employees at work, which themselves were grounded in the Treaty changes agreed upon at the signing of the SEA. On other social and employment policy issues, progress was more limited. As the Community Charter did not have the force of law, and decisions concerning its implementation were left to the Member States, the driving forces behind the integration momentum were soon to dissipate. Second, in terms of creating a level playing field, disagreement remained in the Council on whether the levelling should be one of an increase or decrease in standards – a question that has always surrounded negotiations in the field and hindered progress. As noted by Hantrais (2007: 8), the Charter's inclusion of the terms 'adequate', 'sufficient', 'appropriate' and 'satisfactory', used in the Charter to refer to the levels to be achieved, are indicative of the problems of reaching agreement over the definition of targets. This lack of precision left open the possibility that some states would seek competitive advantages by not offering the same level of social protection to their workers, resulting in what has become known as 'social dumping'. That is, the completion of the Single European Market gave concerns that the free flow of goods, capital, services and workers would result in a gradual and indirect process of social and employment policy erosion (Leibfried and Pierson 1992: 350). With capital able to move freely within the Single European Market, there were fears that Member States with high levels of employment protection, wages and employer social security contributions would be 'dumped' in favour of cheaper and more flexible Members. Social dumping is, of course, a more complicated issue and is not determined by costs alone. Other factors can also determine capital remaining in a location or moving to another, such as labour productivity and skills, as well as infrastructure and geographical proximately to the market.

There are two further important things to note about the momentum surrounding the European social dimension in the late 1980s and early 1990s. First, while the political efforts of the Delors' Commission made some progress pursuing deeper integration in the field, the Community Charter of Fundamental Social Rights of Workers and the broader political developments continued with a preoccupation on employment rather than the broader welfare concerns of its citizens. President Delors may have had a much broader vision of a European social dimension but policy outcomes represented the 'lowest common denominator'. Second, the political momentum, while not producing much in terms of concrete policies that harmonised the employment and social policies of the Member States, created considerable noise that was to feed into the Maastricht Treaty negotiations and the formation of the European-level social dialogue. By 1992, the efforts of the Commission to strengthen the capacity of the ETUC paid off, and the EU-level social partners reached an agreement on the basic parameters of social dialogue. Behind this agreement had been concerns by the employers (UNICE) that if it did not get involved, the EEC would initiate a swathe of employment directives over which it would have no control (Copeland 2014a: 12–13). The Social Dialogue Committee (SDC) was established as the main forum for bipartite social dialogue at the European Level, with the European Commission required to consult the social partners on the preparation of legislation in the European social dimension. It also provided for the possibility of the social partners being able to negotiate framework agreements at the Community level (European Parliament 2017). To date there have been some important policy agreements that have emerged out of the social dialogue. The social partners concluded framework agreements on parental leave (1995), part-time work (1997) and fixed-term work (1999). These were ratified by the Council of Ministers and are now part of the *acquis communautaire*. However, since the late 1990s, the conclusion of further agreements has been difficult, as the employers were less motivated to forge agreements at EU level. That is, disagreements in the Council and the resultant political stalemates throughout the 1990s meant that the threats of the Delors Commission were relatively toothless – the EU was unable to agree legislation in the field, which meant that there were no obvious consequences if the employers did not participate in the SDC.

The Maastricht Treaty negotiations

The principles of the Community Charter were taken up during the Maastricht Treaty negotiations. Both the Commission and a group of Member States (led by the Mediterranean states) aimed to give the Community Charter full legal recognition in the Treaty. A problem was that opposition by the UK meant that the agreement could not be included in the main body of the Treaty. The result was a separate Protocol on Social Policy that was annexed to the Maastricht Treaty. By doing so, the 11 other Member States could proceed to integrate in the field and make decisions without the UK. Article 1 of the agreement amended Article 117 of the EEC Treaty which claimed that improvements in the social systems of the Member States would automatically follow from market integration. Instead, specific objectives covering the promotion of employment, living and working conditions, social protection, social dialogue and the development of human resources to secure employment and the combating of exclusion, were included. The latter is particularly interesting, given that the focus on the EU from the mid-1990s onwards was on the supply-side policies of the labour market, including the need to increase the rate of employment, as well as labour productivity and education and training. Furthermore, the objectives of the Protocol were to be achieved via measures designed to take into account national diversity. In this regard, the Social Protocol presents the beginning of the EU's drift away from the harmonisation of policy within the European social dimension, as well as traditional Keynesian-inspired welfare policy. Meanwhile, the ambition of integration within the field was not to jeopardise the competitiveness of the Single European Market.

Article 2 of the agreement assigned a complementary role for the EU in the areas of health and safety at work, working conditions, information and consultation of workers, equality between men and women, and the integration of persons excluded from the labour market (Hantrais 2007: 11). To minimise deadlock in the Council, the 11 Member States could agree directives by QMV. Importantly, any agreement needed to ensure that it did not constrain the creation, or impede the development of, small- and medium-sized enterprises (SMEs), as SMEs were regarded as the future engine of growth and jobs. Other policy areas were identified as being the responsibility of both the EU and the Member States, including social security and social protection of workers, the protection of workers made redundant, representation and collective defence of workers and employers, the conditions of employment for third-country nationals and financial contributions for job promotion. The distinction between the policy areas featuring QMV was important, since it reflected the topics where a considerable degree of consensus already existed (Hantrais 2007: 11). The Protocol can therefore be regarded as an attempt to nudge the European social dimension into further integration, by capitalising on policy areas where there was broad agreement with the hope that the integration momentum would spillover into fields where there was less consensus.

While the Protocol was heralded as the social dimension to the Single European Market, further Treaty changes agreed at Maastricht were to curb the integration momentum in the field. The Treaty on European Union (TEU) introduced the Principle of Subsidiarity and the principle of proportionality to govern the exercise of the EU's competences. In areas where the EU does not have exclusive competence, the Principle of Subsidiarity seeks to safeguard the ability of the Member States to take decisions and formulate policy by the EU when the objectives of an action cannot be sufficiently achieved by the Member States but can better be achieved at the EU level, 'by reason of the scale and effects of the proposed action' (European Parliament 2018). The purpose of including this in the EU Treaties is to ensure that powers are exercised as close to citizens as possible, but it also serves to act as a powerful break on the process of European integration, including within the European social dimension.

The burden of proof is on the EU's institutions to demonstrate a need to legislate at the EU level with the most binding governance instruments being used as a last resort – the latter known as the Principle of Proportionality. While the Principle of Subsidiarity serves to justify whether or not the EU should formulate action, the Principle of Proportionality requires the most legally binding instruments to be used as a last resort. In short, the Treaty changes introduced in 1992 were something of a mixed bag for the European social dimension, as they served to both extend the EU's remit in the field, while simultaneously curbing the extent of integration. By incorporating the Principle of Subsidiarity, Member States seemingly confirmed their reluctance to develop a substantive European social dimension that would harmonise policies across the EU.

The early 1990s witnessed the continuation of political activity surrounding the European social dimension, albeit with very little in terms of concrete policy outcomes. The European Commission launched the 1993 Green Paper – a scoping exercise that sought views and opinions from a broad range of EU actors regarding the objectives and targets of the European social dimension. On the back of the Green Paper, the Commission subsequently published a White Paper '*A way to follow for the European Union*' (1994), which referred to a 'European social model' based on a set of shared values, held together by the conviction that economic and social progress must go together. The White Paper set the scene for the policy field through to the end of the decade by providing a comprehensive statement of policy direction and goals. As with all previous initiatives, job creation remained the EU's top priority. By the time of the Treaty of Amsterdam negotiations in 1997, there had been several important developments in the European social dimension. The first was that despite the Treaty changes at Maastricht, the launch of the various initiatives that aimed to move the process of European integration forward in the field, and the legal provision that enabled agreements to be made without the UK, progress in the field was slow. It was seemingly difficult to reach agreements with 11 Member States. Meanwhile, the number of Member States involved in the decision-making process was to increase, following the accession of Austria, Finland and Sweden in 1995 – three Member States with some of the most comprehensive social and employment standards on the Continent. The Scandinavian members, in particular, wanted the EU to go much further in the field of employment and social policy through fear that the lower social and employment standards in other Member States would erode the generosity of their welfare states (Johnson 2005; Velluti 2010). However, it should be noted that the egalitarian nature of the Swedish welfare state that existed during the Bretton Woods era had been severely curtailed by the early 1990s and had succumb to the forces of neoliberalism (Pontusson 1997: 55). A result was a decrease in the generosity of welfare payments and rising levels of inequality in Sweden. Despite this change, relatively speaking the Scandinavian welfare states are much more generous than their European counterparts and perform more favourably on almost all indicators.

The second issue is that by the early 1990s, the nature of the welfare state across Europe was changing – that is, traditional post-war Keynesian welfare policies were proving themselves to be incompatible with the Single European Market. Given that Keynesian macroeconomics had been replaced with neoliberalism across the EU and enshrined within the Single European Market, an ideological and policy disjuncture had occurred between European neoliberal macroeconomics on the one hand and the Keynesian welfare state on the other. Within this context, the traditional tools of government policy to reduce unemployment had either disappeared or had been seriously eroded. EU competition policy meant that governments could no longer subsidise industry, as it would create an unfair competitive advantage within the EU's economic space. Meanwhile, with capital moving more freely around the global economy than it had during Bretton Woods, tax decreases or increases to government spending to counter a cyclical economic downturn can not be guaranteed to produce the desired reflationary effect. Under a system of floating exchange rates without capital controls, any associated economic boost such policies can generate may simply be spent on imports, rather than generating domestic demand (Mishra 1999). Meanwhile, in a neoliberal macroeconomic setting, the Keynesian logic of paying the unemployed welfare benefits, without the requirement that recipients should look for work, is incompatible. Under Keynesian Macroeconomic policy, unemployment benefits can be paid to workers until the government pulls the various levers of the economy to improve the economic situation. However, under neoliberalism the levers of macroeconomic control are less effective and the open-ended payment of unemployment benefits can become a problem. The stimulation of the economy to reduce unemployment becomes a more complicated endeavour and focusses on the ability of governments to attract and maintain mobile capital. The indefinite entitlement for the receipt of unemployment benefit risk straining public finances, while also potentially contributing to the unemployed becoming long-term unemployed with the associated economic and social costs. The varieties of capitalism literature refers to the compatibility of different strands of political economy, such as macroeconomic policy and the welfare state, as 'institutional complementarities', understood as the efficiencies gained from complementarity enabling nations to specialise in particular products, activities and services, and thereby giving rise to comparative institutional advantages. Institutional practices in political economy are said to be complementary when each raises the returns from the other (Hall and Gingerich 2009: 151). For Hall and Soskice (2001: 18), 'nations with a particular type of coordination in one sphere of the economy tend to develop complementary practices in other spheres as well'. This also extends to social and employment policy and the welfare state, as Huber and Stephens (2001: 199) observe: 'within each country certain – although not all – aspects of its welfare state and production regimes do fit each other'. This tells us that to maximise growth and jobs, the different constituents of political economy need to be coherent with each other and in the early 1990s, it was becoming clear that the EU political economy was experiencing institutional/ideological incompatibilities. EU leaders were therefore grappling with the challenges of the new global order for welfare policy, following the enshrining of neoliberalism in the Single European Market and the realisation that the structural purpose of the welfare state needed to change.

The third development within the European political space is the shifting position of the UK following the election of New Labour in 1997. During the 1997 UK election campaign, the Labour Party pledged that if it formed the next government, it would develop a more cooperative relationship between London and Brussels; believing that it was better to be at the negotiating table for EU employment policy, rather than to have an empty chair (Labour Party 1997). In a matter of days after taking office, the new Minister for European Affairs went to Brussels to announce the UK's commitment to 'sign up' to the Social Chapter (Barnard 1997: 275) and this paved the way for the Treaty changes agreed at Amsterdam. All EU Member States would therefore be involved in progressing integration in the European social dimension. The shift in position of the UK's approach towards the EU created a level of optimism around both the process of European integration and the forwarding of the European social dimension (Copeland 2016).

Finally, the 1992 decision at Maastricht to progress with the launching of a single currency, which would eventually be known as the Euro and its associated Member States as being part of the Eurozone, was also influencing developments within the welfare policies of the EU. The Maastricht Convergence Criteria required participants to have a budget deficit of no more than 3 per cent of Gross Domestic Product (GDP), a public debt at or below 60 per cent of GDP and an inflation rate of no more than 1.5 per cent above the average of the three lowest countries (Schmidt 2002: 46). In April 1994, none of the EU states had fulfilled the convergence criteria, not even Germany. In November of that year, ten states had suffered from excessive deficits (Chang 2009: 52). The prospect of being denied membership of the Euro encouraged debt reduction and a balancing of budgets by governments, which resulted in cuts and reforms to public spending, including the welfare state which for some at the time, threatened to undermine the pursuit of a European social dimension (Teague 1998). The broader political economy of European integration was therefore providing 'indirect' or 'backdoor' integration pressures on the welfare states of its members. This, and the previous three developments combined with high levels of unemployment in Europe in the mid-1990s, were to provide the impetus for the Treaty changes agreed at Amsterdam.

The Amsterdam Treaty changes (1997)

The Amsterdam Treaty (1997) negotiations ushered in a significant change for integration in the European social dimension. In the run-up to the agreement, the political positions of both the European Commission and the Council were being influenced and inspired by the reforms that had taken place in the Scandinavian Members to focus on supply-side policies to boost employment. Such supply-side policies had been 'proven' in Scandinavia and provided a credible solution to combating unemployment under neo-liberal macroeconomics. The basic principle of the supply-side approach to employment policy is to make labour more attractive so that employers are motivated to recruit workers. This is fundamentally different from the Keynesian policies of stimulating the economy with monetary and fiscal policy or subsidising industry to generate domestic growth and the demand for labour. For Velluti (2010: 114), the EU's new approach to employment crystallised at the 1994 European Council meeting in Essen which drew up five priorities:

• Improving job opportunities for the working population by promoting investment in educational training, particularly for the young;
• Increasing the intensity of the work content of economic growth (macroeconomic policy);
• Reducing unsalaried labour costs, particularly for non-qualified workers (labour market policy);
• Improving the efficiency of employment policies by avoiding measures that negatively affect the availability for work and by replacing passive unemployment policies with active ones (flexibility);
• Improving the measures concerning the assistance to groups that have been most affected by unemployment such as young people, long-term unemployed workers, women and older employees (social inclusion).

This position had also been incorporated into the approach to employment by the Organisation for Economic Cooperation and Development (OECD). The OECD Jobs Strategy was first established in 1992 following the persistence of high unemployment in most European countries and focussed on the adoption of supply-side policies. The shift to supply-side policies to improve employment within the EU therefore had broader structural connections to the reconfiguration of the welfare state in accordance with neoliberalism. The Commission took advantage of the political opportunity by launching a medium-term social action programme for 1995–1997 in which social and employment policy was argued to be a productive factor rather than a burden of growth. The mid-1990s represent a significant turning point within the development of the European social dimension. What emerged from the European Commission and the European Council was a policy blueprint capable of reforming and restructuring the Keynesian welfare state more in accordance with neoliberal macroeconomics. The new vision of the welfare state was not born out of the victories gained in the struggle for European integration by social democrats/Keynesians over neoliberals; rather, it was born out of the restructuring of the left to embrace neoliberalism. This new vision of political economy, epitomised by the Third-Way in the UK as well as 'Neue Mitte' in Germany and the 'Polder Model' in the Netherlands sought to bridge the divide between neoliberalism and social democracy (James 2012). In short, the Third Way vision of political economy was to embrace neoliberalism, albeit to intervene in the market to support economic and social fairness by ensuring that individuals had the necessary opportunities and skills to participate in the market. In this regard, the Third Way is about embracing the neoliberal market while simultaneously reducing some of the more extremes of purely commodified labour markets (cf. Giddens 1998; Painter 1999). The Third Way was a post-Keynesian solution for the reform and reconfiguration of the Keynesian welfare state, as well as a welfare state model that candidate countries in Eastern Europe could aim towards in their preparations for EU membership. However, it should be noted that while the Commission was an important player in the European social dimension in the 1990s, the European Council remained in the driving seat, as centre-left governments were in a majority across the Member States and were willing to move forward on the European social dimension.

At the 1997 Amsterdam European Council Summit, it was agreed to amend the EC Treaty and launch the EES (1997). The amendments included inserting a new title on employment into the EC Treaty and to amend the old title on social policy, education, vocational training and youth. Article 145 of the Treaty on the Functioning of the European Union (TFEU) obliges the Member States to work towards developing a coordinated strategy for employment, particularly for promoting a skilled, trained and adaptable workforce and labour markets. Crucially, there was no longer a consensus around the use of hard law and a harmonisation of employment and social policy across the EU. Articles 146–150 outlined the governance processes for the EES, which drew inspiration from the governance processes of the single currency. The political agreement at Maastricht had resulted in a pooling of sovereignty in monetary policy, but economic policies were to be governed more intergovernmentally with the EU providing a coordinating role. Article 121 of the TFEU stipulates that 'Member States shall regard their economic policies as a matter of common concern'. To this end, the Broad Economic Policy Guidelines (BEPG) are adopted by the Council as non-legally-binding recommendations which guide annual economic policy in both the Member States and the EU. This iterative governance process involves the adoption of common guidelines and the annual reporting of progress by the Member States to the Commission and the Council. In areas of policy weakness, the European Commission and the Council can issue CSRs, which a Member State is required to act upon over the next annual governance cycle. Importantly, should Member States fail to comply, there are few immediate consequences, although it was hoped that peer pressure would generate sufficient incentives for Member States to follow the rules and conduct any necessary reforms. This mode of governance was to be used in the EES, where it was believed that EU targets, annual reporting by the Member States and the issuing of CSRs would both modernise and result in a convergence of the EU's welfare states. The governance mechanisms were also specifically designed to encourage the cooperation between Member States and to support their action in the field of employment through initiatives aimed at developing exchanges of information and best practice (Ashiagbor 2005; Caune et al. 2011; Copeland and ter Haar 2013; Trubek and Mosher 2003; Velluti 2010). To this end, the Employment Committee (EMCO), comprised of representatives from the European Commission and the Member States, was established to guide and monitor progress within the EES. Meanwhile, the flexibility of the mode of governance would respect national diversity in the field and overcome the difficulties posed by the harmonisation of policy.

The EES was greeted with considerable optimism when it was launched, particularly by those who advocated for a stronger European social dimension; after a decade of high expectations, but low capabilities in the field, it was believed that the innovative mode of governance would finally deliver the desired progress in the field (cf. Rhodes 2005). The 1997 EES was based on a four-pillar structure, with the employment guidelines relating to one of the pillars:

- Improving employability;
- Creating a new culture of entrepreneurship;
- Promoting and encouraging the adaptability of firms and their workers;
- Strengthening equal opportunity policies.

The main objectives were higher employment participation, increasing active employment policies, increasing the number of highly skilled workers, to help to ensure the low-skilled remain in employment, find the correct balance between employment flexibility and employment security, promote entrepreneurship, and to promote gender equality (Velluti 2010: 129). Ashiagbor (2005: 317) notes this represents a shift of focus from 'social law and legislative initiatives, towards soft law, or rather policies aimed at employment creation, which for the most part eschew legislation'. While this shift represents an important moment within the development of a European social dimension, it is worth reiterating that economic integration remained the EU's number one priority, with the legal status of employment policy having changed very little. Furthermore, the independence of the EES, and thereby the autonomy of actors to pursue their own goals, was severely clipped – the

Treaty amendments agreed at Amsterdam establish an asymmetrical dependency between macroeconomic policy and the EES, which favours the former. Article 146 of the TFEU states that the achievement of employment policy should be done in a manner that is consistent with Article 121 – the BEPG. Importantly, Article 121 makes no reference to the need for macroeconomic policy to accommodate the employment situation, as outlined in Article 146. This legal arrangement therefore clarifies the secondary importance of the EES vis-à-vis the EU's macroeconomic objectives.

The Lisbon Strategy

Following the launch of the EES informally referred to as the Luxembourg process, in 1998, the UK Presidency of the European Council launched a light reporting procedure to stimulate structural reforms in the product and capital markets, often referred to as the Cardiff process. Meanwhile, in 1999, the German Presidency of the European Council introduced a stronger macroeconomic dialogue between the EU social partners, known as the Cologne process (Linsenmann et al. 2007). What connected these three initiatives was a preference for soft modes of governance, similar to the EES which were designed to facilitate coordination and reform (James 2012: 13). Simultaneously, the Commission and the Council became increasingly aware of the EU's competitive lag, added to which the constraints imposed by Economic and Monetary Union in the form of the SGP 'constitute[d] a significant change in the macroeconomic policy environment' and further narrowed the policy options of the Member States (Begg and Berghman 2002: 187). A coordinated response to modernising the European economy and improving its competitiveness based on coordination and legally non-binding agreements appeared to be a viable solution to the multidimensional problem. The Lisbon European Council built on the political momentum as well as the new governance processes in operation and launched the EU's Lisbon Agenda that aimed to make the EU: 'the most competitive and dynamic knowledge-based economy in the world capable of sustainable economic growth with more and better jobs and greater social cohesion' (Council of the European Union 2000a: 5). According to James (2012: 13), the Lisbon Agenda constituted the final logical stage in the integration of Europe's economic and social objectives by attempting to construct a new hybrid political economy.

   To achieve these aims and targets, the EU institutionalised the new governance arrangements that had been established for the BEPG and the EES and for the purposes of the Lisbon Agenda, it was referred to as the OMC. A legally non-binding cycle of governance in which the archetypical version was the EES. However, different policy areas within the Lisbon Agenda – such as education and training, pensions, social inclusion, healthcare, research and development – developed their own variant of

---

Box 1.1: The aims and targets of the Lisbon Agenda 2000

The Lisbon Agenda had the following aims:

*   To prepare the transition to a knowledge-based economy and so-ciety by better policies for the information society and research and development, as well as stepping up the process of structural reform for competitiveness and innovation and by completing the internal market;
*   To modernise the European social model, investing in people and combating social exclusion;
*   To sustain the healthy economic outlook and favourable growth prospects by applying an appropriate macroeconomic policy mix.

To these ends the EU set itself the following targets to be achieved by 2010:

1   Annual economic growth of around 3 per cent of GDP;
2   The creation of 20 million new jobs;
3   Raising the employment rate from 61 per cent to 'as close as pos-sible' to 70 per cent;
4   Raising the employment rate for women from 51 per cent to 'more than' 60 per cent;
5   Raising the employment rate of older workers to 50 per cent;
6   Raising research and development spending to approach 3 per cent of GDP.

Sources: Council of the European Union (2000b, 2002),
European Commission (2000), James (2012: 17).

---

the OMC to accommodate the needs of the policy area, the latter reflect-ing Treaty provisions and the extent to which the Member States were prepared to accept EU interference (Copeland 2012a: 234). For example, while there was an annual reporting cycle for the EES with the issuing of CSRs, for social inclusion the reporting cycle was every two or three years and did not issue CSRs for areas of policy weaknesses. A further impor-tant observation of the governance of the Lisbon Strategy was the planned 'openness' of the OMC. In generating structural reforms, actors were to be drawn from the various levels of governance across the EU and were to include both state and non-state actors; the idea being that the reform process would be generated and sustained by broad coalitions of diverse actors from across the EU's political space. The Lisbon Agenda would not only modernise and reform the European economy, but it would serve to improve its democratic credentials and legitimacy. Lisbon was therefore a very ambitious programme that would seemingly tackle a multitude of problems linked to EU competitiveness and democracy. The level of optimism in the EU at the time should not be underestimated. In 2002, Barnard and Deakin argued that the Lisbon Agenda and the OMC were to be seen as a way of regulatory intervention which attempts to provide space for experimentation in rule-making and to encourage regulatory learning through the exchange of best practice. Rhodes (2000: 3) went much further and claimed that providing the political will exists, 'Lisbon may one day be considered Europe's 'Maastricht' for the Welfare State'.

Despite the optimism and initial political activity surrounding the Lisbon Agenda, the reform programme was soon to stall. By 2004, actors within Brussels and across the Member States were frustrated by the slow pace of reform and increasingly complex processes of governance. Not only were governments engaging with the OMCs to varying degrees, but they could also avoid domestically contentious reforms with very few short-term consequences. Simultaneously, the political composition of the EU institutions had shifted to the centre-right, which culminated in the appointment of José Manuel Barroso as President of the European Commission in the Autumn of 2004. 2004 also witnessed the accession of ten new EU Member States, following the 'big bang' enlargement. President Barroso appointed the former Dutch Prime Minister, Wim Kok, to evaluate the Lisbon Agenda. The Kok Report (2004), as it became known, argued that the Member States were failing to achieve the targets because of policy overload (for example, there were some 50 benchmarks to be achieved in employment and social policy alone), poor coordination, conflicting priorities and weak national ownership. The Kok Report, as well as the shifting political tendencies of the EU, provided sufficient justification to relaunch the Lisbon Agenda, which became known as Lisbon II or, more commonly, the Lisbon Strategy. The relaunched Lisbon Strategy signifies the end of the EU's experiment with the Third Way and a turn to purer neoliberal tendencies of employment and social policy. The relaunched Strategy refocussed itself around the priorities of growth and employment to 'renew the basis of its competitiveness, increase its growth potential and its productivity, and strengthen social cohesion, placing emphasis on knowledge, innovation, and the optimisation of human capital' (Council of the European Union 2005). The result was a 'meta-OMC' in which the BEPG and the Employment Policy Guidelines (EPG) were merged into a single guidelines package structured around macroeconomic, microeconomic and employment pillars (Tholoniat 2010: 107). The OMCs of social protection and inclusion, pensions, and education and training, were separated from the main governance processes and were to be organised independently, albeit they were to feed in and out of the meta-OMC. This reconfiguration represented a desire to not only improve the governance processes but also to shift the agenda away from one in which economic growth was to be combined with social cohesion, to one in which economic growth was to create social cohesion (ter Haar and Copeland 2010). In other words, rather than being an independent objective in its own right, social cohesion in the Lisbon Strategy became a function of, and dependent upon, progress made within the economic pillars.

The broader policy environment surounding the political economy of European integration was also indicative of the shift to the centre-right during the middle of the decade, including within the European social dimension. During the final months of the Prodi Commission (1999–2004), the Commission released a draft proposal for the reform of the EU service sector. The reform of the EU service sector was perceived as being a key stepping stone towards achieving some of the ambitious targets of the Lisbon Strategy. The Commission argued that integration within the service sector had been piecemeal and that 'a decade after the envisaged completion of the Internal Market, there is still a huge gap between the vision of an integrated EU economy and the reality as experienced by European citizens and European service providers' (European Commission 2002: 9). The need to reform and integrate the service sector was further justified in the context of the size and significance of the sector to the EU's economy. In terms of employment, in 2000, services accounted for 116 million jobs in the then EU-15 Member States, which represented 72 per cent of the active workforce. In comparison, manufacturing jobs – where the Single Market is complete – accounted for 33 million jobs or 19.45 per cent of the total workforce. Meanwhile, between 1997 and 2002, services accounted for approximately 11.4 million jobs in the EU, representing 96 per cent of total net job creation during the period (Kox et al. 2004: 10). The draft proposal realised to the EU had been penned by the Commissioner for the Internal Market, Frits Bolkestein – a former Dutch Cabinet Minister who made no secret of his neoliberal preferences for the EU (Clift 2009; Höpner and Schäfer 2010). Bolkestein favoured the rapid liberalisation of the EU service sector that had a horizontal approach to reforming the sector, which was to be combined with administrative cooperation, the application of the country of origin principle and the harmonisation of some basic requirements for services (European Commission 2004b: 27–28). In short, to aid the freedom to establish services (permanent establishment of a service provider in another Member State) certain barriers and authorisation schemes were prohibited and Member States were to create single points of contact for service providers to assist their completion of the necessary administrative procedures. To improve the freedom to provide services (temporary cross-border services) providers were subject to the laws of their country of establishment, except for the Posting of Workers Directive. The ensuring debate across the European political space focussed on the consequences of the proposed directive for the European social dimension.

The main concerns of actors within the regulatory coalition, a group of Northern and Southern Members, as well as organisations such as the ETUC focussed on two issues. First, the broad scope of the directive included Services of General Economic Interest (SGEI) and thereby healthcare and social services. The coalition argued that this would result in the introduction of market principles to European healthcare systems that could create pressures for privatisation. By easing the restrictions on EU patients receiving treatment in another Member State, patients would be able to shop around for the best treatment which could potentially open up healthcare systems to competition, and inadvertently undermine the provision of healthcare in some Member States (ETUC 2005). Second, the use of the country of origin principle for temporary cross-border service providers created complexity and potentially undermined the generosity of the European social dimension. Temporary cross-border service providers were to follow the law of their country of origin, except for the Posting of Workers Directive. The problem with this approach is that the latter Directive covers minimum standards. At the time of the negotiations, there was no nationally agreed minimum wage in Member States such as Germany and Sweden, as collective agreements were used to agree sectoral and regional minimum wages (as a result of the debate on the Services Directive Germany introduced a minimum wage in 2015). As such agreements are not universally applicable, they are not covered by the Posting of Workers Directive. This legal arrangement would provide temporary cross-border service providers with a potential cost advantage vis-à-vis local service providers and could place a downward pressure on Member States with more extensive social protection systems (ETUC 2005). For the regulatory coalition, the proposed directive, particularly the application of the country of origin principle, would result in social dumping as EU companies flocked to establish themselves in Member States with the lowest levels of social protection.

While the proposed directive therefore aimed to complete a single market for services, the political debate focussed on the consequences of the proposal for the European social dimension. The negotiations took many twists and turns with public protests in Brussels being the largest ever organised against the EU – for example, on 19 March 2004, an estimated 75,000–100,000 trade unionists protested in Brussels against the proposed directive (Kowalsky 2005: 7). After two years of negotiations and political uproar, the final agreed version of the Services Directive removed SGEI from its scope, as well as the country of origin principle which was renamed the freedom to provide services. The 2006 agreed Directive also explicitly states that labour law and working conditions would not be affected with temporary cross-border service providers having to adhere to all the employment regulations and conditions of the host country. The political debate and division surrounding the Services Directive should not be underestimated, but the timing of the debate was also hugely significant for the process of European integration and the European social dimension. The negotiations for the Services Directive were situated in a broader political environment in which Lisbon II was launched and the EU was failing to reach an agreement on the revision of the Working Time Directive – one of the cornerstones of the European social dimension (Copeland 2012a). These events severely damaged the reputation of the Barroso Commission and the ideological shift to the centre-right did not sit well with the broader set of stakeholders within the EU's political space including the trade union movement, the social NGOs and think tanks. The ETUC, for example, became a staunch critic of Lisbon II, arguing that the EU failed to meet its targets 'largely because essential social and environmental objectives ... [were] being sacrificed to short-term economic demands' (ETUC 2012).

Progress within the Lisbon Strategy stalled and so too did the deepening and widening of the European social dimension. The broader political environment was also influenced by the 2004 EU enlargement, which, except for Cyprus and Malta, saw the EU expand into predominantly former state-socialist countries that had very little political preference for a Keynesian-inspired welfare state. During the transition from state-socialism to capitalist democracy, neoliberalism has formed the ideological cement to which a 'new' political economy could emerge in the region. This transition has been reinforced by EU accession preparations, in that the EU prioritised market-led integration and gave very little attention to the European social dimension. Once these countries became formal members of the EU, their position as more liberal-leaning political economies was reinforced, as they sought to protect their low-cost base for production within the EU's competitive space. The concept of a European social dimension that is not market-driven is perceived by the Eastern Members as potentially increasing the costs of labour and reducing their competitive advantage vis-à-vis the EU-15 Member States. EU enlargement has therefore had a profound impact on the pursuit of a European social dimension, not to mention the practical problems posed by reaching agreements between 28 different Member States (Copeland 2014a: 115–127).

The Lisbon Strategy has spawned an extensive academic literature (e.g. Begg 2007, 2008, 2010; Borras and Radaelli 2011; Collignon 2008; Copeland and Papadimitriou 2012; de la Porte and Pochet 2003; Radaelli 2003; Zeitlin et al. 2005; Zeitlin 2009), but most empirical studies with respect to concrete policy outcomes at the Member State level remain sceptical. Several scholars have taken a much broader understanding of outcomes to conceptualise the impact of the OMC at the national level. Zeitlin (2009) conceptualises substantive policy change in terms of changes in national policy thinking (cognitive shifts), in national policy agendas (political shifts) and in specific national policies (programmatic shifts) and argues that there is evidence of cognitive and political shifts, but little to suggest that there have been programmatic shifts within the Member States. This claim has been subsequently confirmed by the empirical findings of Büchs (2007). But if the Lisbon Strategy was a failure in terms of concrete policy outcomes, it was also a failure to enshrine the post-Keynesian centre-left vision for the EU that emerged during the late 1990s, which became easily moulded into a centre-right vision during Lisbon II.

Europe 2020

While the relaunch of the Lisbon Strategy in 2005 goes some way to explaining its failure, the use of the OMC was also a contributing factor (Copeland 2012a). Optimists, such as Maria João Rodrigues, current Member of the European Parliament (MEP) and former political advisor to the Portuguese Prime Minister Antonio Guterres, who launched the Lisbon Agenda during Portugal's Presidency of the European Council in 2000, claim that while Lisbon had failures, it also had successes (Notre Europe 2010: 5). In 2007, for example, the average GDP growth rate was 2.7 per cent and 16 million jobs had been created. However, what this fails to mention is that these positive economic conditions had nothing to do with the Lisbon Strategy, rather as explained in Chapter 3, the economic boom of the Lisbon decade was generated by access to cheap credit, which generated spikes in government borrowing/spending, consumer spending and asset bubbles. Cheap credit enabled some governments to postpone structural economic reforms, thus creating the perception that the European economy was being reformed and generating growth and jobs because of structural reforms. However, the positive economic conditions stemmed from the governance of the Eurozone, which was not fit for purpose and created economic distortions. Meanwhile, access to cheap credit was to fuel current account divergences within the Eurozone and structural imbalances. Broadly speaking, Northern Member States with their export-driven economies were posting current account surpluses; meanwhile, the debt-fuelled economies of the South were posting current account deficits.

Further evidence regarding the limits of what was achieved during the Lisbon decade can be drawn from pace and scale of Europe's recovery from the financial/Eurozone crisis. While the EU's pursuit of austerity made the economic situation much worse by deepening the economic recession, had the EU achieved at least some progress towards its Lisbon targets, the economic recovery would not have been as prolonged. The envisaged 'dynamic, flexible, and knowledge-based economy' would have enabled the European economy to recover much quicker than was hitherto the case. The latter would have been achieved by the attractiveness of European labour to employers, who would have more readily hired workers due to their high level of skills, flexibility and competitive costs. Meanwhile, an army of entrepreneurs would have come to the rescue of the European economy. Neither of these situations occurred, rather EU-inspired ALMPs forced the unemployed to continuously search for a decreasing pool of job vacancies or risk losing access to unemployment benefit. The only alternative to this option is for the unemployed to participate in education and training programmes, even though individuals may already have sufficient skills.

Despite the clear flaws and shortcomings of the Lisbon Strategy, the EU decided to replace Lisbon and launch a new economic reform strategy for the decade, known as Europe 2020. For Borrás and Radaelli (2011), the EU's economic reform strategies should be understood as a governance architecture, comprised of political and institutional elements. For these authors, governance architectures, such as the Lisbon Strategy and Europe 2020, represent 'strategic and long-term political initiatives of international organizations on cross cutting policy issues locked into commitments about targets and processes'. In the Borrás and Radaelli framing, governance architectures are situated at the meso-level between the multi-level governance of an international institution and an individual policy programme. Such architectures are conceived as comprising ideational and organisational components. The ideational component is defined as: a set of fundamental ideational repertoires, expressed in notions such as 'governance', 'competitiveness', 'sustainability', 'knowledge-based society', the 'market' and a discourse that uses the ideational repertoires to discipline, organise and legitimise the hierarchical relationships between the goals and the policy instruments. Taken together, ideas and discourses give shape to the overall attempt to socialise actors into a specific frame of reference that is supposed to make sense of a complex world of cross-cutting policy problems. The organisational component comprises formal and informal organisational arrangements (politico-organisational machinery) where the ideational repertoires and discourses are defined and patterned through complex political processes of a multi-level nature and the selection of policy instruments and their procedural requirements. This is a major contribution that takes the field forward in several ways. In the first instance, Borrás and Radaelli aim to provide an integrated or encompassing framework that takes account of both the many fields in which the EU is now active and the EU's attempt to integrate these through innovations in policy and governance. Furthermore, the arrangements for governance are to be simultaneously considered with and analysed in relation to the ideas and discourses involved in the policy portfolio, making for a more interactional and dynamic approach. In many ways, its integrated framework – melding ideas, culture and norms with political and organisational factors – mirrors the breadth and integrational ambition of the Lisbon Strategy and Europe 2020.

The complexities of Europe 2020 will be analysed in Chapters 3 and 4, so the concern of the discussion here is of the relationship between it and the European social dimension. The Commission's draft proposals for the Europe 2020 strategy, agreed by national leaders at European Council summits in March and May 2010, constituted a revision of the EU's economic and social reform agenda. Both Europe 2020 and the numerous reforms to EU economic governance were forged and agreed during the EU's response to the 2007/2008 financial crisis and the beginnings of the Eurozone crisis – a period in which the centre-right remained dominant. The various aspects of Europe 2020 that concern the European social dimension therefore cannot be understood without considering the broader structural political dynamics of the process of European integration. Like Lisbon, Europe 2020 is guided by a series of headline targets and 'thematic' priorities related to employment policy, poverty reduction, research and development and climate change, aimed at raising Europe's competitiveness (Copeland and James 2014; European Commission 2010a,b). The Flagship initiatives give a thematic focus to reform efforts. In some areas like the initiative on the digital economy, there is significant space for legislative action. In areas like the Innovation Union, the emphasis is also on EU research expenditure and structural funds towards the objectives of Europe 2020. As for the European Platform Against Poverty, there are less precise proposals for 'initiatives' combined with aspirations to build on the concepts of active inclusion (Armstrong 2012: 219–220). With respect to the individual targets for Europe 2020 concerning the European social dimension, in employment, the aim is to increase the number of individuals in work to 75 per cent (age 20–64). In the field of education and training, the aim is to reduce school drop-out rates to less than 10 per cent and to increase the share of the population aged 30–34 who have completed tertiary education to at least 40 per cent. While in poverty and social exclusion, the target is to reduce the numbers poor across the EU by 20 million. Note that for the latter policy area, this is the first quantitative target in the field and on paper represents significant progress, even though the EU's legal competence in the field has remained unchanged.

Despite the ambition of the Europe 2020 targets for the European social dimension, it is worth mentioning the broader structural macroeconomic context within which they are situated. Compared to the Lisbon Strategy, the governance of Europe 2020 represents a step-change in policy coordination with the overall emphasis being on budgetary discipline and fiscal consolidation (Armstrong 2012; Copeland and James 2014). While Member States are to report their progress in the Europe 2020 guidelines in an annual National Reform Programme (NRP), this reporting is explicitly linked to a broader annual governance cycle known as the European Semester. The European Semester tightly couples the policy objectives of Europe 2020 with those of the SGP, the latter having been reformed in the wake of the Eurozone crisis with the aim to strengthen Member State compliance to the rules on government borrowing and national debt. As explained by Dyson and Quaglia (2012: 202), the European Semester developed a new architecture to integrate the surveillance of structural reform policies (Europe 2020), greater fiscal discipline (the reinforced SGP and new national fiscal rules) and macroeconomic imbalances (focussing the BEPG on competitiveness and current account developments). The various elements of the European Semester remain legally separate but are aligned in timing through the governance cycle.

This OMC-inspired system of governance aims to create stronger synergies and linkages between the various aspects of the political economy of European integration.

Conclusion

Prior to the 2010 Eurozone crisis, the European social dimension was therefore not a priority for the EU and remained on the margins of the overall integration project. It was also clear that the political debate within the EU was shifting and the left had fractured. On the one hand, some actors on the left have remained steadfast to the ideology of post-war Keynesianism, such as the ETUC and the European Anti-Poverty Network (EAPN), and those MEPs on the left of the Members of the Progressive Alliance of Socialists and Democrats (S&D) in the European Parliament. The position of these actors is influenced not just by the institutional legacies of Keynesian institutions across Europe but also by a desire to provide a genuine alternative to neoliberalism on the left. Meanwhile, those who identify as being more centre-left have embraced neoliberalism, albeit a version in which the edges of the market are smoothed-out. These are two very different and incompatible positions. To take one example, consider the welfare state and the role of commodification. Keynesian macroeconomics aims to limit the commodification of individuals, while neoliberalism aims to extend commodification. On the left, those who adopt a Keynesian position focus on debates and policies regarding the extent to which individuals and daily life should be commodified. Meanwhile, those of the centre-left focus on the extent to which the state should support individuals during their commodification. This division is fundamentally important to understand division within the European social dimension. It also means that ideologically, the centre-left has more in common with the centre-right, than it does with Keynesianism.

The main division within the European social dimension prior to 2010 was a political battle between a centre-left vision of the EU versus that of the centre-right. To call this, an ideological battle would be something of a stretch, as the division centres around being given a choice between policies that provide for more neoliberalism or those that offer ever so slightly less. The institutional and political setting of the debate is one in which the fundamental purpose of the EU is to make markets and to push for deeper and wider economic integration in the name of neoliberalism. The EU's left has been able to make some progress in the construction of the European social dimension, but it has done so by accommodating neoliberalism, not by altering the fundamental logic of EU integration. Pre-crisis EU political contestation within the European social dimension is therefore between actors who pursue policies that serve to enable the efficient functioning of labour markets, versus those who wish to smooth the edges of such extreme neoliberalism and to support individuals during the pursuit of efficient labour markets. Importantly, the continuous tussle between the centre-left and the centre-right for the European social dimension rests in part because over the last two decades the EU has opted for legally non-binding modes of governance. The fluidity of this form of governance is both a blessing and a curse. On the one hand, it allows for a diverse EU in terms of welfare states and income levels to reach agreements, but on the other hand, the flexibility of the governance arrangements means that they are constantly evolving, depending on the political dynamics of the EU at any one time. The question is: how do these political dynamics play out in a post-2010 EU in the European social dimension? This question will be addressed in the chapters that follow.

Note

1 In 2007, UNICE changed its name to BusinessEurope.

2 Governance in advanced European integration

Introduction

The specific choice of theoretical lens through which to analyse the EU depends on two main points. The first is the ontological and epistemological position of the researcher. In its crudest simplification, theoretical approaches can be positioned along a spectrum. At one end is the positivist tradition, whereby the researcher considers the mode of social enquiry to be scientific and capable of producing rules and laws that explain the topic under focus. These rules and laws can then be used to explain developments in other case studies. At the other end of the spectrum is the interpretivist approach, which claims that the principles of science cannot be adapted to human behaviour and human interaction, and as a result, we can only ever really understand phenomena and draw generalities from events (Furlong and Marsh 2010). The second guiding factor in adopting a theoretical lens is that of the topic or case study under discussion, as some topics lend themselves more easily to certain EU theories and approaches over others. For example, multi-level governance has its origins in EU regional policy, and is frequently used in case studies analysing the policy area, while research into Treaty revisions and other decisions made in the Council that use unanimity voting often use Liberal Intergovernmentalism to explain outcomes. As scholars of EU studies, we probably do not talk about these basics as much as we should, especially compared to other sub-disciplines of the social sciences, e.g. international relations (IR), but it is important to emphasise that theory is not just chosen at random – it is based on an interaction between the position of the researcher and the topic under analysis.

In the case of the European social dimension and as discussed in the previous chapter, research is predominantly situated in the governance approach. This is because the barriers to integration via more traditional means, i.e. hard law, have resulted in legally non-binding modes of governance being used that are flexible and respect the diversity of welfare states found across the EU's members; such flexibility has helped to overcome resistance from the Member States in the Council. Such innovative modes of governance, although not exclusive to the European social dimension, have developed their own analytical framework over the past three decades as part of the governance turn in EU studies. Broadly, governance sees policy as being developed, agreed and implemented by a broad range of state and non-state actors thereby gaining the consensus and expertise necessary to identify complex policy problems and their solutions in contemporary capitalism. The governance approach has made a significant contribution to the analysis of European integration and the European social dimension, and the approach has the added benefit of being sufficiently broad enough to incorporate the range of ontological and epistemological positions found within the social sciences. For example, there is a tendency within the governance approach to draw from the new institutionalists approaches of rational, sociological, historical and discursive institutionalism (Hall and Taylor 1996; Schmidt 2008).

This chapter provides the necessary theoretical lens through which to analyse post-2010 developments within the European social dimension. It situates itself within the governance approach, but overcomes some of the inherent weaknesses found within existing frameworks: that of the absence and thereby the inclusion of issues of power and politics within contemporary governance frameworks. The decision to side step power and politics from EU governance owes much to the early governance literature, which claimed that relations between actors in governance were non-hierarchical, thereby suggesting that different groups of actors were near equal. However, this decision has also been influenced by a rejection within EU scholars to the grand debate on European integration. The grand debate had drawn inspiration from very traditional theories of IR and was obsessed with the sovereignty and thereby the power of the nation state during the integration process. On the one hand, intergovernmentalists argued and continue to argue in the form of Liberal Intergovernmentalism, that the EU does not erode national sovereignty as it is an international organisation whereby the Member States remain in the driving seat. Neofunctionalists argue that regional integration in the form of European integration will develop its own momentum and undermine state sovereignty. The governance turn in EU studies shifted analysis into what Caporaso (1996) referred to as a 'post-ontological' phase and was an antidote to a grand debate that was suffering from fatigue. By shifting the analysis away from questions of sovereignty and power to how the EU works, much has been learnt about the processes of European integration, but, I believe, much has also been lost. The absence of the concepts of power and politics within mainstream governance approaches to EU studies creates a tendency towards apolitical findings. This is a problem in the sense that such research generally supports the status quo of the political order. The approach developed in this chapter responds to this weakness and proposes a governance framework through which to analyse developments within the European social dimension. I refer to this approach as '*governance in advanced European integration*'. The approach developed is much closer to interpretivism than positivism, and while this may be a less fashionable position than has previously been the case, it is nevertheless one that remains useful to understand European integration and to frame analysis.

This chapter is divided into four main parts. The first section reviews the grand debate. While the reader may be all too familiar with it, it is important to underline what the debate was ultimately concerned with. It is only then that we fully appreciate how and why the governance approach emerged and what it does differently. The second section focusses on the main weakness of the grand debate: that it failed to acknowledge the changing nature of the state and the changing nature of the European integration project. From 1986 onwards, European integration as a peace-building project for the European Continent was replaced by the need for a European project to transmit and manage neoliberalism. The latter having filled the ideological void left from the demise of Keynesianism and the collapse of the Bretton Woods System. The new *raison d'être* of European integration generated alternative theoretical approaches to study the EU, much of which stepped away from IR-inspired theory and borrowed the tools of comparative politics. The governance approach is one such framework and its emergence and main tenants are outlined in the third section. However, as explained in the final section of the chapter, the moving away from the grand debate towards governance has also had its problems. It too has failed to fully grasp the purpose of European integration post-1986, the reconfiguration of the state, and the power and politics attached to this process. By doing so, the governance approach in its existing form provides a one-dimensional understanding of developments within the EU. The remainder of the section is devoted to correcting this deficiency by outlining 'governance in advanced European integration'.

The grand debate – neofunctionalists versus Intergovernmentalism

The grand theoretical debate on European integration – neofunctionalism versus Intergovernmentalism – has its origins in IR theory and, prior to the mid-1990s, had dominated the debate on the process. Both theories attempted to explain the character of European integration, albeit they drew two very different conclusions on the process. At the heart of the grand debate was the central concern of the role of the nation state and the question of state sovereignty or power – in other words, the ability of a nation state to determine and execute its own autonomous decisions. The neofunctionalist theorisation that regional integration would result in the erosion of state sovereignty by nation states was juxtaposed with the intergovernmentalist position that integration would not result in an erosion of state sovereignty, and that nation states would remain fully in control of the process. The peaks and troughs of both these theories corresponded with actual developments within the process of integration. Readers of this chapter will be familiar with the grand debate, but it is worth briefly considering the nature of the beast.

For Haas (1964), the founder of neofunctionalism, the process of European state cooperation was conceived as one in which the integration of one policy area would create pressures in a neighbouring policy area and ultimately lead to further integration. Initially, integration would proceed in the areas of 'low politics' – key strategic economic sectors such as coal and steel – with the creation of a high authority to oversee the integration process. The integration of economic sectors across nations would create functional pressures for the integration of further sectors. This momentum is likely to continue, especially with the guiding role played by the high authority. The result is a chain reaction of integration driven by continued 'spillovers' (Rosamond 2000: 50–51) and such 'spillovers' come in three different forms.

1   Functional spillovers, where one step towards cooperation functionally leads to another. An example being the spillover of the Single European Market (SEM) into the area of health and safety. The different standards that existed between the Member States distorted competition and as a result, governments accepted the need to harmonise health and safety standards with the creation of EU directives, even though this had not been their original objective.
2   Political spillovers stem from the gradual shift of national political elites and interest groups to argue that supranational cooperation is needed to solve specific problems. Overtime, interest groups and national actors begin to shift their loyalty to the supranational level.
3   Cultivated spillovers refer to situations in which supranational actors – especially the European Commission – push the process of integration forward when they draft policy proposals or mediate between the Member States, by pushing for policy solutions that favour supranationalism (Strøby Jensen 2016: 57–58).

As a result of the various spillovers stemming from the regional integration process, the Member States experience a reduction in their sovereignty and ultimately lose some control over an 'inevitable' process. Despite the relevance of neofunctionalism in the immediate aftermath of the signing of the Treaty of Rome (1957), by the late 1960s it was failing to fully capture the dynamics of European integration. The claim that the process of European integration would be gradual, automatic and incremental toward deeper integration and supranational influence, proved both overly optimistic and inaccurate (Moravcsik 1993: 476). Following the Empty Chair Crisis, whereby in 1965 French President Charles de Gaulle withdrew the French representative from the Council in response to growing supranationalism, the 1966 Luxembourg compromise gave the individual Member States a veto over any decision it believed it to be in its national interest. The compromise resulted in gridlock in the European Council. Research by Lindberg and Scheingold (1970) highlighted that European integration could also 'spill back', thereby retreating to the status quo prior to the initiation of integration. Indeed, the turbulent political and economic conditions of the 1970s seemed to suggest this could be the case. The collapse of the Bretton Woods system of pegging currencies to the US Dollar corresponded with the 1973 Oil Shock, which set the Western economies on a path of recessions and high inflation (discussed below). The ineffectual coordinated response by the EEC to these turbulent conditions undermined the purpose of European Integration (Keohane and Hoffmann 1991: 8). This period corresponded with only limited progress in the deepening of European integration and of muddling through (Armstrong and Bulmer 1998: 15–16).

It is within this context that Intergovernmentalism developed as an alternative explanation to neofunctionalism. Intergovernmentalism has its origins from classical theories of IR, notably realist or neorealist accounts of interstate bargaining, albeit at a very general level (Pollack 2010). Realism views international politics as the interaction of self-interested states in an anarchic environment in which no global authority is capable of securing order (Morgenthau 1985). States are rational, unitary actors that define their interests based on an evaluation of their position in the system of states (Dunne and Schmidt 2011). While negotiation outcomes are shaped by the distribution of state power, whereby the most powerful dominate, states can cooperate, if only as a rational means of state survival. For intergovernmentalists then, state cooperation is about finding common solutions to common problems, but any attempt to build a community beyond the nation state will fail because state preferences or interests rarely converge. Cooperation between states is therefore conservative and pragmatic, and European integration represents a highly institutionalised form of international cooperation that is simply a more advanced form of an international organisation (Cini 2016: 67).

From the perspective of Intergovernmentalism, Member States are the most important actors for determining the speed and direction of European integration, and they remain in control of the process (Cini 2016: 67). European integration implies at most a pooling or sharing of sovereignty, rather than its erosion or loss for the nation state and thereby the transfer from the national to the supranational level (Keohane and Hoffmann 1991: 277). In this frame of thinking, EU institutions are agents that ensure inter-state bargaining commitments are honoured and they are unable to play an independent or autonomous role within the process of European integration. Nation states, therefore, delegate authority to international institutions, and although this will allow cooperation to be more effective, it does not imply a loss of sovereignty – the Member States remain in control of European integration and they have the final say in any developments. Given Member States' preoccupation with the economic turbulence of the 1970s and the limited progress made to deepen European integration, Intergovernmentalism, penned by Stanley Hoffmann (1995, 1966), resonated with the empirical developments of the EEC at the time. Explaining European integration required an appreciation that national interests, underpinned by the cultural differences of Member States, served to check any move towards European federalism, which is the endpoint of the neofunctionalist spillovers. Member State diversity, created from a combination of domestic factors and the situation of the state in the international system, create forces that place limits on European integration (Rosamond 2000: 76). The latter is particularly relevant given the continued expansion of the EU to include Member States with an ever-greater diversified set of interests.

The revitalisation of the European integration project in the mid-1980s gave the grand debate a wealth of empirical evidence from which to mine and claim that one theoretical perspective over the other was more accurate in explaining the process. The signing of the SEA aimed to not only complete the Internal Market for physical goods with the removal of all barriers and tariffs, but there were several changes to the Brussels decision-making process. First, QMV was introduced in the Council of Ministers in several policy areas, effectively speeding-up decision-making. The introduction of QMV offered a more rapid legislative route than unanimous voting in the Council which was one of the root causes of the EU's inability to respond to the conditions of the 1970s (Armstrong and Bulmer 1998: 23). Second, the role of the European Parliament was strengthened with the introduction of the Cooperation Procedure. This gave the European Parliament a voice within policy negotiations relating to the SEM and the working environment. In conjunction with this reform, the Commission's mediatory powers were increased, enabling disagreements between the Council and the Parliament to be resolved more easily. Finally, linked to the institutional reforms were a series of substantive changes to specific policy goals to increase the role of the EU in the areas of social policy, environmental policy, research and technology and cohesion policy (Armstrong and Bulmer 1998: 27–28).

Given such developments the question of whether European integration resulted in a reduction of Member State sovereignty and a loss of control of the process (neofunctionalism) or simply regional cooperation in which Member States remained in the driving seat (Intergovernmentalism) persisted. While the contents of the SEA were rather narrow, according to Armstrong and Bulmer (1998: 2), it 'triggered policy activism in a range of policy areas beyond the Single European Act itself'. A result was the 'spillover' of the Act, which had only concerned itself with the elimination of tariffs and barriers for physical goods, into policy areas such as transport, telecommunications, energy and services (Schmidt 2002). The political energy that surrounded the SEA and the integration project of the late 1980s and early 1990s should not be underestimated, as Member States appeared to signal their desire to move European integration forward. Jacques Delors, the then-President of the European Commission, is often credited with cultivating a desire at the EU level to move European integration much further and deeper than had hitherto been the case with such agency normally referred to as 'Commission entrepreneurship'. However, it is also obvious that there was widespread support across the governments of the Member States in the Council to push for further integration. Commission entrepreneurship versus the preferences and steering of the Member States were to represent the continued dividing line between the two opposing schools of thought in the grand debate.

Developments from the Maastricht Treaty changes continued the theoretical divide. Maastricht is credited with setting out the timetable for Economic and Monetary Union, but it contained several important reforms and revisions that both extended the Community's powers and served to limit its expansion. The three-pillar structure grouped EU competences into areas with each pillar having different roles for the institutions, thereby striking different balances between Intergovernmentalism and supranationalism. Pillar I mainly related to the SEM and predominantly used the Community Method of Decision-Making, while Pillars II (Common Foreign and Security Policy) and III (Justice and Home Affairs) consisted of intergovernmental cooperation. The Community was given new competences in areas of education, culture, public health, consumer protection, trans-European networks, industry and cooperation (Phinnemore 2016: 21). However, the Maastricht Treaty changes also introduced the Principle of Subsidiarity for areas where the EU does not have an exclusive competence. The Principle of Subsidiarity states that the EU may only make legislation where the action by individual countries is insufficient. In other words, action by the EU can only be taken when the objectives of an action cannot be sufficiently achieved by the Member States alone – the aim being to have decisions made as close to EU citizens as possible. Therefore, should a Member State or a group of Member States wish to put a brake on, or oppose, a proposed policy in an area of shared EU policy competence, they can refer to the Subsidiarity Principle.

Further brakes on European integration by the Member States were also apparent at Maastricht. During the negotiations both Denmark and the UK secured legal opt-outs from Economic and Monetary Union. The Social Chapter, which formed the basis of integration for the European social dimension, did also not to apply to the UK, while Denmark was granted a de facto opt-out from involvement in the elaboration and implementation of foreign policy decisions and actions that have defence implications. A further complication for the grand debate was that while the Member States had agreed to move towards supranationalism in monetary policy with the formation of a single currency, in the areas of budgetary and fiscal policy, they opted for intergovernmental arrangements with the Member States 'retain[ing] ultimate responsibility for their economic policies' (Article 103). Under Article 103, the Member States are required to regard their economic policies as a matter of common concern and are obliged to coordinate them with the Council. A crucial role was attributed to the formation of the BEPG, which constitute a reference frame for conduct, and regular monitoring and assessment by the Commission and the Council in the areas of budgetary and fiscal policy (European Commission 1995: 7).

Theoretically, the grand debate was reaching its limit, as it was unable to fully explain the process of European integration. This did not stop the emergence of Liberal Intergovernmentalism, a more refined version of Hoffmann's Intergovernmentalism, penned and staunchly defended by Moravcsik (1993, 1998, 2018). Liberal Intergovernmentalism rests on two basic assumptions: first, that states are actors and achieve their goals through intergovernmental negotiation and bargaining, rather than through a centralised authority making and enforcing political decisions; and second, that states are rational and calculate the utility of alternative courses of action and choose the one that maximises their utility under the circumstances. Decisions to cooperate internationally can be explained in a three-stage framework (Moravcsik 1998). First, state preferences, which centre on economic interests and geopolitical considerations, are determined by national governments (not international institutions) as an aggregate of the interests of domestic constituents (Moravcsik and Schimmelfenning 2009: 70). Second, bargaining between states reflects an asymmetrical interdependence; that is, states that are least in need of a specific agreement are best able to threaten others with non-cooperation and thereby force them to make concessions; those who gain the most economically from a proposal compromise most of the margins to realise such gains, whereas those who gain the least tend to enjoy more clout to impose conditions and extract concessions (Moravcsik 1998: 3). For the bargaining theory to hold, negotiations are required to take place in a non-coercive, unanimous voting system where transaction costs are low and asymmetrical interdependence defines relative power (Moravcsik and Schimmelfenning 2009: 63). Third, once the Member States have reached an agreement, they delegate authority to (EU) institutions which increase the credibility of mutual commitments and reduce the temptation for Member States to cheat or defect. In this context, the role of institutions is limited and 'supranationalism is a controlled means of implementing intergovernmental bargains' (Wincott 1995: 602).

While Liberal Intergovernmentalism generated theoretical debate, scholars of EU studies began to shift their attention away from the grand debate. Arguably, the contents of the Maastricht Treaty (1992) fundamentally shifted the nature of European integration – it was beginning to resemble a fuzzy mix of supranationalism and Intergovernmentalism and it was clear that the dichotomy of the grand debate could not fully capture the essence of the European project. The debate has experienced something of a renaissance since the financial crisis and the Eurozone crisis (Bickerton et al. 2015). Much of the focus and attention within this research, but not all, is on the EU's response to the Eurozone crisis and the preference for intergovernmental decision-making and policy outcomes. In other words, research has focussed on the explanatory causes behind the absence of pooling of sovereignty in response to critical juncture that has been the Eurozone crisis. Fabbrini (2013) argues that EU policy areas can be identified as being either supranational or intergovernmental and the situating of policy areas in one or the other is the norm within European integration. Importantly, for those areas that are intergovernmental, Member States have continued to prefer intergovernmental solutions to common problems with a preference for 'coordination', rather than the pooling of sovereignty. Up until 2012, the EU's response to the Eurozone crisis was driven by the relationship between Angela Merkel, the Chancellor of Germany, and Nicholas Sarkozy, the President of France (Schoeller 2018). Merkozy, as they were often referred to, both preferred intergovernmental solutions to the situation, rather than the drift towards supranationalism. Guided by the Presidential style of politics in France, Sarkozy preferred the crisis to be resolved by the exclusive hands of the governments within in the European Council and the ECOFIN Council (or the Euro Summit and the Euro Group regarding the Euro-Area Member States), rather than involve the broader set of EU institutions. This position also suited Merkel and reflected a shift in the German position towards European integration. Having been open to further integration within the European project as a means to achieve reconciliation and atonement in post-war Europe, Germany, under Merkel, became more concerned with protecting and defending German interests. For Fabbrini (2013), this shift represented a new post-war generation of German politicians. Furthermore, intergovernmental solutions to the Eurozone crisis would prevent Germany from having to fund and subsidise other EU Member States when governments have not taken responsibility for their macroeconomic policies.

While Fabbrini (2013) aligns himself with Liberal Intergovernmentalism *a la* Moravcsik, Bickerton *et al.* (2015) provide a modified version of Liberal Intergovernmentalism, known as 'new Intergovernmentalism'. The authors argue that since the signing of the Maastricht Treaty, the basic legal parameters of the EU and hence the sovereignty of the Member States have remained stable. Meanwhile, EU activity has expanded by an unprecedented degree, albeit there has been a preference for Intergovernmentalism rather than supranationalism in such policy areas. For the authors, the unravelling of the post-war compacts, such as the Keynesian welfare state, have resulted in a convergence of interests and a desire for European solutions to common problems. However, this integration momentum is contained by the breakdown of the 'permissive consensus' in which people deferred decisions regarding the pooling of sovereignty to elites (Lindberg and Scheingold 1970; Lahr 2002: 248). The rise of Euroscepticism is given as one of the main reasons for the breakdown of the consensus. As a result, Bickerton *et al.* prove six hypotheses in which, while they acknowledge the intergovernmental nature European integration, wish to distance themselves from Liberal Intergovernmentalism. The claims are as follows:

- Deliberation and consensus have become the norm during the EU decision-making process;
- Supranational institutions are not hard-wired to seek ever-closer union;
- When delegation occurs, governments and supranational actors prefer new bodies, rather than an increase of powers by, say, the European Commission;
- Domestic preference formation is complex;
- The differences between high and low politics have become blurred;
- European integration is continuously influx and unstable.

Drawing from these newly formed principles of new Intergovernmentalism, Hodson and Puetter (2019) account for how the process of European integration has been able to accommodate the Eurosceptic movement since the signing of the Treaty of Maastricht. This new wave of academic research is somewhat different to the work put forward by Moravcsik, as it is much more critical about the process of European integration and argues that the EU's tendency is to produce policy outputs that polarise politics in ways that cast doubt on the future of the EU. This disequilibrium is the product of dysfunctional outputs by integrationists and consensus-seeking elites on the one hand, and dysfunctional inputs, including public scepticism about the benefits of European integration and declining trust in the EU and national political systems on the other. For Hodson and Puetter (2019), the current disequilibrium in the EU is a real cause for concern and the future of the EU is uncertain. Nevertheless, this strand of literature is an attempt to catch up with the reality of European integration in the context of multiple crises and possible disintegration.

The limits of the grand debate

The strengths and weaknesses of the grand debate are well documented and for the reader, they should not need repeating in their entirety (Pierson 1996; Stone Sweet and Sandholtz 1997, 1998, 1999; Wallace et al. 1999; Wincott 1995). However, this section will argue that the main reason the grand debate reached its limit is because, from the mid-1980s, the nature and focus of European integration shifted from regional cooperation as a peace-building project for the European Continent, to one in which European integration was to serve, and continues to serve, as a regional solution to the changing structural conditions of the global economy. Such structural conditions reflected the decline of the post-war Keynesian consensus and their replacement with neoliberalism. The replacement of the former with the latter was by no means a straightforward process, but as will be discussed below, the European regional structures that had been in place during the Keynesian consensus (1946–1971) proved themselves to be adaptable for the new neoliberal global order. European integration therefore became a regional solution to manage neoliberalism and the result is that the nature and power of the nation state fundamentally shifted. The grand debate therefore became obsolete because of its fixation with an out-of-date concept of the state. It is worth exploring this issue further.

The post-war Keynesian state, as featured across the Western Continent until the late 1970s and referred to by Ruggie (1982) as 'embedded liberalism', enabled countries to build their economic policies around the protective barriers of capital exchange controls, fixed but adjustable exchange rates to the US Dollar, and optional barriers to trade – referred to as the Bretton Woods system. While capital controls mainly applied to companies, such was the extent of these controls that they could also apply to citizens who were travelling abroad and were exchanging their domestic currency for a foreign currency. These controls were necessary to keep national currencies pegged to the dollar and thereby avoid significant swings in exchange rates. What differentiated Western capitalist states from one another was the level of state involvement within the economy which the Bretton Woods system afforded. As the varieties of capitalism literature have illustrated, the actual level of state involvement across the European Continent varied from country-to-country (Bohle and Greskovits 2007; Hall 2007; Hall and Soskice 2001; King 2007; King and Sznajder 2006; Rhodes 2005). Significant differences existed between the German model of Ordoliberalism, French dirigisme, Scandinavian corporatism and UK liberalism – each striking a different balance between state involvement in the economy, the role of the trade unions and employers associations, as well as cultural-historical practices of economic policy.

The period also witnessed a progressive expansion of the welfare state 'from cradle to grave', although as with economic policy, countries developed their own distinct models that should be regarded as complementary to their varieties of capitalism. Ebbinghaus and Manow (2006) suggest that welfare state-economy linkages within varieties of capitalism manifest themselves in the relationship between social policy and the system of industrial relations, production systems and employment regimes and financial and corporate systems. The complementarity between the welfare state and a variety of capitalism enables a particular model to maximise its efficiency in terms of the sectors or industries that a country specialises in. For example, the long-term perspective often taken by German industry, the cooperative relations between employers and employees and a supportive vocational and training system directly linked to industrial development have historically enabled the German economy to specialise in the manufacturing of high-value export-oriented products. Meanwhile, the German welfare state provides for several supportive formal and informal structures, such as extensive dismissal protection and an insurance-based model of welfare run by semi-autonomous non-state bodies and administered by employers and employees. As a result, German labour tends to be less mobile between employers and more likely to switch roles within an existing organisation, thus ensuring that employer investments in education and training are more likely to be recuperated in productivity gains. All of this suggests that from a political economy perspective, the varieties of capitalism/varieties of welfare state literature, which often differentiates between the two, are different sides of the same coin.

Bretton Woods partly reflected the decision to sacrifice financial liberalisation in the interest of creating a stable exchange rate system and a liberal trading order to avoid the economic instability of the interwar period. Such certainty also served to encourage international trade with Helleiner (2000: 165) suggesting that 'finance could be said to have held a kind of second-class status in the post-war vision of a liberal international economy'. The impact of capital controls had a direct consequence on the ability of countries to exercise government self-determination (sovereignty). Governments could set levels of taxation considered desirable by the electorate without the fear of money moving abroad (capital flight). In other words, if income tax or corporation tax increased, individuals or companies could not easily move their investments to another country where taxation was lower and thereby returns on investment potentially higher. Meanwhile, the revenue from such tax increases could be spent by either smoothing out the peaks and troughs of the economic cycle or on investments such as the welfare state. Under such a system, government attempts to inflate or deflate the economy were more easily controlled and more predictable. A further central aspect of this system was high levels of organised labour, who were included into the decision-making process at various levels of government in the form of social dialogue and/or collective bargaining. As with the level of state involvement in the economy, there were differences in the individual organisation of labour across the European Continent (Hall and Soskice 2001).

The Bretton Woods system was not without its problems, as some countries experienced balance of payments problems for which they were required to borrow from the International Monetary Fund (IMF) and take corrective action, normally in the form of deflation, which was unpopular with the electorate. Some countries also had difficulties in maintaining their exchange rate parity with the dollar (discussed below). But provided a country was prepared to adhere to the criteria of the international system, there was a considerable amount of domestic autonomy exercised by elected governments, particularly in the context of state ownership of industry and the ability of governments to directly create jobs, as well as the independence to determine tax levels and thereby spending on the welfare state. Within this context, it is easy to see why scholars of IR-inspired theory of European integration conceived sovereignty as being solely exercised by the state/elected governments, as relatively speaking, governments had the ability to forge their own domestic priorities and policies.

The transformation of state-centred sovereignty began in 1971 as the Western States proceeded to lift capital controls and promoted financial market liberalisation and deregulation. While there had been tensions between the Bretton Woods members regarding capital controls in the run-up to their liberalisation, the death knell to the system was the USA's decision to end the convertibility of dollars to gold. In keeping their exchange rates pegged to the dollar, countries would buy and sell foreign currency, mainly dollars, to manipulate the market. The USA guaranteed the conversion of dollars into gold (at a rate of $35 per ounce of gold) and it was hoped that countries would hold dollars as they were 'as good as gold'. However, from the 1960s, the US balance of payments deficits steadily got worse, particularly in the context of the Vietnam War. To plug the deficit, the USA printed more dollars, which other countries were prepared to accept as reserves. World liquidity expanded rapidly, thereby fuelling world inflation. Furthermore, the rapid growth in overseas dollar holdings meant that US gold reserves were becoming increasingly inadequate to guarantee convertibility. Some countries, fearful that the USA might eventually be forced to suspend convertibility, chose to exchange dollars into gold. The US's gold reserves began to dwindle, and international speculation regarding the US economy put further strains on the system. As a result, President Richard Nixon announced in 1971 the end of converting dollars into gold, preventing the pegging of the exchange rate to the dollar (Sloman 1995: 1003).

Under the domestically closed economic system of Bretton Woods a definition of sovereignty, understood as the right of a state to govern itself, is convincing. Relatively speaking, elected governments could make some substantial policy changes and the balance of power between labour and capital was more equal than is the case during the post-Keynesian period. But as the varieties of capitalism literature has demonstrated, the demise of the Keynesian consensus also corresponded with a decline of state autonomy over the last four decades. As countries moved from relatively closed economies to more open economies from 1971 onwards, floating exchange rates combined with the eventual removal of capital controls meant that capital could more easily move across international borders and invest in the most profitable places than had hitherto been the case. Capital thus became internationally mobile, thereby undermining the effectiveness of Keynesian demand management. For example, as investment is a key contributor to economic growth, the international mobility of capital can be problematic for governments as there are no guarantees that domestic capital will invest at home. The sensitivity of global capital to taxation and labour costs, particularly corporation tax, often results in capital 'venue shopping' to find the best place in which to invest. This often places a downward pressure on levels of taxation, as demonstrated by the case of Sweden in the 1990s (Pontusson 1997). This, in turn, reduces state revenue and government ability to deliver public services, and this is further problematic given that advanced capitalism is experiencing an ageing population.

The demise of Keynesianism corresponded with a turbulent decade for the global political economy in which stagflation, i.e. low growth and high inflation, became the key characteristic of the day, although the USA and Japan weathered the 1970s more successfully than the major European economies (Sandholtz and Zysman 1989: 109–110). Against this backdrop, the process of European integration stalled, as governments attempted to grapple with the international economic conditions at the domestic level. Furthermore, decision-making gridlock in the European Council and an ineffectual coordinated response to the 1973 oil crisis all seemingly combined to undermine the purpose of European integration (Keohane and Hoffmann 1991: 8). As Armstrong and Bulmer (1998: 15–16) put it, 'the ensuing "dark ages" period was characterised by only limited progress in the deepening of European integration' and 'of muddling through'. Europe was often viewed as politically and economically stagnant with the term 'Eurosclerosis' used to describe its then current state (Keohane and Hoffmann 1991: 6).

By the mid-1980s, the process of economic liberalisation – epitomised by Ronald Reagan in the USA and Margaret Thatcher in the UK – had gained appeal in its position as a credible ideological blueprint to fill the void left by the collapse of Keynesianism. Ideologically, neoliberalism aims to remove direct government involvement in the economy by privatising once state-owned assets, prioritising the needs of capital over labour, and ensuring that markets remain as deregulated as possible to maximise their efficiency. At the heart of this philosophy is a transfer of some state power and responsibility to the decisions and preferences of multinational corporations, such as where to invest and thereby create growth and jobs – an autonomy that the Bretton Woods system, with its capital controls, had curtailed. With the operations of companies more geographically spread across the global economy, the ease of doing business across various geographical locations requires goods, services and capital to be easily transferred from one country to another, all of which is aided by a reduction or elimination of policy differences between countries (Cerny 1994, 1996, 1997a, 1997b). Western adoption to neoliberalism was an uneven process. While certain countries were clearly pace-setters, others were more hesitant. France had blamed international economic conditions for the domestic economic crisis of the 1970s, and in 1981, François Mitterrand was elected President on a platform to revitalise the French economy with Keynesian policies. The policies of the socialist government – nationalisation and increases in public spending both of which were funded by increases in taxation – resulted in capital flight, speculative attacks on the Franc, inflation, and a worsening of the economic situation. As a result, in 1983, Mitterand announced the famous French Socialist U-turn calling an end to socialism in France, the prioritisation of controlling inflation, and the subsequent introduction of monetarist policies (Helleiner 1995; Schmidt 1996). The episode is a textbook example of where power had shifted to in the post-Bretton Woods era.

As neoliberalism was gaining traction across the EEC Member States, the SEA (1986) was presented as an antidote to stagflation by liberalising the European economy. According to Nugent (1999: 49), the SEA was something of a 'mixed' bag in that it contained tidying-up provisions, provisions designed to give the Community a new impetus, and provisions that altered the Community's decision-making system. Firstly, the completion of the Single European Market (SEM) by 1992 was added to the Treaty. This built upon the Milan agreement reached by governments in 1985 and endorsed the Commission's White Paper which contained some 300 proposals (later reduced to 282) and centred on the removal of physical, technical and fiscal barriers (Armstrong and Bulmer 1998: 23). The 1992 deadline and its addition to the Treaty ensured that the completion of the SEM legally binding, thereby providing an added incentive for Member States to adhere to the legislative programme. Secondly, the SEA introduced QMV in the Council of Ministers in several policy areas, effectively speeding up decision-making. The introduction of QMV offered a more rapid legislative route than unanimous voting in the Council which was considered to be one of the root causes of Eurosclerosis (Armstrong and Bulmer 1998: 23). Thirdly, the role of the European Parliament was strengthened with the introduction of the Cooperation Procedure. This gave the Parliament a voice within the negotiations relating to the Internal Market and working environment. In conjunction, the European Commission's mediatory powers were increased enabling disagreements between the Council and the Parliament to be more easily resolved. Finally, linked to the institutional reforms were a series of substantive changes to specific policy goals in the areas of social policy, environmental policy, research and technology, cohesion policy (see Armstrong and Bulmer 1998: 27–28).

Although the contents of the SEA were somewhat narrow, according to Armstrong and Bulmer (1998: 2) it 'triggered policy activism in a range of policy areas beyond the SEA itself'. The SEA greatly boosted integration in many EU sectoral policies with transport, telecommunications, energy and services among the policy areas that were essentially a spill-over from the SEA. The SEM, as it became known, was therefore created by the dynamic spill-over effect of the SEA into several (predominantly) market-making policy areas (Armstrong and Bulmer 1998; Schmidt 2002). For Young (2005: 100), the SEA represented 'a strategic policy change and institutional reform [that] were linked symbiotically and symbolically'. In fact, the SEA represents a seismic shift within the process of European integration. Just as the Bretton Woods system of stable exchange rates was an attempt to globally institutionalise and manage Keynesianism, from 1986 onwards, the process of European integration is an attempt to institutionalise and manage neoliberalism. By the early 1990s, Streeck (1995: 35) argued that the contents of the Maastricht Treaty changes required European integration theory to move beyond the teleological federalism that had informed most of the past debate. The idea that European integration would develop into a federal state misunderstood the role that European integration was playing in the transformation of the post-war Keynesian state. While European nation states were ceding important economic functions, either to the market or to international organisations, they were reluctant to go further. That is, while they had experienced some reduction in their *internal sovereignty* – their ability to formulate and exercise autonomous economic policy decision – Member States had resisted any form of pooling or reduction of *external sovereignty* in the form of IR (Streeck 1995). In this frame of thinking, the end point of neofunctionalism is that a traditional state emerges at the regional level to replace the various states of its members, but the 'state' as a theoretical construct remains the same and it will be a copy of the traditional European state.

The move from Keynesianism to neoliberalism therefore resulted in a shift in the structure of the state and our understanding of sovereignty. Sovereignty, as understood by traditional IR theories of European integration, has seeped from elected governments to the whims and preferences of business and finance. As such, traditional European integration theory has become less relevant to explain the process of European integration because it is attached to a theorisation of the state that no longer exists. In her 1994 article 'Wake up, Krasner! The world *has* changed', Susan Strange vented her frustration at the persistence of realist theory despite, in her opinion, it being outdated for contemporary application. This had similar echoes in studies of European integration as the grand debate originates from realist theory. Strange's solution to this problem, was for scholars to adopt and explore approaches from international political economy. However, in the search for an alternative to the grand debate, we should be cautious of Strange's suggestion that international political economy becomes the only framework through which to analyse European integration. Rather EU studies need to move away from outdated conceptualisations of state sovereignty just as the broader fields of IR and international political economy have been able to do so. In this regard, the more recent literature on 'new Intergovernmentalism' goes some way to acknowledging the changing structural conditions of the state and the impact of this on our theoretical understandings of European integration. In the future, it may prove itself to be a useful framework to analyse the EU, but the elephant in the room with such an approach is that it did not see the various EU crises coming. Meanwhile, new Intergovernmentalism required a reinterpretation of historical events (the post-Maastricht era), thereby demonstrating that the EU theory constantly evolves.

The governance approach

Theoretical debates across the whole of political studies were to change rapidly throughout the 1990s and scholars of European integration could both draw from, and contribute to, this movement. The search for alternative theoretical approaches for European integration was to occur at a time when the disciplines of politics and IR were also experiencing rapid change, along with the integration process itself. The shift away from the grand debate manifested itself in two ways. The first was to reject neofunctionalism and (liberal) Intergovernmentalism but to replace them with a suitable IR-inspired grand theory. With its concern for state power and sovereignty, multi-level governance aimed to move beyond the dichotomous debate on European integration. It was first introduced to capture developments within EU Structural Policy (Eising 2015; Marks 1993; Marks et al. 1996; Piattoni 2009). EU Structural Policy made the administration of the Structural Funds subject to partnerships between local, national and supranational actors – the logic here being that successful policy outcomes require actors from the different levels of government (or governance) to effectively cooperate and coordinate activity. According to multi-level governance theorists, this transformation has eroded the sovereignty of the European nation state from several directions, most notably to the European level and the subnational level (local and regional). The result is a weakened nation state and a strengthening of the European and subnational states.

Beyond the Structural Funds, the multi-level governance approach has been applied to a broader range of EU decision-making areas (Knill and Liefferink 2007; Smith 2011). However, it should be noted that the extent to which the EU is a *genuine* multi-level governance entity, beyond a select few policy areas, is contentious. A second issue is that multi-level governance continues with the 'obsessive sovereignty disorder' of IR-inspired approaches of European integration, but the latter is not all bad news: a valuable contribution of multi-level governance is to highlight that the power of the traditional nation state has been eroded and that power has not only seeped vertically (upwards to the transnational level and downwards to the regional/local level) but also horizontally to non-state actors who are involved in the process of governance. What multi-level governance does less successfully is to acknowledge the fundamental reasons as to why all of this is happening. While it can sometimes be beneficial to leave questions open-ended, thereby allowing individuals to draw their own conclusions, it is disappointing not to see those questions being asked in the first place. The danger here is that not only is the EU some distance from a genuine multi-level governance entity, but that it also cannot be taken for granted that students of multi-level governance see the bigger picture around the process of European integration. As with other IR-inspired theories of European integration, the question as to why it is happening is side-stepped.

A second governance approach has been to abandon any attempt to macro-theorise the process of European integration and to focus on the more day-to-day processes of European integration. For this group of EU researchers, the agenda has shifted to what European policy-processes entail. Given the absence of a single 'ruler' and of a clear dividing line between public and private actors in the EU, some researchers, wanting to distance themselves from state-centric thinking, analyse the EU through a governance lens, which emerged from the late 1980s onwards (Armstrong 2010; Armstrong and Bulmer 1998; Bulmer and Lequesne 2013; Kohler-Koch 1996; Kohler-Koch and Larat 2009; Kohler-Koch and Rittberger 2006). In these works, the Member State is no longer in a situation of monopoly or of hierarchical superiority. The move away from government to governance is conceived as being associated with advanced capitalist democracies. The complexity of contemporary policy problems combined with rising expectations by the electorate of what modern government should deliver requires governments to look beyond the confines of their traditional economic and organisational capacities to meet such challenges. Governments have become increasingly dependent upon the cooperation and joint resource mobilisation of policy actors outside of their hierarchical control. The modern policy-process is therefore one in which numerous different actors from both the public and the private combine to pool resources, identify common problems and find common solutions. In the context of the EU, politics and policies are the results of interactions between the European Commission, the Member States, regions and interest groups. On the one hand, the process of problem definition has been transferred away from national governments to the European level, while the policy-making process at both levels of governance has become more technocratic, with specialist experts exercising more power than the post-war state (Bulmer and Lequesne 2013: 12). However, to group governance researchers as a homogenous school of thought would be misleading, not least because they divide in accordance with the different schools of thought found across the social sciences with the 'governance turn' encompassing a variety of preoccupations and orientations. Before exploring this approach, it is necessary to clarify the difference between government and governance by recalling Gerry Stoker's (1998: 18) five propositions on governance.

1   Governance refers to a set of institutions and actors that are drawn from but also beyond government.
2   Governance identifies the blurring of boundaries and responsibilities for tackling social and economic issues.
3   Governance identifies the power dependence involved in the relationships between institutions involved in collective action.
4   Governance is about autonomous self-governing networks of actors.
5   Governance recognises the capacity to get things done which does not rest on the power of government to command or use its authority. It sees government as able to use new tools and techniques to steer and guide.

Meanwhile, the deepening and widening of the EU's policy competencies drew academic attention to the implementation and impact of EU policy at various levels of government, the role that different actors play in this process, whether they be state or non-state actors, and why sometimes compliance with EU policy varies both within States but also between them (Falkner and Treib 2008; Falkner et al. 2007). Related to this issue was the actual changing nature of the mode of policy that was coming out of Brussels. Up until the Maastricht Treaty (1992) changes, the dominant mode of policy was traditional hard-law, which had a harmonising effect across the Member States and whose implementation was underpinned by the threat of infringement proceedings by the European Commission. Legally non-binding EU policy had started to emerge from Brussels in the 1970s; this mainly took the form of Green and White Papers and European Council resolutions, but from the early 1990s onwards, it was to play an increasingly important role in the development of European integration. Under preparations for Economic and Monetary Union, it was decided that fiscal policy was to be 'coordinated' with clear benchmarks regarding the public finances of the Member States established. A crucial role was attributed to the formation of the Broad BEPG which constitute a reference frame for conduct, and regular monitoring and assessment by the Commission and the Council (European Commission 1995: 7). Such guidelines were to represent 'a distillation of, and a consensus on, the most appropriate macro- and microeconomic policy framework' (ibid 8). Article 103(4) empowers the Council to issue recommendations to individual Member States addressing specific concerns, but it was hoped that 'normal peer group pressure at the Community level will be sufficient to elicit the necessary policy adjustments'. The EU's economic pillar was therefore strongly intergovernmental and the Commission's competences much weaker than in the Single Market, competition, external trade and monetary policy (Dyson 2000; Verdun 1996).

The new policy process of the BEPG, in which tangible threats were limited, was the inspiration from which the EES was modelled, as well as the Lisbon Strategy and Europe 2020. The EES, launched at the Luxembourg Jobs Summit in November 1997, aimed to steer an increase of employment within the Member States (Rhodes 2000). The intergovernmental governance mechanism used commonly agreed targets and benchmarks in the form of the employment guidelines. Progress by the Member States was to be reported in an annual NRP, which is reviewed by the European Commission and the European Council. Following the review, CSRs can be issued in areas of weakness for the individual Member States before the annual cycle recommences (Copeland and ter Haar 2013). The Lisbon Strategy, which aimed to make the EU the most competitive and dynamic knowledge-based economy in the world by 2010, broadly employed the governance method introduced from the EES and it was coined as the OMC. The OMC was applied to numerous policy areas, covering pensions, healthcare, education and training, research and innovation, and social inclusion, to name but a few (Copeland and Papadimitriou 2012). Despite the legally non-binding nature of the OMC, it was envisaged that periodic reviewing of progress and peer pressure would stimulate the necessary reforms across the Member

States. Meanwhile, such reforms required both state and non-state actors to cooperate and guide policy reform, hence the 'Open' Method of Coordination. These non-state actors were to include the broadest possible range of actors, such as social partners, charities, non-governmental organisations, interest groups and policy experts.

The governance approach has had one of the most significant impacts on analysing the EU's social dimension. Indeed, on paper, the EES and the OMC during the Lisbon Strategy epitomised the conceptualisation of governance processes. The shift from government to governance in the European social dimension is given a variety of reasons. In the first instance, the diversity between the Member States presents itself as an obstacle: what is a minimum standard of labour protection in the Scandinavian Member States will be too generous for Eastern and Liberal Member States. The expansion of the EU to include 2004, 2007 and 2013 Member States has increased EU diversity in terms of economic growth, development and employment traditions (Copeland 2012b, 2014a; Menz 2015; Vaughan-Whitehead 2003). A result is that reaching agreements for hard law in the European social dimension is near impossible, although it should be remembered that it was also fraught with difficulties when the EU had 12 and 15 Member States (Copeland 2014b: 13).[1] Related to this is a second point in that within the Council and the European Commission there may have been a genuine belief that the governance arrangements were a viable alternative to the Community Method and that they would deliver the expected results. The flexibility that they provide may have been considered a necessity given the scope and scale of reform required to European welfare states. Third, from 2004 onwards, the centre-right leanings of both Barroso Commissions, as well as the Council tilted the balance towards a liberal coalition of actors at the EU level who favoured minimal, if any, EU policy in the social dimension (Copeland 2014a: 24–27). Fourth, however, we should not discount the logic of Streeck's (1995) argument that resistance within the Council to supranationalism in the European social dimension is because it is conceived by the Member States, either rightly or wrongly, as being one of the few remaining policy areas in which governments can pursue policy independence. There is further pressure to protect the advancing of supranationalism in the field, given that welfare policies are highly sensitive to electoral support.

In accordance with the broader analysis of the governance approach across the social sciences, the EU literature has focussed on understanding and explaining governance processes, as well as analysing their impact. There is a tendency to conduct such research within the Europeanisation approach, although the level of engagement with the framework can vary significantly from a rich empirical and theoretical exploration via case studies, to a mere mentioning that findings represent evidence of Europeanisation. Regardless, the Europeanisation literature has identified itself as a key approach to analyse EU policy formation and domestic policy change during the governance processes surrounding European integration. Europeanisation is conceived as a circular process in which political actors first 'upload' their preferences to the European level and thereby construct EU policy, and second, 'download' Europe's policies, institutions, rules, beliefs and values to the Member State and sub-national level. In theory, the subsequent downloading stage can generate long-term convergence across the EU but may also generate divergence. Radaelli's (2003: 30) well-known definition defines the process as:

> Processes of (a) construction, (b) diffusion, and (c) institutionalisation of formal and informal rules, procedures, policy paradigms, styles, 'ways of doing things' and shared beliefs and norms which are first defined and consolidated in the EU policy process and then incorporated into the logic of domestic (national and subnational) discourse, political structures, and public policies.

During the uploading stage, national actors attempt to export their preferences to the EU level that correspond to a 'goodness-of-fit' with domestic policy. If successful, the downloading of EU policies can be a relatively straightforward and inexpensive process. Börzel (2002) refers to such behaviour as being that of 'pace-setting'. By contrast, actors from the Member States that are unsuccessful during the uploading stage will face high adaptational costs during the downloading of EU policy. They may even attempt to block or delay costly policies in order to prevent them altogether or to achieve at least some compensation for implementation costs: such Member States are known as foot-draggers. In contrast, fence-sitters aim neither at initiating or promoting specific policies nor at resisting attempts by others to do so. Rather they take an indifferent and neutral position, or they build ad hoc tactical coalitions with both pace-setters and foot-draggers, depending on the issue involved (Börzel 2002: 207).

Caporaso suggests that the emergence of the Europeanisation approach is intertwined with the governance turn in EU studies, but that the approach is preoccupied with the Member States (and the EU's neighbours), as the growing impact of EU legislation, such as that from the Single Market Programme, impacted on the domestic arena. Empirical research from the new institutionalist approach has revealed two major findings. First, in cases of policy misfit, the more binding EU policies are (i.e. supported by hard law such as regulations and directives), the stronger the adaptational pressure at the domestic level. Second, the more mediating factors (e.g. domestic actors such as governments, political parties, interest groups, etc.) support EU policies, the more intense and rapid the policy change will be (Graziano and Vink 2013: 46). In EU policy areas that use soft law, such as recommendations and communications, as well as the OMC, mediating factors remain important (Graziano 2011; Graziano and Vink 2007; Green Cowles et al. 2001; Gwiazda 2011; Mailand 2008), but compared to hard law, the legally non-binding nature of such governance tools creates weaker adaptational pressures. A result is a much greater degree of uncertainty surrounding the effects and outcomes of Europeanisation in soft law and the OMC vis-à-vis directives.

Given the dominance of soft law in the European social dimension, the process of Europeanisation is a more complex affair and the literature has developed its own conceptual toolkit to understand engagement and impact. For example, analysing the impact of the EES requires research to conceive Europeanisation through several different variables, as Europeanisation that results in programmatic shifts – understood as the introduction of new policy or reforms to existing policies in response to engaging with the OMC – are unlikely. In the context of OMC-inspired Europeanisation, *Agenda shifts* refer to the ability of the OMC to place new issues onto a national political agenda, such as the EES's policy objectives of activation, lifelong learning and gender mainstreaming (Barcevičius et al. 2014). *Procedural shifts* focus on the changes in governance and policy-making and can result from the need to strengthen the horizontal integration of interdependent policy fields through the creation of new formal coordination bodies and inter-ministerial working groups (Zeitlin 2005). They can also enable the creation of formal structures for closer cooperation between national and regional/local administrations in policy-making and coordination (Hamel and Vanhercke 2009). Finally, the 'openness' of the OMC can create or reinforce consultative and participatory structures (Zeitlin 2005). *Cognitive shifts* refer to changes that occur within the mental frameworks of domestic political actors. The OMC has helped to reframe national policy thinking by incorporating EU concepts and categories into domestic debates; exposing domestic actors to new policy approaches, often inspired by foreign examples; and questioning established domestic policy assumptions and programmes (Zeitlin 2005). Mutual learning of developments within other Member States is one of the key achievements of the OMC (2004; Zeitlin 2005). The construction and diffusion of EU ideas and the socialisation provided by EU institutions and policies have constituted a motor of change (Graziano and Vink 2013).

Governance in advanced European integration

Over the last six decades, numerous critiques of the main theoretical approaches have been made and despite claim and counterclaim, theories come and go and often mirror the European integration process. Given that (1) the empirical concern of the research is with developments at EU level in the European social dimension since 2010 and (2) the obvious limitations of the grand debate with its outdated conceptualisation of the state; the research situates itself within the governance approach. However, the constructed approach known as *governance in advanced European integration* responds to a fundamental weakness within the mainstream EU governance literature in the EU's social dimension: that of an almost complete absence of the notion of power and politics and thereby a tendency towards apolitical findings from research. A key contributing factor to this has been the assumption within the governance literature that governance relations are non-hierarchical. Relationships between all actors, regardless of time and space, feature power relations and power asymmetries that produce and reproduce hierarchy, priority and privilege. As power is the currency of politics, governance arrangements are also inherently political. The basic assumption of non-hierarchy has been the single biggest misconception within governance and EU studies over the last two decades. It has resulted in research claiming that anything suggesting an outcome for the European social dimension is considered a positive outcome, regardless of the politics of that outcome and the actors involved.

A second factor creating this tendency is that the governance literature has lost sight of the 'bigger picture' that surrounds the process of European integration and is therefore witness to an academic silo. The governance approach in EU studies has unwittingly failed to grasp the purpose of European integration post-1986, the reconfiguration of the European state, and the impact this has on how we understand governance. Admittedly, the difficulty for researchers is that the process of European integration is something of a moving target – the 'end-point' is unclear and could be one of the numerous possibilities. The EU could evolve into a federal or multi-level state, it could remain a fuzzy mix of Intergovernmentalism and supranationalism, or it could disappear altogether. Often scholars deal with this by claiming that the EU is *sui generis* because it does not fit perfectly into the theories inspired by IR or political studies. While this is indeed the case, the governance literature is limited when it comes to reflecting on the consequences of this assumption. While the framework developed in this section assumes that the EU is *sui generis*, it also assumes that it is *sui generis* because it represents Europe's attempt to respond to and manage neoliberal globalisation and the reconfiguration of the capitalist state. This may sound like the banging of an old drum, but it is *fundamental* to understand EU governance and the process of European integration. To paraphrase Strange (1994), the process of European integration *has changed* and to adopt the current mainstream within the EU governance literature without acknowledging the bigger picture is to provide a one-dimensional understanding of the topic under analysis. The below outlines the main tenants of the framework to understand governance during the advanced stages of European integration and broadly draws from political sociology. It aims to bring power and politics back in from the margins in the analysis of EU governance and will be used to guide analysis during the remainder of the book. It makes the following claims.

1   European integration is a regional response to manage neoliberal globalisation and the associated reconfiguration of the European state.

2   At the centre of this reconfiguration are the shifting power relations between different groups of actors. Such power differentials are materially
and ideationally determined and there is fierce rivalry between groups
of actors for the control of the policy agenda.

3   In advanced capitalist democracy, grand macroeconomic decisions predominantly favour the operations of the business community, but more
specifically, global capital. In second-order issues, understood as policy areas such as education and training, social policy and employment
policy, there is significantly more contestation and policy can potentially diverge from a dominant macroeconomic paradigm.

4   Governance arrangements therefore feature a hierarchy in which some
issues – grand-order issues – are prioritised and given more attention
and resources than others – secondary-order issues.

5   Within this hierarchy policy areas do not operate in isolation of each
other, rather governance arrangements feature high levels of policy interdependence in which decisions in one area can have consequences for
other policy areas. The power relations and thereby the direction of flow
between interdependent policy areas is normally, though not always,
influenced by the governance hierarchy.

A first point to note is that the framework assumes that from 1986 onwards,
European integration is a regional response to globalisation. Governments
of European states used the structures of the EEC to 'manage' neoliberalism
at a regional level. While contemporary political sociology normally links
developments within political economy to neoliberal globalisation either
implicitly or explicitly, given the above critique made regarding the governance approach it is essential to explicitly make this point, even if by now
the reader is aware of the claim. For political sociologists, it is necessary
to establish the symbiotic causality between neoliberalism and European
integration not because it foretells all aspects of European integration, but
because it alludes to why European integration is occurring, the structural
conditions in which decisions are made, and the broad parameters in which
the process moves forward. By outlining the structural conditions of European integration, we are then able to draw attention to the issue of power
and hierarchy within the integration process– that is, who has power, how
that power is distributed, how that power can be used, and how groups of
actors can attempt to challenge that power.

Underpinning the power of actors are material and ideational differences between different groups. While the process of European integration is fundamentally a market-making one, the European political space
is one in which different groups of actors will have different ideas on how
best to govern. To understand the broad contours of political division between actors, we can refer to the EU clash of capitalisms approach (Callaghan 2008; Callaghan and Höpner 2005; Clift 2009; Copeland 2014a;

Hooghe 1998; Hooghe and Marks 1999). Accordingly, actors within the EU's political space can be positioned along a two-dimensional axis. The horizontal axis is the classic political spectrum which ranges from left to right and concerns economic equality and the role of the state. Alongside the left-right dimension is a vertical axis with a spectrum of nationalism versus supranationalism and concerns the role of the nation state as the supreme arbiter of political, economic and cultural life. The nationalism versus supranationalism distinction has its origins within the Eurosceptic versus pro-European dimension that is evident within political arenas. At the one extreme are those who wish to preserve or strengthen the nation state; at the other extreme are those who wish to press for ever-closer European integration and believe that national identities can co-exist with an overarching supranational identity (Hooghe and Marks 1999: 76). Within the EU's political space attitudes within the two dimensions coalesce to form a dominant political cleavage ranging from leftist orientations and supranationalism which support traditional social democracy to right-wing orientations which support nationalism and neoliberalism. Put simply, divisions exist over whether the EU should be a simple market-making process inspired and guided by a neoliberal ideology with minimal regulation and the promotion of competition between the Member States; or whether it should enhance more market-supporting policy to create a competence in the European social dimension (and eventual European social model) (Copeland 2014a: 41). However, it should be noted that in the context of the European social dimension and the EU's left, actors further divide into those who accommodate neoliberalism and those who remain steadfast to post-war Keynesian social democracy. The broader political environment in which governance is situated therefore features such divisions between EU actors. Inspired by Lipset and Rokkan (1967) with their more classic analysis of cleavages, the more recent literature on post-functionalism theorises and analyses the establishment of new political cleavages across the EU, as the reconfiguration of the state (to that of a multi-level state) and the disruption of traditional party cleavages may even conflict with the functional pressures of European integration (Hooghe and Marks 2009, 2019). While this is an important development and can be accommodated by the theoretical approach put forward in this chapter, the main focus of this book is on developments at the EU level. These new post-functionalist political cleavages have yet to coalesce around the European Semester, albeit they may do so in the future.

In terms of the decision-making process of governance, those who have the most resources normally have the most influence on political decisions. This point was made by Charles Lindblom (1977) when he argued that business leaders have a privileged position within market economies (advanced capitalist democracy) such that they are a second set of leaders in government.

As the independent decisions of business are responsible for the health of the economy, government and business must collaborate and to make the system work. The key to understanding this relationship is the role of private enterprise in a market economy, whereby the decisions of its leaders in the form of investment, ordinarily determine economic growth and the rate of job creation. However, these are also issues for which political parties can win or lose elections and as a result, government leadership must ordinarily defer to business leadership regarding any major decisions within political economy; collaboration and deference between the two are at the heart of politics in market economies for 'grand-order issues'. For Lindblom (1977), the relationship between government and business is therefore necessary for a market society, and while government exercises broad authority over business activities, this is curbed by its concern for possible adverse effects on business for fear of creating unemployment. However, business does not always have its own way, particularly when it comes to secondary issues, that is, those which do not concern the fundamentals of the macroeconomy and the operation of business. On such secondary issues, business leaders are themselves in disagreement on them and often subdivide along sectors, size, geographical location, and so forth. This subjects citizens to competing messages and may allow for some interest groups other than business to influence decisions. Secondary issues may relate to policies other than those of macroeconomic policy, such as the employment policy found within the European social dimension.

When it comes to the ideational influence of business, business leaders of global capital ordinarily coalesce around a blueprint or script for macroeconomic decisions, although this is not always a straightforward process (Bieler 2008, 2005a, 2005b; van Apeldoorn 2002). We can refer to such a blueprint as an ideology, and while capitalism is a system of political economy in which primacy is given to private property and the role of free enterprise, it has proved itself to be an adaptable system of governance coalescing around different ideologies of a market economy at different times, e.g. Keynesianism, neoliberalism, etc. Given the ascendency of neoliberalism within the European business community, particularly multinational corporations, there is an obvious tilt towards the process of European integration, particularly regarding macroeconomic decisions within political economy. It is around the secondary-order issues that a greater level of contestation will take place and policies and interest groups are more likely to deviate from the script of a dominant ideology. As discussed above, the European political economy has substantially changed since Lindblom (1977) was penning his work, both in terms of its ideological underpinnings and what we now consider to be dominant business actors. First, there is the well-documented ascendency towards neoliberalism in macroeconomic decisions within business leaders and governments, as well as the process of European integration (Schmidt and Thatcher 2013; Thatcher 2013). A second point is that the financial sector is a more influential sector on government decision-making than it was during the 1970s. The steady removal of capital controls has given capital the ability to move freely around the world and to invest in the most profitable places. Meanwhile, the creation of ever-complex financial products that are subsequently globally traded as though there are physical goods, has resulted in a ballooning of the financial sector which employs an increasing number of workers and accounts for an ever-greater proportion of tax returns to government. The global mobility of this sector and its preference for geographical locations that have low levels of taxation and light regulation creates a downward pressure on government finances. Meanwhile, governments are simultaneously dependent on the financial sector to fund shortfalls in government spending and to refinance their debt. Central to the cost of issuing government bonds are calculations that the (private, not public) financial industry makes regarding the long-term health of an economy in question and the likelihood of a default on debt. Higher than perceived acceptable levels of debt-financed government spending and/or higher than perceived acceptable national debt are considered risky for financial investors, regardless of the cause of the problem, and the result will be higher borrowing costs for government. This set of macroeconomic conditions within advanced capitalism constructs a political decision-making process in which, based on the argument put forward Lindblom (1977), the financial industry has a privileged position within the decision-making process of government and thereby in the process of European integration.

Engaged in the process of European integration, individuals and groups mobilise available resources in their struggle for power and influence. However, the scope of action for agents is always constrained by a variety of social, economic, technological and other factors (Kauppi 2011: 152). In the context of the political economy of European integration, the interests of capital and the structural conditions of the European economy exercise a constraining influence on agents and decisions. However, it is important to understand that this influence is 'constraining' rather than determinant, which would lean towards overt structuralism within the analysis. To understand the relationship between structure and agency, it is necessary to draw from the critical realist perspective on the issue and to relate this to the concept of grand and second-order issues in advanced capitalism. A critical realist perspective disentangles the relationship between structure and agency as a continuous interplay between the intentionalist agency of political actors and the structural context of institutions (Bulmer and Jonathan 2016; Dessler 1989; Wendt 1987). Social structures pre-exist the agents who act within their field and are relatively enduring and thereby provide constraints upon the exercise of agency. Meanwhile, agents possess their own irreducible powers, notably intentionality, reflexivity, consciousness and capacity for strategic action. They may not choose the structures in which they operate, but they are aware of their environment and have an ability to take this into consideration when exercising agency. This approach recognises that, while political agency can, and does, have an impact on policy decisions, it does not foretell the extent to which agents can take forward their aims and objectives because this depends on the procedures and agentic possibilities obtaining within the governance structure. Policy outcomes therefore occur in a context where the structural properties of enablement and constraint combine with the agential powers of action and purpose to produce outcomes.

The previous point can be fleshed out further by incorporating the argument made by Lindblom (1977). In the context of the grand- and secondary-order issues of EU policy, grand-order issues will more than often reproduce and favour the current status quo. It cannot be ruled out that they may not favour the status quo, but for the most part, they do. There is often fierce competition between actors to dominate the grand-order ideology and thereby control and domination the political agenda. Against this backdrop, there will be competing projects of European integration and thereby competing ideas and ideological blueprints, but one of them will emerge as the dominant ideology within the political hierarchy for grand-order issues. For example, in the context of Europe 2020, the EU's reform strategy for 2010–2019, it aims to make 'smart, sustainable and inclusive growth'. However, these aims are not all equal and 'smart growth' dominates the governance agenda – broadly understood as maintaining budgetary discipline and Member States remaining within the parameters of the SGP (Copeland and Daly 2014). This priority thereby structures the governance hierarchy and it is the priority from which all other policy priorities stem from. However, when it comes to secondary-order issues such as those of the European social dimension (education and training, employment and social policy), we need to consider the more dynamic nature around secondary-order issues. As such, there is often uncertainty surrounding outcomes – they may favour the ideological dominance evident within the grand-order issues or they may be able to deviate from the script – the possibilities here remain more open-ended compared to grand-order issues and are context specific.

The history of European integration is littered with advances in the European social dimension that represent the policies of the left and the right, and often an agreed policy can incorporate both perspectives, as is the case with the EPG or the Europe 2020 poverty and social exclusion target. However, as discussed in the previous chapter, over the last two decades the European social dimension has experienced something of an ideological narrowing around the neoliberal ideology.

Indeed, secondary-order issues may become the battleground through which the grand-order ideology is challenged or it may become the battleground through which actors attempt to assimilate secondary-order issues with a grand-order ideology. Much of this depends on the politics and interdependence surrounding these secondary-order issues. Within the decision-making process of EU secondary-order issues, social actors can and do forward their agenda, but outcomes are therefore the result of a complex interplay of politics and power on the one hand and policy inter-dependence on the other. It is worth briefly expanding on these two points. First, the politics surrounding secondary-order issues in the context of the EU decision-making process points to an often-overlooked feature: that the decision-making process is something of a revolving door and thereby dynamic. Elections in the Member States take place at different times, resulting in the political configuration of the European Council continually changing and thereby influx between a majority of centre-left governments and a majority of the centre-right. Council Presidencies can also make modifications to decisions affecting day-to-day governance processes and policy and will have their own aims which may or may not materialise. The European Commission will also have its own initiatives, particularly when it takes office. Whether the Commission can influence the outcome of EU decisions remains disputed, but at a minimum, it is a powerful agenda setter. Related to the politics of governance are the opportunities that are subsequently given to actors within the governance mainstream. For example, actors may be strategically locked out of the decision-making process or they may, via changing political dynamics, be given the opportunities to have their voice heard – although we cannot rule out skilful actors exercising their agency and being able to seize opportunities and to gain influence. Related to the political dynamics of the EU is the organisation of actors around second-order issues. Their organisation and resources will be dependent on the political situation, and the better organised they are, the more likely they are to have their voice heard and to gain prominence within the decision-making process.

Second, the decision-making process around secondary-order issues is also related to the independence and interdependence such actors have to make decisions. As well as governance arrangements featuring hierarchy, they also feature policy interdependence whereby policy areas overlap and there is contestation for their control. Analytically, researchers often put policy areas into neat little boxes, but the reality is very different. In their search for power and influence, actors engaged in the grand-order decisions will try to influence, either directly or indirectly, the secondary-order issues. They may even be able to 'capture' some secondary-order issues and to assimilate them with the grand-order ideology, but in a capitalist democracy, they will be unable to capture all the secondary-order issues. Take, for example, the issue of the welfare state. Social actors will have a variety of ideas on how best to tackle social and employment problems, but such policies will ordinarily involve spending and for this, they will be reliant on the decisions made in grand-order issues to take them forward. Social actors may need to compromise on what they can achieve, and the ability to take policy forward may come with conditions that money is spent in a particular way, thereby predetermining outcomes. Grand-order issues and the actors involved in their governance may act as powerful veto-players over agreements in secondary-order issues. Furthermore, anything that fundamentally challenges the status quo may be regarded as inappropriate or too risky. Alternatively, actors involved in the governance of second-order issues may be given some freedom and space to determine outcomes, but much of this depends on the context.

Conclusion

For the research that follows, EU governance is therefore understood as featuring power relations and power asymmetries that produce and reproduce hierarchy, priority and privilege. The political hierarchy that exists during the advanced stages of European integration can be divided into grand-order issues and secondary-order issues. Grand-order issues are those that determine the macroeconomy and are strongly associated with the business and financial community. Such grand-order issues will produce and reproduce their own dominant ideology and in the context of European integration, the dominant ideology is neoliberalism. While secondary-order issues concern policy areas such as education and training, social policy and employment – in other words, policy areas of the European social dimension. Whether secondary-order issues conform to grand-order issues depends on a variety of factors and is context-specific, but in general, they relate to the extent to which policy interdependence is exercised, and thereby the degree to which secondary-order actors have autonomy to make decisions.

The following chapters analyse developments within the secondary-order issues of European integration – the European social dimension – since 2010. Chapter 3 analyses the governance architecture from which post-2010 policy within the European social dimension is predominantly made. Europe 2020, the EU's economic and social reform programme for the decade outlines the objectives for the social dimension, the governance of which is to be achieved via the European Semester. The European Semester is an annual governance cycle, something of a macro-OMC to govern all previous open methods of coordination and includes the EU's grand and secondary-order issues. Attention is paid to the politics, priorities, power relations and policy interdependencies within the European Semester. The fourth chapter analyses the outcomes of the European Semester and assesses the extent to which social actors have been able to advance their cause. The fifth chapter analyses how actors from the European social dimension navigate and negotiate the European Semester in the context of the constraints and challenges they have faced.

Note

1 For example, between 1997 and 2017, only a handful of directives in the social dimension were negotiated and given the various provisions in the EU Treaties, the directives concerned employment policy and not social policy. These included the revision of the Working Time Directive which ended with no agreement, the temporary agency work directive (2008) and the revision of the Posting of Workers Directive (2018).

3 EU economic governance and Europe 2020

Introduction

That there are significant power asymmetries between economic and social actors at the EU level is well documented and has been analysed in the previous chapter. Post-1986, the *raison d'etre* of European integration shifted from being a peace-building project on the Continent to one in which regional integration was to manage the new neoliberal global order. Hence, the abundance of literature exploring and confirming that the process European integration predominantly concerns itself with making markets and the free flow of goods, services, capital and labour (Bieler and Morton 2001; Scharpf 1996, 2002; Schmidt 2002; Schmidt and Thatcher 2014). In this regard, the development of a European social dimension is a secondary-order issue in the process of European integration, or an add-on or afterthought (Daly 2006: 462–465). Developments within the European social dimension therefore need to be understood within the broader context within which they are situated. That is, they need to be considered against the purpose of European integration, who has power and who has less power, and the politics of the social dimension and how all this influences outcomes.

Europe 2020, the vehicle taking forward the EU's economic reform strategy and policy commitments for the decade, including those within the European social dimension, rests on three economic reform objectives that are designed (in theory) to be mutually reinforcing: 'smart growth' based on a knowledge economy; 'sustainable growth' promoting resource efficiency; and 'inclusive growth' focussing on high levels of employment and social cohesion (Copeland and Daly 2014: 355). Within the European social dimension, Europe 2020 contains the first quantitative EU commitment to reduce the number of people living in poverty and social exclusion by 20 million by 2020, the target population being identified via a multidimensional approach to defining poverty and social exclusion. The strategy also contains the employment guidelines that aim to increase EU employment rates to at least 75 per cent of the working population during the same period. As well as containing market-making policies, the employment guidelines also aim to regulate against the worst excesses of the free market, for example, by curbing precarious employment conditions. In this regard, the Europe 2020 guidelines for the European social dimension continue with the EU's tradition of compromise between the centre-left and centre-right within the EU's political space.

The agreement of Europe 2020 by EU leaders dovetailed with the EU's response to the Eurozone crisis, and this was to have significant consequences for the EU's new economic reform strategy (Armstrong 2012; Copeland and James 2014; Degryse 2012; Dyson and Quaglia 2012). To improve the functioning of the Eurozone and to prevent a future similar crisis, the EU introduced the European Semester – an annual governance cycle in which macroeconomic policy is scrutinised and corrected to ensure that the Member States remain within EU benchmarks. There were also several other reforms to EU economic governance designed to improve the functioning of the Eurozone and to reinforce budgetary and fiscal discipline. The objectives of Europe 2020 were included into this governance mainstream and the purpose of this chapter is to analyse and explore the priorities, political hierarchies and power relationships underpinning the EU's economic governance since 2010. During the uncertainty surrounding the Eurozone crisis, financial actors within the Council and the European Commission exploited the opportunity, dominated the reform agenda, and recast the strategy and various governance reforms on their own terms. As a result, social actors were marginalised during the early years of the European Semester and were further disadvantaged in the EU's political space. The reforms to EU economic governance thereby further strengthened the asymmetries between economic and social actors within the EU and the political environment within which the social actors were to achieve their goals, including the Europe 2020 guidelines. This chapter analyses these developments and the structural conditions of the EU's post-2010 economic governance. The first section of the chapter analyses the causes of the Eurozone crisis and the EU's initial attempts to address it. The second section of the chapter focusses on the formation of Europe 2020, as well as the aims and objectives of the economic reform strategy. The governance arrangements introduced to govern EU fiscal policy and Europe 2020, as well as to improve the policy interdependencies between the various policy areas are interrogated in the third section. The final section of the chapter outlines the political hierarchy of the post-2010 governance arrangements and thereby the structural conditions within which social actors are required to operate and achieve their aims.

The Eurozone crisis and its impact on EU economic governance

The financial crisis that started in 2007/2008 revealed the limitations of the governance processes of the Eurozone. The collapse of the US sub-prime mortgage market and the subsequent near meltdown of the global financial system provided the Eurozone with a 'large symmetric shock with significant asymmetrical effects [on its members]' (Hodson 2010: 225). How developments in the US economy came to jeopardise the financial system, the existence of the Eurozone, and the broader economies of both Eurozone and non-Eurozone EU members is a tale of the increasing risk taken by the financial sector, ever greater global economic interdependence, and poor regulatory oversight of the activities of financial institutions (Acharya and Richardson 2009; Bellamy and Magdoff 2009; Carmassi et al. 2009; Crotty 2009; Dyson and Quaglia 2012). Scholars have long identified the post-Bretton Woods era as one of 'Casino Capitalism' (Strange 1997) thereby highlighting the growing dominance of financial markets in determining the macroeconomy, but the decade prior to the crisis is particularly notable for the rapid expansion of the sector and its willingness to take ever greater risk in the pursuit of creating more complex financial products which could be bought and sold for profit (Crotty 2009; Ivanoa 2011a, 2011b). The crisis originated in the US housing market whereby a significant number of mortgages were granted to households with risky/poor credit ratings in the belief that the economic boom and bust cycle had been eliminated and that house prices would continue an upward trajectory. Typically, these sub-prime mortgages – a somewhat derogatory term given to the lending of money to individuals in a precarious financial situation – were for 100 per cent of the market value of a property which further increased the risks to the lender should repossession occur (foreclosure). As interest rates began to rise from 2004 onwards, borrowers in the sub-prime mortgage market began to face increasing difficulty repaying their mortgages. By the end of 2007, the number of home repossessions had spiked and there were serious concerns that banks would have to write-off a significant amount of bad debt, but a problem for Europe was that its banking system was also exposed to developments in the US. Such exposure was a result of the process of securitisation whereby sub-prime loans were repackaged into bundles with other loans and sold or resold to investors, such as European banks and their investment arms. Such was the scale and complexity of the trading in securities that it took months for banks to calculate their overall exposure to the sub-prime market and thereby their losses.

The uncertainty caused by the evolving collapse of the sub-prime market dented market confidence and thereby the interbank lending market, the latter being a crucial mechanism for financial institutions to lend from each other on a short-term basis to plug gaps in their liquidity. The crisis was therefore initially one of liquidity caused by a significant drop in market confidence. In September 2007, Northern Rock, a former UK Bank specialising in mortgage lending and reliant on short-term financing for 75 per cent of its funding, faced a (re)financing crisis as fears grew among potential lenders over whether the bank would be able to repay new short-term loans when they matured and whether the lenders themselves might face liquidity shortages in the interim (Quaglia et al. 2009: 65). This financial model was not confined to Northern Rock, as in 2007, bank deposits funded less than half of the assets of the five largest banks in several European countries meaning that they were overly reliant on foot-loose wholesale funding (De Grauwe 2008). By February 2008, the UK government had been forced to nationalise Northern Rock, thereby placing the bank into state ownership. Despite the unfavourable financial environment, it was believed that the European economy would be largely immune to the financial turbulence that began in the late summer of 2007 (European Commission 2009: 8).

The optimism in European capitals was to change dramatically in September 2008 with the rescue of Fannie Mae and Freddy Mac, the bankruptcy of Lehman Brothers, and fears that the collapse of the insurance giant AIG would take down major US and EU financial institutions. In the Autumn of 2008, several European banks were to receive bailouts from their respective governments including the UK's Royal Bank of Scotland Group, Lloyds TSB, Halifax and Bank of Scotland, Belgium's Fortis and Germany's Hypo Real Estate Group. For a moment, there were concerns that financial markets would collapse, but government intervention adverted the crisis (Copeland 2014a: 474–475). In October 2008, the then UK government announced details of its financial rescue plan. The British Plan was articulated on three points: liquidity provision to the financial system, through the special liquidity scheme operated by the Bank of England; banks' recapitalisations, whereby the government would buy banks shares; and government guarantees of new debt issued by banks (Quaglia 2009: 1069). In response, the Eurogroup of Member States approved a concerted action plan modelled on the UK plan and urged all EU countries to adopt its principles (Quaglia 2009: 1072). Meanwhile, to avoid or minimise an economic recession, the EU simultaneously negotiated and agreed the European Economic Recovery Plan in November 2008. The Plan aimed to encourage the EU and its Member States to inject the European economy with €200 billion (1.5 per cent of GDP) to boost demand and governments could exceed the parameters of the SGP for up to two years, i.e., national debt could exceed 60 per cent of GDP and the annual budget deficit could also exceed 3 per cent of GDP (European Commission 2008). The Plan also aimed to guide the investment into areas such as workforce skills, energy efficiency, low carbon technologies and infrastructure. The Commission's document regarded such 'smart investment' as being crucial for the long-term growth of the European economy.

Despite various national plans from the Member States (France, Germany, Italy, Netherlands, Spain, UK), the European Economic Recovery Plan failed to prevent a recession, although it may have helped to reduce the severity of it, albeit the extent to which is unclear (Hodson and Puetter 2016: 367–368). For several authors, the European Economic Recovery Plan and the various government interventions into the financial markets were representatives of a Keynesian turn within national governments (Degryse 2012; Gamble 2013; Newell and Paterson 2010; Watt 2009).

However, as discussed below, this development was a temporary response to exceptional circumstances and did not give rise to any long-term changes to the EU's economic paradigm of promoting market efficiency, deregulation, free competition, non-intervention by the state in the economy (Degryse 2012: 20). The reversion came from the pressure exerted by financial markets in response to the ballooning public debt and deficits across both Euro and non-Eurozone Member States that were a result of the various bank bailouts/nationalisations, the fall in tax receipts and rise in costs to unemployment support because of the economic slowdown, and the funds required for the European Economic Recovery Plan. The government deficit to GDP ratio for EU-27 increased from 2.3 per cent in 2008 to 6.8 per cent in 2009; meanwhile, government debt to GDP ratio increased from 69.4 per cent to 78.7 per cent. The downgrading of government bonds from the credit-rating agencies for some Eurozone countries resulted in a spike in costs for such countries when it came to financing government deficits and refinancing national debt. The brief Keynesian turn within European capitals had therefore not been shared by the broader set of actors involved in the governance of the European political economy, particularly those in the financial community who wished to maintain the ideological dominance of neoliberalism and to 'correct' any deviation from the script (see Schmidt and Thatcher 2014: 1–52). The rules, which had been established to govern the Eurozone in the form of the SGP, which the Member States had only broadly followed during the Lisbon decade and, in any case, were arbitrary benchmarks/rules, were now being used by the financial markets to discipline the Eurozone.

The financial crisis, which originated in the private sector, had therefore spilt over into a sovereign debt crisis and was about to threaten the very existence of the Eurozone. 2009 signifies the beginning of the Eurozone crisis, sparked by the exceptional circumstances of 2007/2008 but, more broadly, a result of the poor institutional design of governing the Eurozone. In other words, given the governance arrangements of the Eurozone and the lack of reform to some economies during the Lisbon decade, a crisis for the Eurozone was always a question of when, not if, it would happen. Prior to the crisis, Eurozone governance had paid little, if any, attention to the issue of macroeconomic imbalances between the Member States; rather, it was fixated with a very narrow definition of economic governance in the form of maintaining within the public borrowing and debt-levels of the SGP, and the result was to be catastrophic. Southern (or peripheral) Eurozone Members benefited from a sharp fall in borrowing costs under the euro and this stoked-up inflation, economic activity and generated asset bubbles – especially house prices. Meanwhile, slow-growing, low-inflation countries were in a mirror-image vicious circle, facing slow growth and low inflation with relatively high interest rates. The situation was exaggerated by the one-sided nature of the SGP: slow-growing economies were prevented from pursuing expansionary fiscal policies, while faster-growing economies were not constrained. This situation led to faster nominal wage/price growth in peripheral countries reduced competitiveness in deficit countries while stoking the demand for imports. The reverse situation was to be found in surplus countries, such as Germany, where domestic demand was stagnant and economic growth was driven by exports, some of which went to deficit countries (Frieden and Walter 2017: 373–374; Leschke et al. 2012: 258–259).

The turning point for the sovereign debt crisis came from developments in the EU's periphery. The Panhellenic Socialist Movement (PASOK) won the 2009 Greek elections and in October 2009, George Papakonstantinou, the new finance minister, announced that budget deficit for 2009 was triple than previously thought. The figure of 3.6 per cent of GDP reported by the previous government of Costas Karamanlis (New Democracy) was in-accurate: it was upgraded to 12.8 per cent of GDP, then increased further to 13.6 per cent when further calculations were made in 2010. The credibility of Greek statistical data, as well as its ability to repay its debt, was called into question. All three major credit-rating agencies further downgraded Greece's status, with Fitch leading the way on 8 December 2009 and Standard and Poor eventually judging Greek bonds on 27 April 2010 to have 'junk status'. As Greece faced the maturation of a sizeable portion of its foreign debt on 19 May 2010, the sequence of downgrades greatly exacerbated its position (Featherstone 2010: 199–200). According to Featherstone (2010: 200), 'the role played by the credit-rating agencies brought into sharp relief their highly influential role in a changing international political economy'.

Given the approaching deadline for the refinancing of debt, as well as an over reliance on running a budget deficit to maintain the flow of money, by early 2010, the Greek government found itself in an untenable financial situation: not only could Greece default on its loans, but there was also a strong chance that it may run out of money. Over the first few months of 2010, the EU's response to the situation, however, was one of near absenteeism, as Greece was simply told to drastically reduce spending and to get its public finances in order (Featherstone 2010). The institutional design of the Eurozone had included the 'no-bailout clause' meaning that should a Member State finding itself in a financially difficult situation, other Member States would not step in and foot the bill. Such a clause was designed to discipline members to remain within the parameters of the SGP, although such discipline clearly had not worked. Meanwhile, financial markets were happy to lend to Southern Eurozone Members, as they believed that the interdependence of the Eurozone economies would mean that states were likely to be bail each other our during financial difficulties (Frieden and Walter 2017: 375). A further problem with the Greek crisis is that it had a contagion effect as Spain and Portugal were also targeted by investors who were increasingly calling into question the ability of the Southern European Countries to finance their government deficits, as well as the level of solidarity between the

Eurozone Member States to tackle the crisis (Degryse 2012: 22). A problem for Spain (and Ireland), however, was that during the Lisbon decade, they had not overspent; rather, their national finances were some of the best in the Eurozone. Their economies had been hit hard due to the near collapse of the financial systems and the bursting, with spectacular effect, of asset bubbles. The different reasons behind the various crises across the Member States served to highlight not only the inadequacies of Eurozone governance during the Lisbon decade but also its naivety: members could get into financial difficulty even when they had followed the rules, but regardless, would not be helped.

Despite delay and dithering by EU leaders and some division over how best to proceed, by the end of March 2010 the leaders of the Eurozone, under the direction of 'Merkozy', the German Chancellor Angela Merkel and the French President Nicholas Sarkozy, had agreed a system of bilateral loans for Member States in financial difficulty that could be called upon in conjunction with financial assistance from the IMF. Greece applied to use this facility in April 2010 and emergency loans were activated the following month. The bailout package included €80 billion from the EU and €30 billion from the IMF, although EU leaders preferred not to use to term 'bailout' and insisted that the arrangements were simply loans. The cost of the bailout was an austerity plan that cut spending, increased taxation, introduced structural reform of the economy and privatised government assets. Against a backdrop of continued market turbulence in May 2010 regarding the speculation that other Eurozone members would require bailouts, the EU agreed the European Financial Stabilisation Mechanism (EFSM) and the European Financial Stability Facility (EFSF). These were two temporary funds that made (symbol for euros) 750 billion available to states in financial dificulty.[1] These two programmes were replaced by a permanent intergovernmental arrangement in 2012, known as the European Stability Mechanism (ESM) (European Stability Mechanism 2017).

For Germany and to a lesser extent France, the bailout of Greece and the EFSM and EFSF were conditional upon a strengthening of budgetary surveillance in the Eurozone. In a joint letter by 'Merkozy' on 6 May 2010, the two EU leaders committed themselves to the stepping-up of budgetary surveillance in the Euro Area including more effective sanctions for excessive deficit procedures, the strengthening of the link between national budgetary procedures and the SGP, broadening EU surveillance to cover structural competitiveness and economic imbalances, and enhancing the effectiveness of economic policy recommendations issued to the Member States when they do not meet EU-agreed benchmarks (Degryse 2012: 25). This agenda was to define the various reforms to EU governance that took place over the next couple of years. As analysed in the next section, reforms to the governance of the Eurozone in the form of greater budgetary surveillance of the Member States by the EU and punishment for those who do not follow the rules were proposed and agreed upon, but this reform agenda became intertwined with formulating a successor to the Lisbon Strategy and thereby the structural reforms of the European economy. Reforms to EU governance were to place a much greater emphasis on monitoring developments across all policy areas to ensure that they adhere to the EU's macroeconomic rules of budgetary discipline. In other words, every policy area that fell within the remit of a successor to the Lisbon Strategy was to be scrutinised much more thoroughly than had hitherto been the case, with the aim of ensuring that government spending got, and remained, under control.

Europe 2020 as a successor to the Lisbon Strategy

Europe 2020, the EU's economic reform programme for 2010–2020, was therefore formulated at a time when the EU was driving forward with its austerity programme and simultaneously initiating reforms to economic governance to ensure that Member States did not overspend in the future. The Eurozone crisis therefore served as a 'focussing event' in which the political climate in the European capitals swiftly changed and the issue of how best to reduce and prevent excessive national government spending and national debt dominated the political agenda. To illustrate this shift in thinking, it is worth considering the ideas that underpinned a successor to the Lisbon Strategy prior to the crisis. In 2008, the European Council endorsed the final three years of the Lisbon Strategy and instructed the Commission to start reflecting on the EU's economic and social priorities beyond 2010 (European Council 2008). Discussion within the European Council focussed on the need for Lisbon's successor to move away from the narrow growth and jobs agenda of Lisbon II (from 2005 to 2010) and to become more social democratic by addressing public concern about energy, the environment and climate change. The Commission also began formulating plans for a more prominent role for employment and social policy as a way of addressing criticism from stakeholders that the strategy had failed to connect sufficiently with society (EurActiv 2008). Despite this initial surge of activity, the momentum slowed, and in March EU leaders decided to postpone further talks. Progress stalled because of an absence of leadership from both the main EU institutions (Copeland and James 2014: 6–7), caused by a preoccupation at all levels of governance with efforts to resolve the financial crisis and to prevent the European economy entering a recession. But as 2008 and 2009 proceeded, there was now a mismatch between the initial ideas and preparatory work the European Commission had been doing on a successor to the Lisbon Strategy and the economic and political environment. In the Council there was little enthusiasm to champion social democracy during a severe recession and the influence of traditional cheerleaders had waned as they were distracted by domestic economic challenges (Martens and Zuleeg 2009). Such cheerleaders are to be found in the Mediterranean Member States, which predominantly aim to balance market integration with a social democratic-inspired social dimension, but during the crisis, they were under significant pressure to implement austerity and to introduce structural reforms to their 'over-regulated' economies. Historically, such countries have aimed to place the issue onto the EU's policy agenda, support the advancement of a social dimension, and to defend any attempt to retrench social and employment standards across the EU (Copeland 2014a, 2014b). The Northern European Member States, all of which were pushing for austerity and providing most the funds for the bailouts were even more lukewarm than usual regarding the advancing of a social dimension. The financial crisis and the subsequent Eurozone crisis therefore derailed the European Council's 2008 consensus that economic reform and economic growth should be more balanced with a social dimension that both protects individuals while creating growth and jobs, rather than simply generating employment and social problems via a dismantling of employment protection. As such, the public consultation issued during the final months of the first Barroso Commission was somewhat vague and lacking in policy substance, but it did reveal how quickly the political climate had changed. The documents of the public consultation put forward by the Commission suggested a successor to the Lisbon Strategy that differed very little to the mantra of growth and jobs that had emerged during Lisbon II Strategy (2005–2010).

It was not until the beginning of 2010 that substantive progress towards Europe 2020 and the reform of EU economic governance was made. Within the EU institutions, the newly elected President of the European Council (November 2009), Herman Van Rompuy, declared that addressing the economic crisis was his priority. Once the second Barroso Commission was finally confirmed on 9 February 2010, the two leaders decided to work together and agreed to establish a series of regular meetings and an informal division of labour through which to kick start the economic reform process (Dinan 2011). The informal division of labour centred on President Barroso's focus on new policy initiatives and targets for Europe 2020, while Van Rompuy focussed on compliance and enforcement of such benchmarks as well as the broader issues around economic governance. The two presidents were to have a significant role in defining the contours of the agenda, particularly given the divisions that existed between the Member States in the European Council. The national position papers submitted during the consultation process for a successor to the Lisbon Strategy reveal support for the Commission's ambition that the new strategy should address the fiscal and macroeconomic challenges emerging from the Eurozone crisis, but beyond this there was division. Southern and Eastern Members called for enhanced governance through binding economic convergence criteria and a strengthened link between Europe 2020 and the SGP – that is the aims and objectives of both were to be given an equal status. Opposition to such substantive reforms was led by Northern European

Members, particularly Germany and the Netherlands who resisted further supranationalism, as well any simultaneous reporting of the SGP with Europe 2020 (Copeland and James 2014: 9). The concern with the Northern Members was that such a move could divert attention away from the SGP and the need for budgetary and fiscal discipline. In other words, such a reform could be strategically used to undermine the requirements of the SGP by highlighting policy areas in which spending should not be cut. The Northern Member States clearly wanted to prioritise the rules of the SGP and to ensure that progress could not be derailed by actors strategically using the objectives of Europe 2020.

Divisions between the Member States enabled the Commission to exploit the ambiguity surrounding both the crisis and the Europe 2020 strategy, and DG ECFIN used this opportunity to strengthen its already-privileged role within EU governance process. DG ECFIN therefore formed strategic alliances with both the President of the Commission, via the Commission's Secretariat General, and the President of the European Council. This had been aided by the appointment of Oli Rehn as the Commissioner for Economic and Financial Affairs in the second Barroso Commission, a Finnish liberal who replaced the Spanish Socialist Joaquin Alumnia and who was a close ally of the President of the Commission. As such, policy entrepreneurs in DG ECFIN seized control of the drafting process of both Europe 2020 and the reforms to EU economic governance. The crisis had provided a window of opportunity to recast Europe 2020 as a bold policy response to the crisis that would provide the EU with the short-term means to exit the crisis, while in the long term, it would provide a framework to continue the necessary reform to the European economy to increase its competitiveness. This recasting would also further embed the EU structural reform agenda within a reformed system of economic governance that enhanced the power and status of DG ECFIN and marginalised other DGS involved in structural reform. During the drafting of Europe 2020 and the European Semester, other DGS for which Europe 2020 contained policy commitments, such as DG Employment, Social Affairs and Inclusion (DG EMPL) and DG Enterprise and Industry (DG ENTR), were side-lined (interviews 2, 16). It is important to note that such side-lining had not occurred during the Lisbon Strategy, even when the Strategy was relaunched in 2005 and less emphasis was placed on the social objectives vis-à-vis 'growth and jobs'. The revised Lisbon Strategy in 2005 established a more central role for the Commission's Secretariat General, while DG EMPL, DG ECFIN and DG ENTR – as well as the corresponding Council committees – we put on an equal footing (Tholoniat 2010: 104).

The pressure of the Eurozone crisis helped to soften the position of governments who were opposed to stronger economic governance (Euractiv 2010), but the proposed Europe 2020 strategy and the resultant reforms to EU economic governance overwhelming favoured economic and financial affairs actors. The broad contours of an agreement were presented to the European Council in March 2010, but discussion of the governance reforms was not presented until the June summit (Zuleeg 2010). To govern the guidelines and targets of Europe 2020, the Commission crafted a new system of governance, known as the European Semester, which featured *ex ante* economic surveillance and proposed that the EU should scrutinise Member State budgets before they were agreed in national parliaments (EurActiv 2010). The European Semester also confirmed and reinforced the reconfiguration of power within the Commission by ensuring that DG ECFIN remained in control of the new surveillance process (Copeland and James 2014: 12). However, as the final agreed version of Europe 2020 reveals, economic and financial affairs actors did not have it all their own way. Importantly, Europe 2020 contained the EU headline target to reduce the number of people living in poverty and social exclusion across the EU by 20 million by 2020. This is something of a surprise, given the political climate across the EU capitals and the capturing of the policy agenda by DG ECFIN. For Copeland and Daly (2012), the inclusion of the poverty target in Europe 2020 was a result of the EU-level social actors lobbying the Commission (such as the European Parliament, the ETUC and the European Anti-Poverty Network) for a successor to the Lisbon Strategy that contained a clear commitment to tackle poverty. In this regard, the target is to be seen as an attempt by President Barroso to appease the social actors and to secure his re-election as Commission President for a second term. Pressure also came from a small group of Member States within the Council which called for a strengthening of the social component in Europe 2020. The position papers of Austria, Belgium, Cyprus, France, Italy, Portugal and Spain all argued that the achievement of the internal market should not be considered as an end in itself. Rather, progress in economic growth and jobs should go hand in hand with the preservation and strengthening of the European social model. These seven Member States lobbied the Commission for the inclusion of a social component to Europe 2020 (interview: Commission 3), and Spain used its strategic position as President of the Council of the EU in the first half of 2010 to put the social dimension on the political agenda with respect to both Europe 2020 and to the broader process of European integration (Spanish Presidency, 2010). A further source of support for this position came from the President of the European Council, Herman Van Rompuy, who was committed to a strong social dimension for Europe 2020.

Despite political division in the European Council, the strongest of which came from Northern and Eastern Members, the June European Council Summit agreement on Europe 2020 included the target headline to reduce the number of people living in poverty and social exclusion by 20 million by 2020 (European Commission 2010a). The target is ambitious in the sense that during the Lisbon decade, when the European economy was growing and unemployment falling, poverty across the EU remained constant.

The only Member State in which poverty fell during the Lisbon decade was Greece and this was achieved in the context of mounting public debt. Reducing poverty by 20 million over a decade, especially against the backdrop of the Eurozone crisis, a severe recession, and EU-driven austerity, is therefore incredibly ambitious. Crucial to the agreement were the assurances given to the Member States that the target would not be legally binding, given the absence of a treaty provision for a quantitative target. Further compromises were also made to ensure that agreement could be reached and included allowing Member States to set their own national quantitative targets for poverty reduction, as well as poverty being defined in a multidimensional manner. The Commission had originally proposed that for the purposes of the target, Member States would define poverty in terms of income poverty – that is a redistributionist definition of poverty based on the classic relative poverty definition whereby those experiencing poverty fall below 60 per cent of the national median income level. But given that poverty is defined differently across the Member States, the final agreement on Europe 2020 included two further definitions: poverty defined as material deprivation; and that defined as being in a jobless household. Poverty as material deprivation refers to an individual being without at least four items of a list of nine 'deprivations'.[2] While poverty as a jobless household is based on the number of months spent at work over the previous 12-month period by household members aged 18–59 (excluding students); for the purpose of the target, a threshold of 20 per cent has been adopted to distinguish 'low' work intensity – for those in households where the relevant members were in work for a fifth or less of the available aggregate time in a year (Nolan and Whelan 2011: 228).[3] Furthermore, should it be justified, Member States can also define poverty using their own definition.

Using such a multidimensional approach to define poverty and social exclusion was necessary to reach an agreement, but it further reveals the complexity of the issue and the lack of coherence on the matter at the EU level. While 'income poverty' is the classic redistributive definition of poverty, the jobless household definition has its originals in neoliberal welfare states such as New Zealand and Australia (Copeland and Daly 2012: 282). In this regard, the two definitions call for very different solutions to tackle the problem of poverty and social exclusion. The former calls for a redistributive welfare state with a progressive tax system, while the latter simply aims to get individuals into work, regardless of the quality work or the pay which they receive. A problem for the jobless household definition is that evidence from liberal welfare states demonstrates that moving individuals into employment as a route out of poverty is alone, an insufficient condition to reduce poverty (Brady 2003). In an era of the liberal welfare state whereby temporary contracts and low pay dominate the kind of work a 'jobless household' person would ordinarily move into, such individuals will often find themselves experiencing 'in-work-poverty' and thereby requiring further assistance. A possible solution is to combine such an approach with

the redistributive policies of the welfare state and a relative poverty definition, but there are several limitations to this. The first is that centre-right
governments are ordinarily opposed to such redistribution or at least they
resist any further move towards the policy. Second, cash-strapped governments, particularly in the context of Europe's ageing population and the
associated financial costs (healthcare, pensions) have fewer resources for
redistributive policies and those that are available are often channelled
into education and training rather than direct redistribution. While investments in education and training can lift people out of poverty and
social exclusion, there is no guarantee that this approach will work as outcomes are often context specific across a very diverse European Continent.
Third, in an era of austerity, for which the 2010–2019 decade is known
for, governments have even fewer resources at their disposal for direct
redistribution.

Poverty as material deprivation, the third measure of poverty in the Europe 2020 target, is a relatively new understanding of the problem at EU level,
although it dates to Townsend's UK study (1979) in which he developed a set
of 60 indicators designed to capture 11 different types or aspects, since then
there have been extensive studies on the matter (Nolan and Whelan 2011: 14).
The EU's definition was agreed in 2009 and the impetus came from the 2004
EU enlargement and the need to define poverty with non-monetary indicators. The addition of the Eastern European states in 2004 meant that income
levels across the EU varied much more than before – the relative poverty
thresholds in the more affluent Member States were above average income
in the poorest Member States, while those below the threshold and thus 'at
risk of poverty' in some rich countries have higher standards of living than
the well-off in some of the poorer countries (Nolan and Whelan 2011: 47). In
EU discussions, it soon became apparent that statistics on relative income
positions sometimes failed to capture essential differences in living standards across the Member States (Marlier et al. 2007). Furthermore, a material
deprivation definition is thought to address some of the difficulties posed
by relying on adequate current income, as measured by a relative poverty
definition. A lack of essential durables or difficulties in meeting payments
are thought to be a good proxy of persistent poverty since they are measured
overtime. A concept that has gained traction at EU-level, as well as across
OECD countries more broadly, is to measure poverty both via material deprivation and income poverty. The two measurements ordinarily capture different individuals, but they also capture some of the same individuals. It is
the individuals who experience both forms of poverty and social exclusion
that are then identified as being the most in need and policy can prioritise
addressing this group. In terms of a policy response, there is significantly
more literature on how to define material deprivation, the consequences of
different definitions, and the kind of people who experience material deprivation, than there is on how best to address the problem. Evidence presented
by Nelson (2012) suggests that the relationship between social assistance and

deprivation is negative, indicating that material deprivation is less extensive in countries with higher benefit levels. There is no clear evidence that public services or ALMPs help to reduce material deprivation. A conclusion from these findings is that the tackling of material deprivation requires governments to expand their social assistance schemes, thereby requiring increases in government spending. Such a move would clearly have the same problems as those identified for income poverty, i.e. that increases in government expenditure are both out of fashion across the EU and severely restricted within the European Semester.

As well as the poverty target, there are nine other integrated guidelines for Europe 2020 including: guidelines 1–3 covering public finances and macroeconomic imbalances; guidelines 4–6 concerning structural reform of the economy in areas such as research and development and the environment; guidelines 7–9 covering employment, education and training; and guideline 10 being the poverty and social exclusion target (European Commission 2010a). Within these ten guidelines, Europe 2020 has eight quantitative headline targets, one relating to research and development, three for the environment, one for employment, two for education and training, and one for poverty and social exclusion. Importantly, the guidelines are supported by seven Flagship initiatives which are separated into the three themes of (1) smart growth which includes the digital agenda, innovation and youth policy, (2) sustainable growth which includes resource efficiency and green industrial policy, (3) inclusive growth which includes skills and training and poverty and social exclusion. Although the Flagship Initiatives are steered by the European Commission, they are jointly undertaken by EU and national actors. Their purpose is to coordinate activity at the Member State level, as well as serving as a forum to exchange best practice across the EU – a sort of socialisation of actors without the formalities and the reporting processes of the OMC (European Commission 2010).

Except for guideline 10, for which there is no specific legal provision for a poverty and social exclusion target, the remaining nine guidelines draw their legal foundation from Articles 121 and 148 of the TFEU. Article 121 provides that the Council is to adopt BEPG, while the Employment Guidelines are drawn from Article 148. Both Articles require the Council to coordinate activity within the Member States as they are matters of 'common concern'. Guidelines 1–6 concern the BEPG and the EU's obsession with public finances and fiscal discipline. Guideline 1 aims to ensure the sustainability of public finances by budgetary consolidation under the guidance of the SGP. It calls on the Member States to improve the sustainability to public finances by fast pace debt reduction, reforming age-related public expenditure, such as health spending, and raising the age of retirement. Guidelines 2 and 3 concern macroeconomic imbalances, guideline 2 more broadly while guideline 3 is specific to Eurozone members. For guideline 2, imbalances are identified as coming from current accounts (by the running of a current account deficit), asset bubbles, and household and corporate debt. The prosed solution for a current account deficit is an internal devaluation in the form of making wage bargaining systems more flexible, keeping wage costs in line with productivity and ensuring that wages serve to correct the situation. Furthermore, it calls for wage developments to take into account differences in skills and labour market conditions; thereby further emphasising the need for the employment and social conditions of EU citizens to be wholly determined by the market. Guideline 3 further emphasises the importance of current account imbalances as a matter of common concern for the Euro Area and gives the Eurogroup a role to regularly monitor the situation and propose remedial action. Importantly, it also mentions the need for members with current account surpluses to remove any structural impediments to domestic demand, thereby highlighting the problem of large current account surpluses for the stability of the Eurozone.

Guideline 4 calls on the Member States to invest 3 per cent of their GDP into research and development by 2020. This guideline existed under the Lisbon Strategy, but little progress was made towards the target with EU spending rising only marginally from 1.8 per cent (2000) to 1.9 per cent (2009) (Edler 2012). Guideline 5 aims to reduce greenhouse gasses by at least 20 per cent compared to 1990 levels or by 30 per cent 'if the conditions are right'. It also calls for the EU to increase the share of its renewable energy to 20 per cent of final energy consumption and to increase energy efficiency by 20 per cent. This climate change guideline chimes with the EU/Member State commitments and obligations under the United Nations' Climate Convention and the Kyoto Protocol. Finally, guideline 6 concerns the improvement of the business and consumer environment calls on the Member States to ensure that markets remain open and competitive, administrative burdens are reduced, and that further support is provided for SMEs. In comparison with the first three guidelines of the BEPG, which are very precise about what should be achieved and how this should be done, guidelines 4–6 provide only general advice on how such challenging structural reforms can be achieved. While this general advice may be regarded as a necessary condition to achieve consensus and agreement in a diverse union of Member States with their own varieties of capitalism, such generality stands in contrast to the sheer scale and ambition of the three guidelines which would, more than often, require a once-in-a-generation structural reform of the economy to be achieved in most Member States. The generality of the subtext of guidelines 4–6 versus the very specifics of guidelines 1–3 should also be read in the context of the EU's then priorities when Europe 2020 was being drafted and agreed – that in the short-term, Member States need to get their public finances under control and within the benchmarks of the SGP.

As with guidelines 1–3, guidelines 7–9 on employment, education and training are very specific about what Member States should be doing to reform their labour markets. Central to these three guidelines are the EU's long-held principles of 'flexicurity' based on the Danish model of the 'golden triangle' of labour market flexibility, combined with sufficient social security provisions and an ALMP (Viebrock and Clasen 2009). In this regard, the Member States are encouraged to introduce a combination of flexible and reliable employment contracts, ALMPs, effective lifelong learning, policies to promote labour mobility and adequate social security systems to secure professional transitions accompanied by clear rights and responsibilities for the unemployed to seek work. Despite the push to create labour market flexibility, there is a genuine commitment to tackle some of the more extreme forms of labour market flexibility, most notably the tackling of labour market segmentation in the form of precarious and temporary employment, fighting low wages, and ensuring that vulnerable groups are incorporated into the labour market. Meanwhile, the Member States are to introduce various reforms to education and training to ensure that participation is increased, standards are raised, and that human resources match the needs of the labour market and the modernisation of the industrial base. While the employment guidelines contain elements of both centre-left and centre-right policies, the main solution to the problem of unemployment is a further intensification of supply-side policies and very light-touch labour market regulation if, and when, it is required. In this context, individual rights and responsibilities are emphasised with the unemployed required to seek work and improve their skills, while the state provides the necessary support to do so. A failure to meet the requirements of such employment programmes can result in the withdrawal of state support in the form of benefit cuts – a controversial policy even when there is an abundance of jobs. A reading of the employment guidelines in the context of the economic crisis is even more revealing given that this agenda was pushed at a time when unemployment was rising and there were fewer jobs available to those who were seeking work. In the short-term, supply-side policies are of little help when there is a lack of aggregate demand in the economy – an especially important point given that Southern Member States that were worst affected by the crisis have demand-driven economies, while Northern economies are export-driven. Under such conditions, governments find themselves with few options other than to place a downward pressure on wages and employment conditions with the expectation that it will encourage employers to hire workers and generate economic growth and jobs.

Governing Europe 2020

To fully understand the Europe 2020 guidelines, it is essential to explore the governance processes within which they exist. It is only within this context that we can appreciate the relative importance of each of the guidelines and the priorities which the post-2010 governance architecture promotes. As mentioned in the previous section, the reforms to EU economic governance, for which Europe 2020 became intertwined with, proposed a step-change in economic policy coordination through reinforced mechanisms of budgetary discipline and fiscal consolidation – known as the European Semester. To bring about the changes, the European Commission introduced the six-pack via the Ordinary Legislative Procedure in 2011, consisting of five regulations and one directive (Official Journal of the European Union 2011a–2011f). The six-pack enshrined a new preventive system of *ex ante* surveillance, the centrepiece was a new annual 'European Semester', which provides a framework of surveillance for fiscal policy and macroeconomic imbalances for the Member States and came into effect during December 2011. Regarding imbalances, the six-pack introduced a broader understanding of economic imbalances beyond fiscal imbalances and introduced what is referred to as 'global macroeconomic imbalances'. This has introduced a scoreboard of initially 11 (later extended to 14) macroeconomic indicators covering issues such as public/private debt, net investment position, real effective exchange rates, export market share, house prices, the current account balance, credit flows in the private sector, labour costs, the unemployment rate including a separate indicator for youth unemployment, and the employment rate. Each of these indicators has its own benchmark and should it be breached, the Macroeconomic Imbalances Procedure (MIP) is triggered. It should be noted that it cannot be triggered if the employment indicator is breached, as its purpose is to serve as guidance and information (Eurostat 2017). Following an extensive review of the data by the European Commission, a Member State can either be placed into the preventive arm or the corrective arm of the MIP. The preventative arm is used for imbalances that are not excessive and corrective action forms part of the CSRs that are issued under the European Semester. The European Commission also conducts an in-depth review of the situation and should it find the existence of an excessive imbalance, this can trigger the corrective arm of the MIP, also known as an Excessive Imbalances Procedure (EIP). If the Member State in question has not already initiated corrective action, they are required to submit a 'corrective action plan' to both the Council and the Commission outlining the action that will be taken to resolve the problem. Should a Member State fail EU make sufficient progress the Commission can request the state deposit an interest-bearing deposit of 0.2 per cent of GDP. A failure to further respond to the recommendations can result in the deposit becoming non-interest bearing and eventually converting into a fine (2011b). These rules include the introduction of a Reverse Qualified Majority Vote (RQMV) meaning that to undo corrective action measures proposed by the Commission, the European Council would be required to achieve a QMV. The six-pack also included further reforms to the SGP. In theory, the SGP provided for corrective action if the annual budget deficit of a Member State breached 3 per cent of GDP, although as explained above, this rule was not enforced during the Lisbon decade.

While government debt was also not to exceed 60 per cent of GDP, there was no official corrective action should this rule be breached. Under the six-pack, a breaching of either of these limits is now meet with preventive and/or corrective action via the MIP. The final aspect of the six-pack is the issue of *ex ante* surveillance whereby Member States present their Stability and Convergence Programmes-the annual reports submitted to the European Commission and Council before major decisions are taken concerning national budgets.

At the end of 2011, the reforms to EU economic governance introduced by the six-pack were regarded as being insufficient to respond to the crisis. The backdrop to this was the continued economic uncertainty surrounding the crisis and the need for the EU to demonstrate that it had the matter under control. The six-pack was therefore followed by the two-pack consisting of two regulations which came into effect in 2014 (Official Journal of the European Union 2013a, 2013b). The two-pack introduced a common budgetary calendar for Eurozone Member States by allowing for better synchronisation in the preparation of national budgets. Within the European Semester, Eurozone members are required to present their budgetary plans for the forthcoming year no later than 15 October. The Commission is then able to assess the draft budgets in accordance with the SGP as well as any CSRs that were introduced in the previous year. While the Commission cannot infringe on national sovereignty on budget issues (it only provides opinion), it does provide further information which can be later used to place a Member State in the excessive deficit procedure (Bauer and Becker 2014: 221). On a second level, the two-pack requires Eurozone members who have an ongoing EIP to enter 'enhanced surveillance', which requires quarterly reporting of progress and enables the European Commission to issue possible warnings to national parliaments about missed compliance with programme targets.

The European Semester begins in November with the publishing of the European Commission's Annual Growth Survey (AGS) and the Alert Mechanism Report (AMR). The former sets out the Commission's economic and social priorities for the next 12 months while the latter is the starting point for the annual MIP to identify potential risks in the economies of the Member States. Their publication also corresponds with the Recommendations for the Euro Area and the Joint Employment Report analysing the employment and social situation in the EU (European Commission 2017a). Once the terms of reference of the AGS and the AMR have been agreed, they are adopted by the Spring European Council after which Member States publish their Stability/Convergence Programmes (budgetary policies) alongside their NRPs (economic policies). In these programmes, countries report on the specific policies they are implementing and intend to adopt in order to boost jobs and growth, prevent or correct macroeconomic imbalances, and on their concrete plans to ensure compliance with the outstanding EU's country-specific – and where applicable Euro Area – recommendations and fiscal rules. In May, the European Commission proposes CSRs for budget-ary, economic and social policies, which are endorsed by EU leaders at the June. The Semester ends in September/October and from 2013 onwards, it ends with the Member States presenting their draft budgetary plans for the following year. These plans are reviewed by the Commission and the Coun-cil, with opinions being released alongside the documents that kick-start the next European Semester (European Commission 2017a).

There are several important points relating to the operation of the Euro-pean Semester. The first is that at the heart of the Semester is a strengthen-ing of the linkages and synergies, albeit they maintain their separate legal entities, between the Stability and Growth Pact (SGP) and the Europe 2020 National Reform Programmes (NRPs), both of which are compiled by the Member States and submitted to the European Commission. Although the trend of synchronisation between these two separate documents/pro-cedures began during the Lisbon Strategy, the aim of the Semester is to ensure symmetry between the fiscal situation within a Member State, the broader macroeconomy, and selected Europe 2020 thematic issues (such as microeconomic and employment/social areas). The second point to note is the level of scrutiny now given to the Member States at all levels of the governance process. Throughout the Semester, the Commission contin-ues its process of surveillance with regular meetings with representatives from the Member States regarding the progress being made and areas of imbalances or policy weaknesses. The reforms leave the Commission's assessments and recommendations with more power, as it is now, for in-stance, able to issue early warnings to Member States if expenditure grows faster than GDP. The introduction of the MIP and its ability to conduct in-depth reviews when certain statistical thresholds are breached is more than the European Commission simply 'doing the numbers'; they leave the European Commission with strong interpretative powers and if a Member State is found to have excessive imbalances, the Commission is responsi-ble for the drafting of a recommendation for corrective measures (Bauer and Becker 2014: 220). Third, in comparison to the Lisbon Strategy, the forming of Country Specific Recommendations (CSRs) has substantially changed. They were initiated in 1999 by the Commission without the au-thority of the European Council, but governments clawed back some con-trol over the process by negotiating with the Commission to soften the recommendations (de la Porte 2011: 496–497). During the Lisbon decade, the CSRs were negotiated between the Commission and the Employment, Social Policy, Health and Consumer Affairs Council (EPSCO). By contrast, their formation under Europe 2020 is not a negotiated process, and while the Member States will have an idea as to the recommendations they will receive, particularly given that imbalances/areas of policy weakness will have been discussed during the various bilateral meetings with the Com-mission in the European Semester, they cannot influence the area in which they are received nor the content of the CSRs. The only way that a CSR can be changed or overruled is by an RQMV in the European Council. Fourth, for national budgets, while the European Commission does not have formal powers to intervene directly in the budgetary policies of the Member States of the Eurozone, their scrutiny before adoption at national level and the use of such information for the Alert Mechanisms Report provide an additional layer of checks and balances to discipline the Member States around EU rules and benchmarks.

From the above, it is clear to see why Bauer and Becker (2014) argue that the European Commission has increased its powers and influence since 2010. The various reforms to EU economic governance have resulted in the soft tool of the OMC becoming more prescriptive and coercive, meanwhile, it is the European Commission that monitors developments in the Member States and is able to initiate corrective action and monitor state. The European Semester essentially cobbles together different EU policy areas with different Treaty provisions and legal mandates into a single streamlined governance process. For Armstrong (2012: 225), the European Semester represents not just an enhanced coordination of economic governance, but also a 'coordination of coordination' across economic governance and Europe 2020. In the years immediately after the launch of Europe 2020 and the European Semester, they were both steered by the strategic alliance between the Commission's Secretariat General and DG ECFIN.

However, reforms to EU economic governance have not just been focussed on the emergence of the European Semester and an enhancing of the Commission's role in the process, as there have also been various intergovernmental agreements within the European Council which attempt to further discipline the Member States to adhere to the reformed SGP and Europe 2020 – these included the Euro-Plus Pact and the Fiscal Compact. The former adds a further layer of complexity to the new economic governance and was agreed in 2011 by the EU Member States, except for the Czech Republic, Hungary, Sweden and the UK. The Pact was driven by French and German concerns that at least part of the financial and economic fallout was due to underlying factors that had not been sufficiently addressed by the EU's response to the crisis – such as unit labour costs and employment rates (European Commission 2017b). The underlying rationale of the Pact is that the deteriorating cost of competitiveness is an important factor behind the accumulation of current account deficits and financial vulnerabilities and the agreement will increase fiscal and economic discipline and reduce such vulnerabilities. The Pact focusses on five main areas: competitiveness, employment, sustainable finances, fiscal sustainability and tax policy coordination. Members of the Pact set annual targets in the five areas and engage in the necessary domestic reforms; they are also to justify when action in an area is not required. Progress in the Pact is reported in the Europe 2020 NRPs and for employment policy, governments are to increase labour productivity, reduce public sector pay and to reduce labour costs by weakening 'the degree of centralisation in the bargaining process'. For the latter, the Pact therefore calls for a move away from national collective bargaining to more regional and local agreements reflecting differences in labour costs and productivity. The ETUC was particularly critical of the call within the Pact to dismantle national wage bargaining as it would force the Member States to enter a downward spiral of undercutting each other's wages and working conditions (Degryse 2012: 45).

The Treaty on Stability, Coordination and Governance or the Fiscal Compact represents an additional lever in the strengthening of economic governance centring on budgetary discipline and surveillance (European Commission 2012a). Although the Fiscal Compact is compulsory for the Eurozone members, non-Eurozone states can also participate with only the Czech Republic and the UK declining to join when it was agreed in 2012 (the Czech Republic eventually joined the Fiscal Compact in March 2014). The Compact requires Member States to introduce the 'balanced budget rule' either in their constitutions or quasi-constitutional sources of law that bind the budgetary process. The rule states that national budgets should either be in balance or surplus and can only be in deficit during exceptional circumstances. The Fiscal Compact constitutionalises, at the Member State level, the fiscal benchmarks of the SGP and its debt-brake, which defines the levels at which debt should be reduced (budget deficit not exceeding 3 per cent of GDP and debt levels not exceeding 60 per cent of GDP).

Governance, power and politics

The guidelines of Europe 2020 need to be considered in the context of the priorities of both it, and the European Semester. It is therefore necessary to analyse the political hierarchy of Europe 2020 and the European Semester to situate the relative power of the different actors and the possibilities of what can be achieved. As argued in the previous chapter, governance arrangements are not value-free arenas in which agreed objectives and policy instruments are given an equal weight. Rather, they are embedded in political strategies that privilege certain interests and actors over others, create hierarchies of priority, and reflect a broader set of sociopolitical inequalities among actors and interests. *Governance in Advanced European Integration* sees governance arrangements as featuring hierarchy and priority in which actors navigate and negotiate the opportunities and constraints to achieve their objectives. EU employment and social policy within the European semester therefore faces numerous obstacles. In the first instance, the legal framework of the Semester prioritises the need for governments to remain within the legally binding benchmarks of the SGP. This is overseen by the European Commission and is underpinned by the ECJ. More broadly, within the European Commission the strategic relationship between the Secretariat General and DG ECFIN, and the side-lining of the social actors ensures a rather narrow-focussed interpretation of the rules – that is, austerity takes priority over any other objective.

The main documents released at the launch of Europe 2020 further reveal the hierarchy of priorities within the governance architecture. The formation of the European Semester is intended to ensure that governments adhere to fiscal discipline and developments within Europe 2020 are to remain within this overriding aim. Progress in the strategy's microeconomic and employment pillars are to be much more tightly linked to macroeconomic developments. In other words, developments in the thematic components of Europe 2020 are rendered a function of progress in the macroeconomy (Copeland and Daly 2014: 151). This principle was further emphasised by the Commission which proposed that selected secondary-order issues 'could also be addressed to the extent that they have macroeconomic implications through the recommendations under the BEPG (European Commission 2010b: 28). Underpinning this position, and exploited at the time by DG Economic and Financial Affair are the Treaty Provisions between macroeconomic policy (the BEPG) and (DG ECFIN) employment policy. Article 148 of the TEU provides the employment guidelines of Europe 2020 with their legal mandate. Importantly, it states that such guidelines should be 'adopted pursuant to Article 121' – that is, the BEPG used to govern macroeconomic policy. However, there is no mentioning under Article 121 of the need for the BEPG to simultaneously consider the Employment Guidelines and thereby employment policy. This Treaty provision, while long established in the EU, was strategically used by actors within DG ECFIN to establish a clear priority for the European Semester. While the European Commission argued that the Member States 'must find room in their budgets' for thematic issues (European Commission 2010a: 3), should macroeconomic conditions become unfavourable (through excessive government deficit or debt levels), then spending on the thematic components of Europe 2020 should be restricted until 'sound' public finances are re-established. Both the 2011 and 2012 AGSs produced by the Commission provide an insight into the EU's then priorities. Both surveys make fiscal consolidation the number one priority to be followed by the second-order priorities of promoting growth and competitiveness (i.e., microeconomic reforms) and promoting employment (European Commission 2010a). This represents a clear privileging of activity and progress in the macroeconomic pillar over other pillars of the Semester and thereby empowers actors within DG ECFIN, as well as the Economic and Financial Affairs Council and actors in finance ministries operating at the national level, over any other grouping of decision-makers. This point has been further made by Maricut and Puetter

(2018) who argue that the asymmetry that favours economic actors and their policies over social actors and social policy has been a key feature of the European Semester. Not only are finance ministers better placed to conduct policy dialogue, but they also control the European Semester priorities more effectively than employment and social actors. Finance Ministers are also more closely linked to discussions at the highest political level, the European Council.

Actors in DG ECFIN, national finance ministries, the Economic and Financial Affairs Council, as well as Heads of State/Heads of Government are primarily focussed on achieving the EU's macroeconomic objectives and the European Semester serves to both guide, reinforce, and discipline this prioritisation. Central to the prioritisation of the macroeconomic objectives is the further disciplining of government behaviour exerted by the financial markets which Member States are dependent upon to fund short-term borrowing to plug budget deficits and to refinance long-term debt. The ability of a country to repay its debt is a key determinant behind the interest rate at which a government can borrow. Given that Eurozone governance is not underpinned by guarantees from the other EU Member States should a Eurozone member default on its debt obligations – known as the no-bailout clause in the Treaty – financial markets react to macroeconomic developments in a Eurozone Member State as if it were entirely sovereign in monetary policy. Both the European Semester and the financial markets establish and reinforce the priorities within the governance of the Eurozone.

Attached to the prioritisation of 'sound' macroeconomic policy is that of the long-term stability of the pension systems. Guideline one of Europe 2020 – ensuring the quality and the sustainability of public finances – calls on the Member States to 'reform age related public expenditure, such as healthcare spending, and contributing to raising effective retirement ages to ensure that age-related public expenditure is financially viable, socially adequate and accessible' (Official Journal of the European Union 2010). The call for sustainable pension systems stems from Europe's ageing population and the BEPG serves to focus attention on the need for urgent reform. The secondary priorities of Europe 2020 are that of microeconomic policy, the employment guidelines, and the poverty and social exclusion target. The Treaty provision and the situating of employment as a second-order priority stem from the broader pressures on governance architectures to generate economic growth and jobs. Governments at the national level are acutely aware of the electoral sensitivity of the issue of employment and unemployment and thereby strive to ensure policies that create jobs. An important observation here is that 'active ageing' – essentially policies to promote the labour market participation of older workers – forms part of the employment guidelines, while the issue of age-related public expenditure forms part of the macroeconomic policy guidelines. The separation of the ageing population issue into two sub-policy areas is not only indicative of the complexities of policy issues, but also demonstrates which aspects of the issue are a priority. In the case of Europe's ageing population, pension reform in the context of sustainable public finances is prioritised over active-ageing and financial actors are firmly in the driving seat of the reform process.

Although the poverty target forms part of the Semester's secondary-order priorities, the target is deemed less important to EU actors relative to other secondary-order issues. In the first instance, it should be noted that the target represents Scharpf's (1996) lowest common denominator in terms of its coherence and its ability to produce change in the Member States. As explained above, given that there is limited Treaty provision for an OMC and the issuing of CSRs by the European Commission and European Council in poverty and social exclusion, its inclusion into the Semester came with guarantees that the target was legally non-binding, and thereby the CSRs were to serve as 'guidance'. This suggests that EU activity in the other Europe 2020 guidelines receive more attention and resources relative to the poverty target and the governance arrangements put in place for its realisation were both weak and poorly defined. Within the Council, both employment and poverty and social exclusion are the responsibility of the Employment, Social Policy, Health and Consumer Affairs Council (EPSCO), but within EPSCO, they are governed separately by the Employment Committee (EMCO) and the Social Protection Committee (SPC). This essentially creates a division, and sometimes tension within the EU's social actors even though some national representatives sit in both committees (interviews 21, 26). A problem for the actors within the Social Protection Committee and discussed above was that in the first year of the European Semester, the OMC for social exclusion, which had been a focal point of governance activity for the Social Protection Committee prior to 2010, was suspended. To fight its corner within the European Semester the Social Protection Committee was forced to communicate with DG ECFIN, the Secretariat General and the Economic and Financial Affairs Council via the Employment Committee. The Economic and Financial Affairs actors initially refused to give the Social Protection Committee a voice within the Semester by claiming that while the Committee had legal recognition in the TEU, Article 160 only gave it 'advisory status'. This stands in contrast to the the Employment Committee whereby Article 148 provides it with the authority to draft the Employment Guidelines, which are to be consistent with the BEPG. Article 148 also provides for the Employment Committee to monitor progress of the Employment Guidelines in the Member States, issue CSRs in areas of policy weakness and to draft an annual Employment Report reviewing the current situation. In the eyes of the Economic and Financial Affairs actors, article 148 thereby provided for the justification for the Employment Committee to be incorporated into the processes and procedures of the European Semester, but not the Social Protection Committee. As a way of compromise the Social Protection Committee was given its own subsection in the Employment Report and it is little coincidence that this section is the final section of the report. The poverty target therefore got off to a weak start as the social actors, stripped of the OMC and denied access to the key decision-making process, were considerably disadvantaged in championing their cause.

While Europe 2020 and the European Semester therefore construct a governance hierarchy, the priorities and power asymmetries within the hierarchy are not just about which policy areas receive the most attention and have the most developed and coercive governance instruments. Such an understanding of governance as hierarchy would suggest that groups of actors are relatively independent of each other, able to form and formulate their own agendas, albeit to varying degrees relating to the resources they pertain, and therefore without the need to consider or rely on developments and actors in other policy areas. But governance is more complicated than this. The structural priorities and power asymmetries, in the form of resources and ideas, disseminate throughout governance arrangements precisely because there is a high degree of interdependence between policy issues. The creators of Europe 2020 and the European Semester were acutely aware of this fact. While governance arrangements during the Lisbon Strategy veered more and more towards a tighter coupling of areas such as employment and education and training to the BEPG, Europe 2020 and the European Semester represent the final step in the formalisation of this move at EU level. Documents from the launch of both European 2020 and the European Semester continuously refer to the need for the Member States to strengthen the 'synergies and linkages' between different policy issues, meanwhile, budgetary responsibility and austerity are identified as the overarching priority of the EU for the following decade. Progress in the strategy's second-order issues are to be much more tightly linked to macroeconomic developments and this renders them a function of the macroeconomic situation (Copeland and Daly 2014). This represents a clear privileging of activity and progress in the macroeconomic pillar over other pillars. This privileging extends further into the governance process of Europe 2020 and the European Semester than may first appear. For this, we need to understand how CSRs were drafted and formulated in the early years of the European Semester. The CSRs are initially drafted by the desk officers within the various DGs that are responsible for the individual policies of Europe 2020. Once drafted these are discussed by the Directors of the four core DGS (Secretariat General, Economic and Financial Affairs, Employment, Social Affairs and Inclusion, Taxation and Customs Union) before being sent to the Secretariat General. Once with the Secretariat General, they are redrafted and prioritised in conjunction with DG ECFIN. This powerful screening process by actors in DG ECFIN serves to censor any ambitious secondary-order CSRs that could challenge or contradict the neoliberal mantra of financial actors.

Conclusion

This chapter has concerned itself with the analysing and exploring the priorities, political hierarchies, and power relationships underpinning the Europe 2020 – the EU's economic reform strategy for the decade – and the European Semester – the governance arrangements used to achieve the aims and objectives of the strategy. As argued, post-2010 EU economic governance further strengthens the privileged position of financial actors within the EU, understood to be those individuals in DG ECFIN, the Economic and Financial Affairs Council, and national finance ministries. The financial actors could use the uncertainty surrounding the Eurozone crisis to construct governance arrangements that were to side-line other EU actors, particularly those in the European social dimension. The prevailing structural conditions therefore favour the neoliberal policies of national budgetary discipline and austerity, regardless of the economic situation. A lack of demand within the economy would not serve as a justification to deviate from the script, as demonstrated in the Mediterranean States during the height of the Eurozone and economic recession. Given the history and purpose of European integration the EU's financial actors would have been privileged in the post-2010 economic governance arrangements had the Eurozone crisis not happened, but it is the ratcheting-up of this privileged position vis-à-vis the social actors that is most striking. Europe 2020 and the European Semester appear to give little room for market-correcting policies in the second-order issues. That is, in the area of the European social dimension the evidence suggests a tendency towards policy reform that reduces policy problems to being resolved by introducing ever greater market principles to the labour market. This stands in contrast to resolving policy problems through a broader lens in which reforms may distort the functioning of the market, but are considered necessary to protect certain groups of individuals from the extremes of the market and from having their life chances determined by the market alone.

Progress around the employment and social policy components of Europe 2020 therefore faces considerable obstacles in moving the European social dimension forward in a 'progressive' sense. While the individual guidelines for the social dimension feature policy underpinnings of from both the centre-left and the centre-right, a genuine turn to Keynesian social democracy for the European social dimension is therefore heavily constrained. From the onset of the European Semester, the social actors within the EU's political space found themselves more disadvantaged than had hitherto been the case in terms of getting their voice heard and achieving policy outcomes. However, given the relative fluidity of governance arrangements, as well as the continuously evolving dynamics of the EU's political space, it is important to remember that there will be opportunities for the social actors, which may be seized upon to advance their cause. At a bare minimum, the social actors have a foothold within the European Semester and despite the structural constraints in which they are forced to operate, their remains uncertainty surrounding the extent to which they can fight their corner and champion their cause in unfavourable conditions. The following chapter explores the agency and opportunities of the social actors as they navigate and negotiate the European Semester between 2010 and 2018.

Notes

1 The EFSM mobilises €60 billion with bonds issued by the European Commission and secured against the EU budget, while the EFSF mobilises €440 billion and is secured by the Eurozone Member States in proportion to their share in the paid-up capital of the European Central Bank. The IMF contribution is €250 billion, making a total of €750 billion.
2 For the purpose of the EU's definition, these items are: (1) to pay rent or utility bills; (2) keep one's home adequately warm; (3) face unexpected expenses; (4) eat meat, fish, or a protein equivalent every second day; (5) an annual week of holiday away from home; (6) a car; (7) a washing machine; (8) a colour television; (9) a telephone.
3 Hence, the name of this definition is slightly misleading as individuals defined in this way may be working, albeit a small number of hours.

4 Analysing the politics of the European Semester

Introduction

The previous chapter has focussed on the governance arrangements of the European Semester. Central to this analysis has been to understand the structural power relations within the European Semester and which actors, policies and priorities are privileged over others. While the European Semester prioritises and privileges actors in DG ECFIN, the Economic and Financial Affairs Council and national finance ministries, the European Semester has enabled a ratcheting-up of this prioritisation. Meanwhile, this hyper-prioritisation will clearly have consequences for actors wishing to pursue employment and social objectives. Furthermore, in political economy, policy fields do not exist in isolation of each other, rather they are interlinked and can often crossover each other. It is therefore necessary to unpack the political black box of the European Semester to understand the political direction in which the European social dimension has been travelling.

To analyse the politics of the European social dimension within the European Semester, it is necessary to capture policy outcomes regarding what EU Member States are being asked to do. As explained in the previous chapter, Member States are required to identify their own weaknesses in relation to the Europe 2020 guidelines, to implement national reforms, and to annually report their progress in the two separate, but related documents – the Stability and Growth Programmes for economic and fiscal policies and National Reform Programmes (NRPs) for employment, education and poverty reduction. In areas of policy weakness, the European Commission drafts Country Specific Recommendations (CSRs), which are presented to the European Council. Once the Council has agreed and adopted the Recommendations, Member States are required to introduce domestic reforms; meanwhile, the European Commission monitors progress, or lack thereof, which feeds into the next Semester cycle and future CSRs. The analysis within this chapter focusses on the political direction given by the CSRs. By doing so, it aims to understand how the outputs of the European Semester can be categorised and what this direction reveals. This chapter constructs a coding framework and applies this to the CSRs for the European social dimension between 2011 and 2018. Unlike previous academic research that has coded the Recommendations, the approach adopted in the constructed framework categorises the Recommendations along a five-point continuum ranging from decommodification to commodification. Since the mid-1990s, the conventional concept of decommodification has struggled to find relevance during the reform of the welfare state and the introduction of ALMPs across the European Continent. However, as this chapter will argue the concept remains relevant to understanding the post-Keynesian welfare state, but it requires being placed on a continuum alongside the concept of commodification. Commodification and decommodification are therefore situated at the opposite ends of the continuum, but as the categorisation of employment and social policy is not zero-sum, policy can be positioned at various points along the continuum, as it will most likely feature elements of both concepts, albeit to varying degrees. Understanding whether the majority of the CSRs lean more towards commodification or decommodification will enable us to understand the overall political direction of the social dimension within the European Semester.

The analysis within this chapter reveals that between 2011 and 2018, the vast majority of the CSRs can be categorised as either commodifying or partially commodifying. This finding demonstrates that in reality, EU employment and social policy within the European Semester ultimately aims to create pure, efficient labour markets that treat human beings as though they are pure commodities, such as goods and services that find their price by the laws of supply and demand. To demonstrate this finding, the chapter is divided into six sections. The first section outlines the current approaches to analysing the CSRs and their limitations. The second part of the chapter explores the relationship between commodification/decommodification, the welfare state and ALMPs. The third section outlines the contours of the commodification/decommodification continuum used to code the CSRs, while the fourth section discusses the methodology. The results are presented and analysed in the fourth section. The final section of the chapter analyses the small number of CSRs in the field of health. These are analysed separately to the other CSRs of the European social dimension, owing to the commodification/decommodification continuum not being directly applicable to healthcare. The purpose of this separate analysis is to complete the picture regarding developments in the social dimension. The conclusion reflects on the findings of the chapter.

Current approaches to the analysis of the CSRs

As a dynamic political arena which is constantly evolving, analysing the politics of the European Semester is challenging. This is because governance arrangements represent an interplay between those procedures and practises that are constant and those that remain influx. For example, over the last eight years, the European Semester has remained as an annual governance cycle which has issued CSRs for each year. Meanwhile, against this backdrop, various governance initiatives have been launched which have aimed to feed into the European Semester and thereby steer its direction. Such initiatives include the EU's Youth Guarantee (2013), the Employment Package (2012) and the Social Investment Package (2013). One solution to this difficulty is to analyse the outcomes of the European Semester by capturing their significance. While such an approach is the dominant method in the current academic literature, it divides into two schools of thought. The first focusses on capturing the quantifiable shifts within the European Semester by focussing on the number of CSRs issued for the European social dimension over time. From this approach, the observable trend has been an overall increase in the number of social CSRs, thereby suggesting that the European Semester has been 'progressively' made more social. In this regard, the focus during the early years of Europe 2020 and the European Semester on austerity – understood as reductions in government spending – is slowly being rebalanced by the strategic achievements of social actors and their desire to further advance the cause of a European social dimension. Such a frame of thinking is given by Bekker (2015), Bekker and Klosse (2013), Jessoula (2015) and Zeitlin and Vanhercke (2017) and their work makes some interesting findings and claims regarding recent developments.

In poverty and social exclusion Jessoula (2015) concludes that up to 2014, there has been an increase in the number CSRs surrounding the Europe 2020 poverty target, as social actors became better organised, learnt how to operate within the European Semester, and were thereby able to achieve the aim of advancing their cause. Bekker (2015) takes a broader definition of the social dimension to include employment, pensions, education and training, as well as poverty and social exclusion and finds an increasing emphasis on social and employment issues within the 2013 European Semester, as evidenced by the increased number of CSRs. Such Recommendations are also issued under the SGP and include the accessibility of healthcare and the fight against poverty and social exclusion. Zeitlin and Vanhercke (2017) also find a substantive increase in the number of social CSRs from 2011 to 2014. For the authors, the strategic agency of social and employment actors, reflexive learning from past experiences, and creative adaption of their organisation and practices to the new institutional conditions of EU governance have all served to engineer a 'partial but progressive socialization of the Semester' (Zeitlin and Vanhercke 2017). Furthermore, the streamlining of the European Semester has not hindered the cause of the European social dimension. This streamlining refers to the changes made by the Juncker Commission. In 2014, the incoming Commission was concerned that the growing number of CSRs was resulting in a lack of focus and confusion regarding the prioritisation of reforms in the Member States. It took the decision to reduce the number of CSRs and to simplify their wording. For Zeitlin and Vanhercke (2017), the streamlined CSRs focus more on challenges and outcomes, rather than specific policy measures that prescribe how things can be achieved. Whether this improves Member State engagement with the CSRs remains an open question, but despite the reduction in all CSRs from 2015 onwards, considered in relative rather than absolute terms, the proportion of social CSRs remained relatively stable in subsequent Semester cycles (Clauwaert 2015; Zeitlin and Vanhercke 2017). Zeitlin and Vanhercke (2017) suggest that further advances within the social dimension have been made owing to the more integrated character of the social CSRs with the macroeconomic ones, thereby giving the social CSRs an increased status.

This school of thought regard outcomes achieved in the name of a European social dimension, regardless of the content of such outcomes, as providing sufficient evidence to demonstrate 'progress'. Central to such a perspective is the counting of outcomes from the Semester, such as counting the number of CSRs, to assess for the overall status of the European social dimension. However, there are valid reasons to be sceptical and thereby critical of such claims. The first relates to the naivety of simply counting policy outcomes and then extrapolating conclusions from changes overtime in their annual aggregates. Although the number of CSRs related to the European social dimension has increased overtime, first in absolute and more recently in relative terms, this does not automatically result in the 'socializing of the European Semester' as argued by Zeitlin and Vanhercke (2017). Such a claim has the same redundant logic as suggesting that since France, Germany, Italy, Spain and the UK all spend a similar percentage of GDP on healthcare, they all must have similar healthcare systems. This is clearly not the case. As with using any form of quantitative data used to analyse an issue, the policy specifics are important. For example, there may have been an increase in the number of social CSRs, but this tells us nothing about the content of the CSRs. It is perfectly plausible to envisage a situation whereby an increase in the CSRs is accompanied by an increase in the call to dismantle the welfare state within the EU's members or to change its ideological direction towards a more neoliberal form. One of the most important aspects of Europe 2020 is that the policy guidelines direct developments within policy areas and for the European social dimension, the guidelines represent an ideological mix of both centre-left and centre-right policies. Policy outcomes, then, cannot simply be taken for granted that they represent anything other than what the specific details tell us.

A second point to note relates to the deceptively simple, yet often ignored, issue of hierarchy and priority within governance. The obvious example being the role of the EU's constitutional asymmetry and how this plays within governance arrangements and the day-to-day priorities, processes and practices of EU governance. Take macroeconomic policy within the European Semester. As discussed in the previous chapter, there have been significant reforms since 2010 to its already privileged position within the process of

European integration. The governance of EU macroeconomic policy within the European Semester is operationalised by increasingly stringent tools and greater surveillance of the economic situation of the Member States, particularly the Eurozone. The reforms of the SGP, along with the introduction of the MIP, are designed to incentivise the Member States to adhere to the rules. By contrast within the Semester, the governance tools for the European social dimension remain soft and legally non-binding. There are opportunities for peer pressure and policy learning for social actors within the Semester, but the consequences of Member States failing to make sufficient progress towards the EU benchmark targets or to adequately respond to a CSR do not incur financial penalties. Meanwhile, the employment indicators included within the MIP cannot initiate formal corrective action/proceedings, rather they are to serve as guidance. It is also essential to note that the process of Multilateral Surveillance, whereby the European Commission monitors the progress made by each Member State for every CSR, differs depending on the policy area within the European social dimension. Engagement with the Multilateral Surveillance process in employment policy is compulsory for Member States who have been issued with a CSR, but in the area of poverty and social exclusion engagement is voluntary. If a Member State does not wish to engage in the process of Multilateral Surveillance, the agreement within the EU institutions is that the Member State will receive the Recommendation or a similar Recommendation during the following Semester.

A third claim by Zeitlin and Vanhercke (2017: 166) relates to the argument that progress within the European social dimension has been achieved by the social CSRs becoming more integrated with macroeconomic policy which provides for the better coordination between economic and social policy. This stands in contrast to the early years of the European Semester where social actors found themselves on the margins of the decision-making process and less influential. A result of such shifts within the governance architecture is some internalisation of social objectives when economic policy actors make their decisions. A footnote to this shift is that economic actors formally retain a leading role in some of the CSRs which concern the European social dimension, such as pensions. Again, the claim that this leads to a 'socializing of the European Semester' does not automatically hold. The shifting relations between different groups of actors may result in a closer cooperation between economic and social actors and a further consideration of social issues within the European Semester, but as with the previous point, such a shift tells us very little, if anything, about the politics of what is happening. The ultimate litmus test of whether the European Semester is being 'socialised' should focus on the political content of outcomes. It is perfectly plausible that the agency of social actors, when exercised, is confronted with the structural power of the EU's constitutional asymmetry within the European Semester. A result of the interplay between structure and agency can be unintended consequences whereby the policy aims of social actors become distorted and far removed from their original intention. Social actors may also find that engaging with macroeconomic actors comes at a cost of being co-opted in 'their' ideological position with social and employment policy emulating from the European Semester having a 'market-making' or 'neoliberal' purpose.

The first school of thought is a classic example of the 'problem-solving approach' to European integration, which falls within what Robert Cox (1981: 208) referred to as 'problem-solving theory'. It takes the world as it finds it, with the prevailing social and power relationships and the institutions into which they are organised, as the given framework for action. The general aim of the problem-solving approach is to analyse how existing relationships and institutions are able to work more smoothly by dealing effectively with particular sources of trouble. Since the general pattern of institutions and relationships is not called into question, particular problems can be considered in relation to the specialised areas of activity in which they arise. The strength of the problem-solving approach lies in its ability to fix limits or parameters to a problem area. In the case of the European social dimension, the first approach focusses on how increased policy outcomes for employment and social policy are achieved, with the fix or parameter of the study being that all policy outcomes are regarded as 'progress' regardless of their actual meaning. The final thing to note about problem-solving approaches relates to their ideological underpinnings. 'Theory [or an approach] is always for someone and for some purpose' wrote Cox (1981: 207) meaning that there is no such thing as a theory or approach in itself, divorced from a standpoint in time and space. When any theory or approach represents itself, it is important to examine it as ideology. The problem-solving approach serves a conservative and vested interest that does not aim to challenge the given order, rather it generally supports the given order. It claims to be objective and value-free, thereby presenting the 'truth' of a current topic or case study, but in reality, the truth is embedded in an ideological position that is often obscured by the attempt to completely remove politics and ideology from the picture. An important observation regarding this first group of academics is the close relationship that exists between them and the EU institutions, especially DG Employment, Social Affairs and Inclusion. In the power politics of European Integration, different DGs struggle for prominence and forge close relations with a broad range of actors, including researchers and academics. The European Commission can also be a valuable source of research funding or opportunities for external consultancy, which serve to further the prominence and status of researchers and academics in their field. In this codependent relationship, all parties have a vested interest to put a positive-spin on any situation or outcome and this can influence the supposed 'objectivity' of research.

Fortunately, there are a group of scholars who adhere to critical theory or critical approaches in their study of the relationship between the European

Semester and the European social dimension. These approaches move analysis away from the problem-solving approach and its trappings. They stand away from the prevailing order and do not take institutions and social and power relations for granted, nor do they believe that governance processes are produced and reproduced in non-hierarchical settings. Rather, critical approaches are directed to the social and political complex which empowers certain individuals and courses of action over others. While both problem-solving approaches and critical approaches both begin with the European social dimension as the issue under focus, the problem-solving approach burrows-down and limits its analysis to the issue being dealt with. By contrast, critical approaches lead toward the construction of a larger picture of the whole of which the initially contemplated part is just one component, and it seeks to understand processes of change in which both parts and the whole are involved (Cox 1981: 209). Critical approaches therefore situate developments of the European social dimension within the broader process of European integration; they do not regard the policy area as operating in isolation of developments in other policy areas. Importantly, the analytical lens of critical approaches allows for a reflection on the normative choice in favour of a social and political order (ibid). Although both the scholar and the reader of such research need to regard the feasibility of any proposed transformations.

Crespy and Vanheuverzwijn (2019) analyse the policy content of the European Semester with their main purpose being to focus on the ideas surrounding the role of structural reforms in the European Semester. Their research is grounded in a content analysis of all European Semester documents between 2011 and 2017 and includes AGS, AMRs, Euro Area Recommendations and CSRs. Their findings are complemented by a short series of interviews with European and national officials involved in the European Semester. The authors find that despite the floating meaning of 'structural reform', in the context of the EU it consists of neoliberal policy recipes such as liberalisation of product and service markets, the deregulation of labour markets and public administration reform. At the same time, structural reforms have covered eclectic – if not contradictory – policy ideas, thus accompanying a discursive turn towards fiscal flexibility and social investment. Indeed, one of the most significant findings from their research is that over time, the CSRs increasingly veer away from the policies of social retrenchment towards those of social investment. A note of caution, however, is needed regarding such findings: CSRs framed as social investment are predominantly found in soft law, while those that call for social retrenchment rely on more solid and thereby coercive legal foundations. To put it differently, when asked to implement the CSRs, Member States are faced on the one hand with few but strong recommendations to curb spending or reduce labour costs, and on the other hand, with more numerous but softer requests to engage in social investment (Crespy and Vanheuverzwijn 2019: 107). In this regard, the shifting nature of the politics and ideology of the European Semester needs to be contextualised with the 'bigger picture' surrounding EU governance. To put it differently, when asked to implement the CSRs, Member States are faced on the one hand with few but strong recommendations to curb spending or reduce labour costs, and on the other hand with more numerous but softer requests to engage in social investment.

We should also add a further word of caution to the findings of Crespy and Vanheuverzwijn (2019) and that relates to the concept of social investment. Nolan's 2013 review of the concept illustrates several points that warn of the dangers of ascribing overly positive connotations with the paradigm to reform the welfare state. Social investment is an emerging paradigm across Europe regarding the reform of the welfare state that remains fluid and ill-defined. It has deep historical roots within political economy/welfare state literature (cf. O'Connor 1973) and for this reason, it can be argued that social investment is 'old wine in new bottles' (Nolan 2013). The concept draws from the long-standing Scandinavian emphasis on 'productive' social policy and debates surrounding 'active' versus 'passive' labour market policies. In its purest form, social investment is about distinguishing between welfare spending that enhances productive capacity, such as education and training, and that which is passive and spent on consumption, such as pensions and spending on elderly care. The distinction between these two forms of the welfare state sending is complex and not a particularly straightforward categorisation, as nearly every state expenditure can be regarded as part social investment and part social consumption. Nolan gives the example of capital spending on hospice care which would generate a very substantial social return over a long period, and in that sense could qualify as social investment. There are also difficulties posed by calculating any 'investment' returns from social investment. For example, Germany spends less than the UK on education and training (6.5 per cent of public spending versus 9.5 per cent of public spending), yet German labour productivity is much higher than the UK (66.6 US dollars per hour worked versus 52.4 US dollars per hour) (OECD 2019). A final point is that social investment can be regarded as an attempt by social actors to align welfare policies with that of mainstream economics. The danger here is that by focussing on economic indicators as output, rather than social indicators, the returns of supposed social investment get framed in terms of economic growth, rather than more and better jobs. Social investment then becomes one of those malleable ambiguous concepts (Busemeyer *et al.* 2018). Social investment may simply get hijacked by neoliberalism, despite the original good intentions. In this context, there has been considerable lip-service given to social investment by the European Commission, but in reality, the default neoliberal paradigm of market liberalisation, balanced budgets, hard currency and welfare retrenchment remain dominant characteristics of the EU (Hemerijck 2018). Finally, Ronchi's (2018) research into the relationship between social investment and social protection provides further caution. Ronchi finds that contrary to the situation in European welfare states prior to the crisis, re-source competition has become a matter of concern during the 2010 decade. This poses a politically salient trade-off for governments, whose room for manoeuvre has further tightened because of the financial crisis. A result is that a budgetary expansion of social investment appears possible only when retrenching social protection. For this reason, it seems at least reasonable to raise doubts about the budgetary viability of recalibrating welfare states to-wards social investment, especially given the electoral cost for governments of retrenching social protection.

A number of scholars have moved the debate forward in terms of analys-ing how EU Member States engage with the Europe 2020 targets. Jessoula and Madama (2019) coedited a volume in which they explore and analyse the engagement of Member States in the context of the Europe 2020 poverty target. The findings of the research suggest that a first group of Member States (Germany, Sweden and the UK) reacted against the poverty target to defend national sovereignty, while a second group of countries (Belgium, Poland and to some extent Italy) have been much more engaged with the target and used it to initiate national change. The study thereby highlights the continued tension between political contestation and opposition on the one hand and broad support on the other, within the EU's political space around Europe 2020. The overall result of this process is one a differentiated integration.

In 2018, Mary Daly and I published a paper in which we coded the CSRs of the Semester for the European social dimension (2011–2015), albeit our framework is different to that of Crespy and Vanheuverzwijn (2019). Our coding framework characterised the CSRs as market-making, market-correcting, or mixed. This categorisation draws from Wolfgang Streeck's (1995) differentiation between market-making and market-correcting social policy. Streeck argues that the economic and market nature of European integration, as set out in the Treaties, favours a form of social policy that is oriented to integrating the EU labour market and mandates the use of social policy mainly to enable efficient market functioning. The driving motor of reform here includes the removal of regulations and barriers to trade and unfettered competition, making for a model of social policy that supports a deregulation of employment, cuts back on non-market-oriented benefits and services, downgrades income redistribution and reframes social pol-icy around activation and human capital development. Market-correcting measures, on the other hand, aim at ameliorating market outcomes (or neg-ative externalities) and call for redistributive intervention in line with stand-ards of adequate income, social protection and even social justice. Such policy may be market-distorting (Streeck 1995: 34) in aiming for the 'greater good' of less inequality, compensation and social inclusion. To code, we fo-cussed on the general orientation and policy direction of each of the CSRs and each recommendation was allocated to one category. The result made for an interesting finding: that the degree of progress in 'socialising' EU policy over the last five years has been conditional and contingent. In reality, market-correcting CSRs are few and far between, while any shift towards 'socialising' the European Semester has resulted in a moderate increase in CSRs that are categorised as mixed. In this regard, the struggle to advance the cause of the European social model remains fraught with obstacles.

How, then, can we take the issue of analysing the relationship between the European Semester and the European social dimension further? Indeed, it could be argued that sufficient analyses of the CSRs have been conducted, but to this, I would add two things. First, that more nuance can be brought to the existing analysis of the Recommendations. For example, the more forensic analysis would allow for a greater understanding of the recommendations, particularly with respect to those that are regarded as being 'mixed'. Second, as an individual CSR can contain several issues, it is important to disentangle the various actions and direction that can be found within one Recommendation. Aggregating these findings will provide a more fine-grained analysis.

Active labour market policies and the commodification/ decommodification conundrum

In coding the CSRs, several issues need to be addressed. The first relates to the ideological direction of the policies emanating from Brussels, understood as categorising EU employment and social policy according to the traditional left-right political spectrum. Positioning individual employment and social policies on the classic political spectrum is not an easy task, particularly in the context of the reduced ideological differences between the centre-left and the centre-right across Europe over the last 30 years. For the purposes of analysing the EU employment and social policy within the European Semester, I therefore focus on the concepts of commodification and decommodification. The analytical focus on the two concepts breaks with the academic tradition of welfare studies established by Esping-Andersen's (1990) seminal *Three Worlds of Welfare Capitalism*. In the latter, Esping-Andersen analyses the welfare state via its ability to decommodify the individual, but as I will argue, if we are to fully appreciate the welfare state, we also need to equally consider its ability to commodify, as the contemporary welfare state is a complex machine that has the power to both commodify and decommodify various aspects of an individual's life.

Esping-Andersen bases his concept of decommodification on the works of Karl Marx and Karl Polanyi. The classical view of commodification is understood as policies designed to make wage employment and the cash nexus the linchpin of a person's very existence within the capitalist system of political economy. Individual welfare, if not survival, depends on the willingness of someone to hire one's labour power (Esping-Andersen 1990: 36). The commodification of the individual as a resource strengthens the power of capital over labour, but within the capitalist system, this is justified with reference to the freedom individuals are granted by being able to choose between different job roles/employers and leisure/work trade-offs. However, such freedom is fictitious as workers are not commodities like 'true' commodities, such as physical goods because they need to survive and reproduce. Unlike true commodities, labour cannot withhold its resource until the price being paid for it increases unless there is an alternative means of subsistence. For Esping-Andersen (1990), this is where the welfare state plays an important role – its ability to provide an alternative means of subsistence to paid employment and the extent to which it makes individuals more, or less, reliant of the functioning of labour markets. For Esping-Andersen (1990), the concept of decommodification refers to the degree to which individuals or families can uphold a socially acceptable standard of living independent of the market and it is the process and the extent of decommodification that is the central analytical focus in *Three Worlds of Welfare Capitalism*. Importantly, decommodification should not be confused with the complete eradication of labour as a commodity; it is not an issue of all or nothing as labour is always commodified in the capitalist system. Rather, decommodification refers to the extent to which individuals or families can uphold a socially acceptable standard of living independently of the operation of the market. In other words, decommodification is the extent to which the roof over a person's head, the food they eat and their level of consumption, and the social activities they choose to participate in, are determined by the peaks and troughs of the economic growth cycle and their ability to participate in the labour market. The higher the degree of decommodification, the more likely individuals or families are to be able to uphold a socially acceptable standard of living independently of market participation.

Using the concept of decommodification, Esping-Andersen (1990) analyses different welfare states by focussing on three social and employment policy benefits: unemployment benefits, sickness benefits and pensions. For each of the benefits, a decommodification index is constructed and is comprised of data for: (1) replacement rates – the after-tax benefit paid to a typical worker relative to their after-tax wage gained from employment; (2) qualifying conditions such as the waiting days before one can receive benefit, the duration of the benefit and the number of years of insurance required to receive a standard pension; (3) and finally the coverage rate, which includes the proportion of people who are entitled to claim benefits, such as those covered by an insurance scheme or the principle of universalism. From the decommodification index, three types of welfare state can be identified. The first group of liberal welfare states includes countries such as Australia, Canada and the USA with low levels of decommodification. The benefit system of liberal welfare states is designed to provide low levels of income which in turn encourages individual self-reliance and very short periods of unemployment. The second cluster of welfare states, the conservative and corporatist grouping, includes countries such as Austria, France, Germany and Italy. In such welfare states, social rights are granted to all, but benefits are dependent on an individual's class and status – there overall contribution to the system. Typically, the level of unemployment benefit for an individual is dependent on previous earnings. The conservative corporatist welfare states emphasise the upholding of status differences and limited redistribution. The third cluster – the social democratic countries such as Sweden – feature high levels of decommodification and universalism within the welfare state, as individuals are able to maintain a high standard of living, irrespective of market conditions, with high levels of benefits.

Despite the groundbreaking analysis and perspective offered by *Three Worlds of Welfare Capitalism*, it has been criticised from numerous perspectives (Castles and Mitchell 1993; Gal 2004; Hicks and Kenworthy 2003; Room 2000) not least because Esping-Andersen (1990) neglected the role of women in the commodification of men. Historically, the ability of men to be commodified is dependent on the non-commodified or unpaid work done by women in the household, child-raising, schooling, affective care and a host of other activities that maintain social bonds and shared understandings. Benefits for women were therefore dependent on their husband's performance in the labour market. Importantly, this gendered hierarchy is necessary for labour to produce and reproduce – women are needed as careers and home servants to nurture both current and future labour. However, the feminist critique of Esping-Andersen's (1990) concept of decommodification reveals a further issue with his definition. Female emancipation from the gendered hierarchy of the male breadwinner model of production will inevitably result in them being commodified. Historically, to free themselves from domination women have opposed the oppression that has kept them within domestic servitude and prevented them from selling their labour and gaining independence from men. As noted by Fraser (2014: 7–8), female social rights are therefore secured through commodification and the selling of labour power. Meanwhile, as greater numbers of women enter the workplace there becomes a need for childcare, which ultimately becomes marketised. The unfortunate irony of the situation being that the emancipation of women, secured by their commodification within the labour market, can result in new relations of dependency for some women as the dependency on a male breadwinner is replaced with a dependency on the labour market (Papadopoulos 2005: 7–8). The social liberalism that comes with economic liberalism (neoliberalism) therefore provides both an opportunity and a constraint for women, but it is presented by political elites, particularly those closely connected to capital accumulation, as the 'natural' or 'ultimate freedom' that stems from the neoliberal state. The market is therefore the liberator of oppressed individuals and resistance to such a move is perceived to deny ultimate freedom to women, even though such freedom may represent merely a different prison. Caution therefore needs to be taken when evaluating EU policy in gender equality, particularly that packaged as increasing female participation in the labour market, as it is clearly not a simple extension of social rights. Similar arguments can also be made regarding EU activity to incorporate marginalised groups into the labour market, such as those with disabilities or the Roma population.

The feminist critique of Esping-Andersen's analysis points to a second criticism of the approach adopted in *Three Worlds of Welfare Capitalism* – that little attention is paid to the experience and situation of individuals while they are in work (Papadopoulos 2005). Esping-Andersen's decommodification index centres on 'the extent to which individuals and families can maintain a normal and socially acceptable standard of living regardless of their market performance' (Esping-Andersen 1987: 86). It does not discuss employment protection policy, arguably one of the most important employment protection measures that govern the relationship between workers and capital. However, the experience of individuals when they are in employment, such as the relative ease at which they can be dismissed, rights obtained from redundancy law, contract period (permanent versus temporary), holiday entitlement and parental leave, are just a few examples of employment policies that are clearly linked to processes of commodification and decommodification. Individuals are not simply commodified once they enter the labour market: the situation is more complex than this and there are degrees of commodification. Once an individual enters the labour market, their employment conditions also determine the extent to which they are truly treated as a commodity, not a human being, and are therefore commodified. While Esping-Andersen analyses the different employment regimes attached to welfare states, it is done so through the lens of decommodification and the ability of individuals to exit the labour market. His analysis does not include the other side of the employment coin, i.e. what happens once individuals are in employment and the extent to which they are commodified. Relatively speaking, employment protection legislation across the EU is the weakest in the UK and the strongest in Belgium (OECD 2018). Once in employment, UK workers are therefore the most commodified in the EU in employment protection, relative to other EU countries. It is also interesting to reflect on the approach adopted in *Three Worlds of Welfare Capitalism* whereby the different typologies of welfare state are conceived as creating different employment regimes. In this frame of thinking, the line of causality between the two is unidirectional. However, the line of causality is a two-way process in which social and employment policies influence each other in a complex multidimensional web of policies and processes.

A final criticism of Esping-Andersen's (1990) concept of decommodification relates to its applicability to the contemporary welfare state following its shift to ALMPs. *Three Worlds of Welfare Capitalism* is based on empirical data that capture the essence of welfare states during Keynesianism. Throughout the 1990s, the European welfare state was to shift from passive policies of welfare to activation or workfare where state support primarily focusses on promoting employability in an open market. Passive employment policies of receiving benefits, such as unemployment benefit, regardless of whether an individual is looking for work, are replaced by activation policies whereby benefits are received on the condition of recipients actively seeking work and/or engaging in any necessary retraining. Such a shift is accompanied by restrictions on the length of time benefits can be received, as well as reductions to benefit levels. Meanwhile, the emphasis on human capital development, as a means through which countries can further compete against each other, is given a greater priority with a focus on 'productive' education and training. In a world of mobile capital whereby private investment has few national allegiances, human capital has become one of the few areas where countries can invest to remain competitive. The shift to rename 'personnel' departments as 'human resources' is one example of the changing perceptions and theorisation of labour. This subtle change of wording masks significant structural changes in the commodification of labour. Human self-development, as given by education and training that is increasingly integrated with labour market participation, rather than being an end itself, is regarded as a being capable of minimising social risk. For Huo *et al.* (2008), Esping-Andersen's (1990) concept of decommodification does not capture the importance of human development and skill investment, and for the authors, this renders the concept ineffective. This is an important point as it enables us to reflect on the role of education and training, employment, social policy and the welfare state. However, the wide-scale adoption of ALMPs does not render the concept of decommodification redundant, rather it serves to highlight the importance of conceptualising decommodification on a continuum that also includes commodification. In this line of thinking, education and training within workfare programmes that are linked to competition, production and labour market participation form just as much a part of the commodification of individuals as the level and duration of any benefits they are entitled to receive. It is worth pausing for a moment to reflect on this issue in greater detail.

ALMPs represent a form of welfare policy that is commodifying and thereby political. When it comes to the education and training provided under such schemes, they are narrowly defined as a productive factor. It has a means to an end, i.e. for the individual to secure employment and is purely associated with labour market participation. It is not associated with the broader educational well-being of an individual. 'Life-long learning', another buzzword within ALMPs, proposes that workers should engage in occupational education and training throughout their working lives to be adaptable to dynamic market conditions. Again, this is not educational enlightenment in the classical sense, rather it serves to ensure that labour, as a commodity, more readily finds its equilibrium within the operation of the free market. As the capitalist economy continues to evolve its industrial and technological base, previous employment roles become redundant and the economy requires workers with new skills and knowledge. Life-long learning is one way in which labour remains mobile and adaptable as if it were a true commodity in a perfect market. It also shifts some of the responsibility for the structural changes within the economy onto the individual, who to survive, is required to remain dynamic and adaptable. This leads to a broader criticism of ALMPs: that they place a disproportionate level of responsibility on an individual to find work, regardless of the economic conditions. If the economy is in recession and unemployment high, the unemployed are still required to search for work and/or engage in further training, as was the case during the Great Recession (2007–2009). The result is an increased number of individuals applying for a dwindling number of jobs. Such policies can lead to a situation whereby individuals who already have sufficient skills are required to engage in further training that simply churns them through the system and does not enhance their employment prospects, as there are currently fewer jobs available. Such a system of governing employment represents a Darwinian struggle of 'hyper-competitiveness' in which only the fittest survive; it is worth reiterating that what we are referring to here are human beings that have emotional intelligence, not physical goods being traded. Added to which such programmes operate on the principle that individuals should take any job, even if such employment represents significant underemployment – i.e., that individuals are over-skilled for the job that they are employed in. The logic here is that as individuals in employment tend to lead healthier and more fulfilling lives relative to those who are unemployed, employment is the route through which health and well-being can be secured. Yet correlation is not always causation and employment does not always secure well-being – nor is it the only means through which well-being can be achieved. One of the most important shifts within the European economy over the last two decades has been the rise of casualisation in the form of temporary and fixed-term employment contracts, part-time employment and low-paid service sector employment. Such vulnerable employment, which is often received by individuals engaged in ALMPs, is unlikely to represent an improvement on simply receiving benefits. Little wonder that countless studies reveal participation in ALMPs to be demoralising, depressing, and unlikely to lead to long-term paid employment (Friedi and Stearn 2015).

The final point to note regarding ALMPs is that as well as emphasising the need for individuals to participate in a very specific form of education and training, in a European context, they also aim to liberalise labour markets to make labour a more flexible and mobile factor of production. The overall result of this liberalisation is the ability of employers to more easily hire and fire employees and to reduce their overall costs. In theory, labour market liberalisation is supposed to encourage job creation. Costly labour market practices, such as permanent employment contracts that give workers morally decent rights, are regarded as inhibiting job creation. When workers resist an erosion of such rights, they are regarded as being selfish and preventing companies from hiring more workers. The replacement of permanent contracts with temporary contracts is argued to encourage employers to hire more workers. This liberalisation of labour markets, whereby hiring and firing becomes more in sync with ups and downs of the economic growth cycle is commodifying. In a somewhat perverse manner, decisions to place employees on temporary contracts are often always made by individuals who are either on permanent contracts themselves or who receive a disproportionate level of remuneration, meaning that periods of unemployment could be sufficiently managed. ALMPs, then, are not a magic bullet that transcends the decommodification/commodification continuum; rather, the very essence of ALMPs is to deepen the commodification of individuals. Importantly, outside of Scandinavia where such policies originate from, their record is patchy at best.

For example, between 1997 and 2010, successive Labour Governments in the UK launched reforms to employment and welfare policy, known as the New Deals, which targeted specific groups such as single-parent families and the long-term unemployment. However, 40 per cent of participants in the various schemes were back on benefits within six months (Toynbee and Walker 2010: 203). Meanwhile, of those that found employment it remains hard to prove that ALMPs were responsible. The Conservative-Liberal Democrat Coalition (2010–2015) responded to the limitations of the schemes by tightening benefit conditionality and renegotiating contracts with service providers. Post-2011 service providers involved in the provision of ALMPs are remunerated solely on results, dependent, not just on individuals entering employment, but also on their ability to remain in employment (Department of Work and Pensions 2012). In other words, the limitations of the various New Deals did not result in a root and branch reform of the approach, rather the perceived solution was to place more pressure on individuals participating in the programmes and to increase the tendency towards commodification. While the UK's decision to tinker with its ALMPs can be regarded as ideological, as the Coalition Government was centre-right while its predecessor was centre-left, there are broader reasons as to why such policies have dominated EU employment policy and these relate to the EU's constitutional asymmetry, which favours market-making integration over market-correcting integration. A problem for EU leaders is that in the context of the constitutional asymmetry, there are very few options for employment policy other than to intensify competition in the labour market. Under EU state aid rules governments are unable to subsidise sectors or industries of the economy, as this would represent anti-competitive practices and distort competition within the Single European Market. But such subsidies may have a broader social purpose by creating jobs and growth in deprived areas that otherwise would remain deprived.

Under such legal constraints, alternative policy solutions to direct state intervention to generate employment are somewhat narrow. ALMPs are one of the few policy options available, as they extend competition without distorting the market. Political contestation around ALMPs is therefore centred on the extent of individual vulnerability, rather than whether such vulnerability should be eliminated and is immoral. Importantly, over the last two decades, EU employment policy has also emphasised the promotion of entrepreneurship as a route out of unemployment, thereby further emphasising personal responsibility as a solution to economic and social problems that are often not the fault of the individual. It should go without saying that there are very few people who are born to be entrepreneurs. Worryingly, self-employment can often mask low pay and underemployment. Entrepreneurship, as a route out of unemployment, is not a solution for the EU's economic growth model.

To summarise, if we are to truly appreciate the politics of ALMPs, we need to delve into broader conceptual understandings than those provided for in *Three Worlds of Welfare Capitalism*. It is within this context that I propose decommodification be considered alongside commodification, with both concepts forming the two extremes of a policy continuum. Therefore, to categorise employment and social policy, it is necessary to not only focus on what happens to individuals when they exit labour markets, but how they are also encouraged to re-enter the labour market, remain in the labour market, their experiences once in employment, the type of education and training they receive, and how wages are determined. The traditional contours of the welfare state form one half of the commodification and decommodification of individuals, while the day-to-day experiences of employment forms the other half. ALMPs therefore do not disrupt the analytical value of commodification and decommodification, rather they are a fundamental component of them. Translating this conceptualisation into a coding framework will enable the capturing of the political dynamics of EU employment and social policy within the European Semester.

Commodification and decommodification of employment and social policy

To categorise employment and social policy in the context of the European Semester, policy outputs can be positioned along a five-point continuum ranging from decommodification to commodification. Table 4.1 illustrates the decommodification/commodification scale used to code the CSRs. Code 1 captures decommodification in its purest form and includes an extension or expansion of social rights and welfare policy which are independent of the need to be in employed or seeking employment. Examples of such policies include a

Table 4.1 The Commodification/Decommodification Index

Code	Definition	Examples
1 Decommodification.	The improvement/extension of employment and welfare rights in the context of making individuals less reliant on the cash nexus of employment for their existence.	Such policies present themselves as an expansion of benefit levels or improved access to benefits, neither of which are conditional upon activation or participation in employment. Included within this category are education and training programmes that do not serve to activate individuals or employment prospects, rather the objective of such programmes is to improve social well-being and social integration.
2 Partial decommodification.	This category includes policies that attempt to address the pure commodification of labour and some of the excessive consequences. Within this category, individuals are required to work, but the state intervenes to ensure that employment is not completely de-humanising.	Examples include concerns over low pay and suggest attempts to correct it via wage increases or reforms to the tax system. It also includes policies designed to move workers from flexible/short-term contracts to permanent contracts. The movement of workers onto permanent contracts is done so without eroding the rights of such contracts. That is, employers are not encouraged to shift individuals from temporary to permanent contracts by reducing the rights of permanent workers, thereby reducing the associated risks and costs of permanent employment.
3 Commodification and decommodification.	Within this mid-range point of the continuum are employment and social policies that target specific marginalised groups and aim to promote social inclusion.	Examples include policies targeting women, the Roma, the disabled, and those with a migrant background. While these policies are concerned with the integration of such groups and a reduction of social exclusion, this is achieved by securing participation in the labour market. A problem here is that the latter may, or may not, lead to emancipation and/or social inclusion. Within this midway point, we also include increased to childcare provision that serves to encourage female participation in the labour market.

(Continued)

Code	Definition	Examples
4 Partial commodification.	The overall concern of such policies is to get previously inactive individuals into employment, as well as to ensure that the unemployed secure employment within the shortest possible period.	Examples of these policies include (a) benefit receipt conditionality in terms of a reduction in the period benefits are received, as well as schemes to ensure individuals claiming benefits are 'engaged' in securing employment; (b) reforms to education and training to improve the functioning of the labour market; (c) reforms to social security and taxation to get the low-skilled into work with the use of buzzwords such as 'to make work pay'; (d) policies that regard the reduction of poverty and social exclusion as being secured via participation in the labour market; (e) the targeting of specific groups such as the young, older workers and the low-skilled under the buzzwords of 'youth policy' 'life-long learning' and 'active ageing'; (f) this category also includes policies to better target welfare recipients in the context of a move away from universalism in the welfare state; (g) finally, this code includes policies designed to promote entrepreneurship as a way out of unemployment.
5 Commodification.	The erosion of employment and social rights that serve to further improve the functioning of the labour market and commodification.	Such policies include (a) the weakening of labour contracts and labour rights, (b) the need to reduce wages in line with productivity, to make national collective bargaining more flexible including the introduction of regional wage variations, (c) to increase in the age of retirement or a reduction in pension entitlements to extend working life, (d) the reduction of benefits and to reduce benefit entitlements.

reduction in the age of retirement and eligibility for a pension and increases to child benefit not conditional upon the labour market participation of the parents. It also includes education and training that is broadly concerned with the welfare and social integration of individuals, rather than serving to secure employment. Code 2 concerns policies to correct some of the worst excesses of the unfettered market, such as concerns to increase the wages of the low-paid and shifting workers on temporary contracts onto permanent or open-ended contracts. An important condition for this type of policy is that the move from temporary to permanent employment contracts is achieved without the dilution of employment rights and working conditions of employees on permanent contracts. Furthermore, concerns over low pay are to be achieved by increases in wages rather than tax deductions – tax deductions may marginally improve pay, but workers remain low paid and potentially trapped in their circumstances. Code 3 is a midpoint between commodification and decommodification and concerns the EU's policies for marginalised groups such as women, the disabled, Roma, and those from a migrant background. Historically, the EU's response to the promotion of equality and integration is for individuals to participate in the labour market and to ensure that they are protected from discrimination in the workplace. In this respect, equality is achieved by commodifying previously decommodified individuals. Whether this represents an improvement for under-presented groups very much depends on the individual. Employment may represent a form of emancipation or it can simply replace one form of domination and marginalisation with another if employment is precarious. For this reason, we need to acknowledge the individual experience of such policies and the need to code this as a mid-point between the two extremes of commodification and decommodification.

Code 4 concerns supply-side policies that serve to encourage (or force) individuals into employment. Examples of such policies include the need for benefit recipients to search for employment or participate in training programmes, limits on the period for which benefits can be claimed, and reductions in benefits to encourage claimants into employment. Such policies may also include targeted groups such as the low-skilled, youth, or older workers. The difference between these groups of people and those identified in code 3 is that motivations for employment for code 4 are fundamentally about getting people into work, rather than employment as a route to greater equality. It is also important to understand some of the terminologies around such policies. In an EU context, 'active-ageing' refers to policies designed to increase the employment rate of older workers and is not concerned with broader issues surrounding the need for older people to maintain active lifestyles to minimise long-term health risks, as can be found in the healthcare literature. The EU promotes an employment-first approach for older people. This code also includes the linking of benefits to activation, such as the aim to reduce poverty and social exclusion by encouraging individuals back into the labour market. Such a narrow interpretation of reducing poverty and social exclusion is problematic given the prevalence of in-work poverty (Fraser *et al.* 2011). Finally, this target also includes education and training policies that are linked to improving the function of the labour market and reforms to social security and taxation to get low-skilled into work or to 'make-work-pay', regardless of employment situation.

Code 5 represents policies designed to fundamentally commodify workers by eroding employment and social rights that previously existed. Examples of such policies include the linking of wage increases to productivity so that workers remain 'competitive' and labour costs low. Should inflation rise above productivity-linked pay increases, workers would experience a decline in real wages and living standards – in the eyes of policymakers, this is unfortunate, rather than a justification for a pay increase. Under such circumstances, the only possible solution to avoid a drop in real wages would be for employees to work overtime, should it be available and they can do it, as they may have caring responsibilities or other commitments. Ironically, longer working hours are known to have a negative effect on labour productivity. The linking of wages to productivity overwhelmingly places the burden of adjusting to economic shocks at the micro or individual level and rising living costs are not a justification for wages to be increased. Within this code, we also find policies designed to curtail or dismantle national or sectoral collective bargaining to make labour markets more flexible and competitive relative to their local conditions. This strategy is designed to place a further downward pressure on wages and undermines the collective voice of labour movements. It pits workers against workers in the competitive struggle for employment and represents a ratcheting-up of the already competitive forces between the EU's Member States. The code also includes cuts to benefits as a blunt instrument to bring government spending under control. It is different to any curtailing of benefits that are linked to activation, which fall under code four, as in theory activation is also supposed to include 'support' from employment services to help individuals find work. It also covers the need to increase the age of retirement to bring pension spending under control, regardless of the complexity that surrounds employing older workers.

Methodology – coding the CSRs

In terms of coding the CSRs, all 899 CSRs issued to the Member States between 2011 and 2018 as part of the European Semester were assembled. The next step was to identify those CSRs that fall within the remit of the European social dimension. The selection was based on whether the general theme of the Recommendation was broadly amenable to social and employment policy within EU terms and conventions. In other words, the key exercise here was to determine inclusion or exclusion based on whether the policy domain or problem was framed within either an employment or social policy domain. The underlying logic is that the comparison would be flawed were it to include problems or areas that are highly unlikely to be addressed by social policy (e.g., budget deficit). The list of areas included within the Recommendations includes employment policy, education and training, poverty and social exclusion, equality, pensions and wages. Importantly, those Recommendations that relate to health and long-term care are removed from the coding database as this policy issue cannot be coded in terms of the commodification/decommodification continuum. To minimise the impact of their removal, the recommendations for healthcare will be discussed in a separate section below. Typically excluded CSRs focussed on budgeting and fiscal governance, banking regulation and refinancing, physical infrastructure and energy, non-labour market-related tax reform, the organisation of trades and the professions, reform of the administrative and legal systems including the undeclared economy, and the opening-up of public services to competition. This left 391 CSRs for the analysis.

Once all the CSRs were identified, the various constituents were disaggregated into individual policy areas/recommendations, thereby giving a much higher number of CSRs. This disaggregation is intended to capture the overall aggregate political direction of the CSRs, given that one CSR can often include numerous policy issues that require action by a Member State. The very specific way the CSRs are written means that each individual policy area/action can be identified. A 2014 CSR issued to Lithuania serves as example. It calls on the Member State to:

> Better target active labour market policy measures to the low-skilled and long-term unemployed. Improve coverage and adequacy of unemployment benefits and link them to activation. Address persistent skills mismatches by improving the labour market relevance of education inter alia based on skills forecast systems and promote life-long learning. In order to increase the employability of young people, prioritise offering quality apprenticeships, other forms of work-based learning, and strengthen partnership with the private sector. Review the appropriateness of labour legislation, in particular with regard to the framework for labour contracts and for working-time arrangements, in consultation with social partners.
>
> (European Council 2014)

The recommendation contains eight policy areas that need addressing: targeting for the (1) low skilled and (2) long-term unemployed; (3) linking benefits to activation; (4) improving labour market relevance of education and (5) promoting life-long learning; (6) improving the employability of young people; and reviewing legislation for labour contracts (7) and working time (8). This one CSR therefore contains no fewer than eight policy areas that need addressing. The first six of the policy issues fall within code number 4, while issues 7 and 8 fall under code number 5. It is not immediately obvious that issues 7 and 8 should be given a code of 5, as the political direction of suggested reforms cannot be inferred from the Recommendation. The problem is not unique to this example and featured in several Recommendations throughout the period of analysis. The solution to this conundrum is to read the Country Reports produced by the European Commission to ascertain the political context within which the reform is proposed. In the case of policy issues 7 and 8, the 2014 Country Report for Lithuania claims that the current legal framework for employment contracts and working time is restrictive and requires reform to improve labour market flexibility. This therefore justifies the two issues being given a code of 5.

Results

The results from the aggregate data of Table 4.2 provide an overview of the content and number of issues raised within the CSRs between 2011 and 2018. Between 2011 and 2014, the number of policy reforms required by the CSRs steadily increased from 103 to 202 and this is accounted for, not by the increased number of CSRs per se, but rather their bloating to include multiple policy issues, as demonstrated by the above 2014 CSRs for Lithuania. The number suggested policy reforms declined to 89 from 2015 onwards and reflected an overall reduction in the number of individual CSRs from that period onwards. In 2017, there was an overall dip in the number of CSRs, as well as suggested policy issues, but their increase in 2018 to 86 suggests that 2017 was an exception, rather than the new norm (Figure 4.1).

It is also interesting to note the aggregate number of policy issues per category during the period. The least number of policy issues are to be found in code 1, the purest form of decommodification. In eight years, seven policy issues within the CSRs can be categorised as decommodifying. All the decommodifying Recommendations are issued to Bulgaria, Cyprus, Hungary, Latvia and Slovakia – post-2004 new Member States whose welfare states contain various weaknesses that are perceived to need addressing. The seven policy issues focus on reducing poverty for the elderly and children, as well as in the need to address persistent inequalities and marginalisation of the Roma community. It is not the only instance in which the three issues are identified as requiring policy reform within the Member

Table 4.2 Aggregate Data of Coded Policy Issues within the CSRs

Year	Decommodification/Commodification					Total
	1	*2*	*3*	*4*	*5*	
2011	0	7	14	50	32	103
2012	1	11	21	64	29	126
2013	1	24	28	92	20	165
2014	2	21	32	107	40	202
2015	0	12	13	43	21	89
2016	0	15	8	40	19	82
2017	0	10	11	35	9	65
2018	3	11	20	35	16	85
	7	111	147	466	186	917

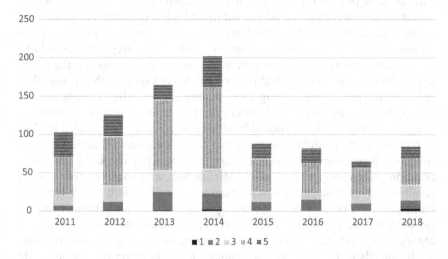

Figure 4.1 Chart showing the aggregate number of coded policy issues found within the CSRs per year.

States, but on these eight occasions, there is no specified linkage to the reforms requiring labour market participation as part of the welfare reform. While each of the issues is important policy objectives, they are very specific issues that require an intervention. The decommodifying CSRs do not suggest a fundamental reorientation of the European Welfare State, rather they suggest that individuals should receive support in only very extreme situations. In other words, the minuscule number of CSRs reflects, not the belief that European welfare states already do a good job of decommodifying their citizens, but that in the few instances they were issued, the situation was so severe that intervention was necessary beyond the dominant theme of activation. A final issue to consider, along with all of the CSRs, is that the Member States have some wiggle room in designing their policy response. A specific ideological direction of a CSR does not always translate in action within a Member State.

The second least popular category of CSRs is those that are partially decommodifying or coded as 2. Between 2011 and 2018, there were 111 issues that required policy reform within the Member States. The highest number of such Recommendations was issued in 2013, while the lowest number of those issued was in 2011. The overall concern of these CSRs is to improve educational outcomes of individuals. While such outcomes are not explicitly linked to activation and labour market policy, it is evident from the broader process of European integration that the EU's obsession with competitiveness provides the context within which they are formulated. Nevertheless, they are coded as 2 so as to air on the side of optimism regarding some of the EU's intentions. Between 2011 and 2018, all the Member States were issued with at least one of these types of Recommendations. This category includes other issues that are addressed to a handful of Member States, such as the need to improve benefit adequacy, as well as improving the take-up rates for those who are entitled to receive them. This category also includes Recommendations that aim to reduce the burden of taxation on the lowest paid. The methods via which this is to be achieved suggest that rather than reducing inequality and taxing high-income earners, the tax base is to be shifted to other areas of the economy. In the earlier Recommendations, it is suggested that taxation should be shifted to consumption, which is likely to have very few positive effects on low-income earners. Taxation on consumption is regressive because all income earners pay the same amount of taxation on a good, regardless of their income, and such tax reforms can result in low-income earners paying more tax, rather than less. Later Recommendations on this issue do not specify how the reduction of income tax for the lowest earners should be reduced, presumably over concerns of regressive tax reforms. None of the 111 recommendations suggest that inequality needs to be reduced, even though it has been on the rise since the early 1980s. The OECD estimates that in the early 1980s, the average income of the richest 10 per cent of the population was seven times higher than that of the poorest 10 per cent; while in 2017, it was around 9.5 times higher. This long-term trend has not been reversed during the recent economic recovery (OECD 2017). A final thing to note about this category of Recommendations is that in a few instances the Member States are asked to ensure higher real wage growth. This issue is targeted to Germany and the Netherlands, where it is believed that the growth of wages below productivity increases has enabled them to gain a competitive advantage vis-à-vis other members of the Eurozone. Germany is also required to improve the transition from temporary employment or mini-jobs to permanent contracts. Presumably, the economic conditions in Germany pertain to such a move, as the recommendations do not call for the transition to be achieved by reducing the rights of employees on permanent contracts, as is the case with the Netherlands and the other Member States. CSRs that call for an improvement of the transition from temporary to permanent employment contracts by ensuring that the rights and costs of employees on permanent contracts are reduced are coded as 4/5.

Policy issues that constitute a midway point and feature both commodification and decommodification are the third most popular during the period of analysis with 147 issued. In terms of the Member States that were issued with these recommendations, during the early years of the Semester, the focus was on post-2004 new Member States, but by 2018 the clear majority of the Member States had received at least one policy recommendation, except for some Scandinavian Members. This category addresses the equal treatment of men and women in the labour market, as well as integrating vulnerable groups by labour market participation. This is to be achieved by providing education and training for women with the specific purpose of enabling them to join the workfare, as well as reducing the fiscal disincentives for second income earners to work. An emphasis is also placed on ensuring the provision of affordable childcare as well as an expansion of pre-school. Policy issues coded at this midway point also include reintegrating vulnerable groups into the labour market, as well as the Roma population. It is not always clear what constitutes a 'vulnerable person', but the logic with the employment first approach adopted by the EU is that a job will help to reduce the numbers of vulnerable people in society. This is not always the case and is overly simplistic, but as discussed above the EU's 'work first' approach to equality may do little to improve the lives of those who it is intended to help.

The second most popular category is policy reforms that push the employment and social policies towards pure commodification (code 5). Between 2011 and 2018, there were 186 policy issues within the recommendations. Again, nearly all the Member States receive several such policy issues to address during the timeframe and there is no patterning regarding the North versus South or the East versus West. This suggests that commodification is a central aim of employment and social policy within the European Semester which should be advanced in all the Member States. This category includes several policy areas that require reform. The first concerns reforming pension systems by increasing the age of retirement. Some of the recommendations go one step further by explicitly calling for the linking of the retirement age to life expectancy – a strategy that is both controversial and complex, as some older workers may be unable to work due to health reasons. A second issue covered includes reducing employment rights to make labour law more flexible to combat 'labour-market rigidity'. In some instances, Member States are asked to either introduce fixed-term contracts or to make much better use of them. In other cases, they are asked to reduce the discrepancies of employment rights between workers on short-term and permanent contracts, but this is to be achieved not by improving the rights of workers on short-term contracts and a levelling up for all workers, but by reducing the employment rights of individuals on permanent contracts and thereby a levelling down. A final topic covered in the category 5 CSRs is the reform to the system of wage bargaining to ensure that wages grow in line with productivity and Member States do not become uncompetitive. A similar logic is also applied to minimum wages, as the Member States are asked to ensure that any increases do not restrict job creation by making workers too expensive.

By far, the most popular theme within the CSRs are those policy issues that are predominantly commodifying and are coded as 4. This code includes policies that serve to 'activate' people to participate in the labour market. Unlike code 3, these policies do not aim to improve gender equality or the situation of marginalised individuals, rather the aim is to simply improve employment rates for the general population, as well as specific groups that include the young, older workers and the long-term unemployment.

There are several policy issues that are identified as requiring reform. First, there is a need to strengthen the link between activation and welfare benefits for a broad range of individuals. Second, such activation also extends to the aim of reducing poverty and social exclusion by encouraging individuals to participate in the labour market as the means to which their situation can be improved. The terminology used for this end is to 'ensure effective activation of benefit recipients' and while this does occasionally incorporate the need to ensure adequate levels and coverage of social assistance, the link to employment is explicit and prioritised. Third, skills and training also feature extensively within this code with the purpose being to improve the employment prospects of individuals, particularly those on the margins of society or those with low skills. By making improvements to education and training, including vocational education, the Member States are required to ensure that such programmes address any skills shortages or mismatches in the labour market. A final policy issue raised within this code is the strengthening of the relevant employment services to provide adequate support for the unemployment during their search for jobs and training. Adequate support also extends to the governance of ALMPs to ensure that benefit recipients are monitored and benefits are withdrawn at appropriate points in programmes, including instances when individuals are disengaged with programmes and need to be sanctioned. The strengthening of employment services is as much about ensuring participants in schemes are monitored and sanctioned, as it is about ensuring any necessary education and training is provided. As with code 5, there is no patterning in terms of the Member States that receive code 4 CSRs with them being given to all Member States. Again, this suggests that activation remains one of the EU's key priorities in employment and social policy. Social and employment policy is afforded and conditioned on the continuous marketisation of labour markets and the commodification of individuals.

Figure 4.2 illustrates the proportion of the five different codes between 2011 and 2018 expressed as a percentage of the total issued per Semester cycle. The results provide an overview of the evolution of employment and social policy within the European Semester and except for 2018, suggest continuity in the EU's approach to reforming employment and social policy across its Member States. The highest percentage of code 4 and 5 recommendations is in the 2011 European Semester with 80 per cent of all issued falling into this category, while the lowest is at 60 per cent for the 2018 Semester. Between the high and low point of these two codes, there is a continuous variation of the percentage of code 4 and 5 policy issues: 74 (2012), 68 (2013), 73 (2014), 71 (2015), 72 (2016), 67 (2017). When it comes to policy issues that are coded as decommodifying or partially decommodifying, the highest percentage issued is in 2016 with 18 per cent of the policy issues being coded as 1 or 2. The lowest number issued is in 2011 with 7 per cent assigned a code of 1 or 2. Between these two periods, there is some modest variation in the percentage issued: 9.5 (2012), 15 (2013), 11 (2014), 13 (2015), 15 (2017), 16 (2018). The trend of policy issues that are coded as 1 and 2 is for a marginal increase over time. This suggests much continuity over time of the EU's approach, rather than any radical departure from a market-led form of integration for the European social dimension. It should also be noted that despite the modest increase overtime, as outlined above, the policy issues that are coded as 1 are issue-specific and do not suggest that the EU promotes decommodification in its employment and social policy; decommodification is pursed in cases when situations have become so extreme, that non-action is deemed to be politically too costly (Table 4.3).

This leaves policy issues that are coded as both commodifying and decommodifying and are midpoint or code number 3 on the continuum. The lowest percentage of those issued was ten in 2015, while the highest

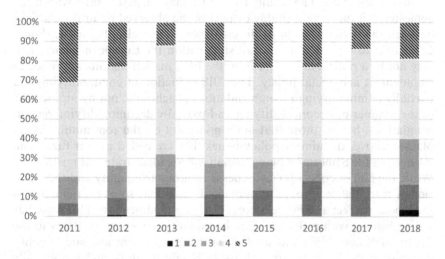

Figure 4.2 Chart showing the percentage distribution of coded policy issues found within the CSRs per year.

Table 4.3 Percentage of Coded Policy Issues within the CSRs

Year	Decommodification/Commodification				
	1	*2*	*3*	*4*	*5*
2011	0	7	13.5	48.5	31
2012	0.8	8.7	16.7	50.8	23
2013	0.6	14.6	17	55.7	12.1
2014	1	10.4	15.8	53	19.8
2015	0	13.5	14.6	48.3	23.6
2016	0	18.3	9.6	48.8	23.1
2017	0	15.4	16.9	53.0	13.8
2018	3.6	12.9	23.5	41.2	18.8

number of those issued is 23 per cent in 2018. As with all the codes, there is some minor variation in the Semester cycles: 14 (2011), 17 (2012, 2013), 16 (2014), 14 (2015), 17 (2017). One of the most interesting observations from the data relates to 2018. While there is a reduction in the number of policy issues that are coded as commodifying (codes 4 and 5), this is achieved, not by increasing the number of policy issues regarded as decommodifying (codes 1 and 2), but by increasing the policy issues that are code 3 or the midpoint. The extent to which this suggests an overall shift in the Semester remains an open question. First, for the period of analysis, the Juncker Commission is responsible for issuing the most policy issues for this category, as well as the least number. The results suggest that minor variations in the categorisation of the policy issues addressed are an inherent feature of the Semester, and care should be given when trying to extract generalisations from the coded results of one cycle. The results from 2018 may suggest a shift within the Semester, but they could simply be part of the observed natural variations between the policy content of different Semester cycles. However, should 2018 come to represent an overall shift within the European Semester, it may not be a radical departure from the EU's market-making approach to employment and social policy. The 2018 reduction of commodifying and partially commodifying recommendations is achieved, not by an increase in the number of decommodifying and partially decommodifying recommendations, but by those that are a mid-point on the continuum. As explained above, the aim of policy issues that are coded as 3 is fuzzy and claims that the Semester is being 'socialised' are inaccurate and misleading. While the aim of code 3 policy issues is to promote equality and the inclusion of marginalised groups of individuals, it is done so by participation in the labour market and hence a process of commodification. This topic has a long history within the EU. Gender equality, for example, dates to the Treaty of Rome (1957) and so shifting the employment and social policy contents of the Semester to such issues is safe territory and a politically realistic solution to slowly shifting the focus of EU employment and social policy. It also reflects the difficulties posed by constructing policy issues that tend towards decommodification.

Health and long-term care

The European Semester has also put healthcare and long-term care on the agenda by issuing CSRs in the field. The most policy issues in this area were 13 (2014) and the least 2 (2011). Other Semester cycles feature variation between the two: 3 (2012), 7 (2013), 6 (2015, 2017), 8 (2016), 11 (2018). Given the EU's relatively weak competence in the field, these results are surprising and at first glance suggest a competence creep in the field. Indeed, much has been made of the fact that the European Semester has expanded into this area, with suggestions that EU involvement is further evidence of progress around a rebalancing of the Semester for the European social dimension. To fully appreciate the CSRs for healthcare, we need to move beyond the above continuum to analyse them. While commodification and decommodification are inherent features of healthcare provision, a reading of the EU's CSRs suggests that they cannot be captured by this framework. For this reason, we need to give a broad overview of the content of the CSRs and thereby the EU's intentions in the field.

During the 2011 and 2012 Semesters, three Member States received CSRs in the field – Belgium, Cyprus and the Netherlands. The recommendation for Belgium clearly states that healthcare spending needs to be curbed to ensure that public spending is placed on a long-term sustainable path, but to fully understand those issued to Cyprus and the Netherlands, it is necessary to delve into the Country Reports. The CSRs for Cyprus (2011, 2012) call on the Member State to accelerate the implementation of the health insurance system, while that for the Netherlands calls on the government to prepare a blueprint for reforming long-term care in view of the ageing population. Initially, both appear to be positive developments in the sense that they may extend rights and coverage for individuals, however, a closer inspection reveals that the intention is for the reforms to curb spending and reduce the pressure on the public finances. Subsequent CSRs in the 2013 Semester Cycle follow the underlying logic in that their purpose is to control or cut public spending. They are issued to Austria, Bulgaria, Czech Republic, Finland, Malta, the Netherlands and Romania. This list was expanded in 2014 to further include Croatia, the latter having formally become a Member in 2014, France, Germany, Ireland, Latvia and Slovenia. The 2014 Latvian CSR is the first to mention the quality of healthcare and accessibility, although these issues are combined with the need to improve cost-effectiveness. In the six CSRs issued in 2015, all concern the cost-effectiveness and efficiency of healthcare systems, while those issued for Croatia, Finland and Romania balance this with the need to improve the quality of provision. Only one of the seven 2016 CSRs in healthcare balance cost-effectiveness with quality and accessibility, with the remaining six solely focussed on cost-effectiveness, efficiency and sustainability. At first glance, the CSRs for Lithuania also suggests that it is concerned with the quality of provision of healthcare, as it calls on the Member State to improve the performance of outpatient care, but a closer inspection of the Country Report reveals the aim to be driven by the need to reduce costs associated with inpatient care. Lithuania is deemed to have too many patients on hospital wards, which is costly. To reduce costs, it is necessary to reduce the number of beds in hospitals and treat patients in the community. While this is not necessarily a bad thing, the underlying rationale for the reform is to reduce costs, not to improve the quality of care for patients. Seven CSRs were also issued in 2017 with those for Bulgaria and Slovenia calling for reforms to improve both the quality of healthcare and the cost-effectiveness of the systems. The remaining five CSRs purely focus on the need to improve the efficiencies and cost-effectiveness of the systems. The CSRs for 2018 also follow a similar pattern; of the 11 issued, only two – Bulgaria and Latvia – balance cost-effectiveness with the quality of provision. The remaining nine CSRs focus on the need to improve the cost-effectiveness of healthcare systems.

In short, while there has been some increased attention on the health-care and long-term care systems of the Member States within the Semes-ter, having grown from two recommendations in 2012 to 11 by 2018, the focus overwhelmingly prioritises financial stability and efficiencies. The EU's competence creeps in the field is one that has been achieved indirectly by linking healthcare expenditure to the BEPG and the need for the Mem-ber States to create 'sound' public finances. It is an attempt to influence the healthcare systems of its Member States by putting pressure on public spending in the field, rather than the need to reform healthcare per se, and is a clear example of issue-linkage within both the process of European In-tegration and the European Semester. The CSRs for healthcare need to be read for what they are, i.e., an overriding concern with public finances and an attempt by the EU to gain ever greater control over the spending of its members, especially members of the Eurozone.

Conclusion

This chapter has analysed the policy issues contained within the CSRs that are issued as part of the European Semester. Given that individual CSRs can contain several policy issues that a Member State will need address, to analyse the trends and overall direction of them, it was necessary to disag-gregate each CSR into its various policy constituents. Once disaggregated, the policy issues were coded according to a five-point continuum ranging from 1 (decommodification) to 2 (commodification). Conventional wel-fare state studies have focussed on the role of the welfare state in terms of its potential to decommodify individuals, as found in Esping-Andersen's (1990) *Three Worlds of Welfare Capitalism*. A limitation of the concept of decommodification is that it does not fully capture the shift in welfare pol-icy that has spread across Europe since Esping-Andersen's (1990) seminal piece. Typically, during the Keynesian era, European welfare states would provide a range of benefits, such as unemployment benefits, that were not linked to an individual searching for work or engaging in education and training programmes. Unemployment benefits served to enable individuals to weather the storm of the boom and bust economic growth cycle. The in-troduction of ALMPs, which requires benefit recipients to either prove they are searching for work or to engage in training programmes, regardless of the macroeconomic situation, is clearly not a policy approach that aims to decommodifying individuals. Hence, arguments that the concept of decom-modification has lost some of its relevance to understand the contemporary welfare state. However, as argued in this chapter, a solution to this con-ceptual conundrum is to also consider how the welfare state commodifies individuals. While it is important to understand the extent to which welfare states can decommodify individuals, it is also important to understand the extent to which the welfare state actively commodifies individuals. Therefore, both decommodification and commodification can be applied to contemporary welfare policy.

The analysis within the chapter provides for some important findings regarding the over direction of the CSRs. Incidences of policies that are either decommodifying or partially decommodifying are the exception within the the European Semester. Furthermore, the EU's motivation within these policy areas, which include marginalised groups such as the Roma, children or the elderly and not the broader population, is that the situation on the ground is so terrible, that intervention would be deemed hard not to defend. In this regard, the EU will only protect individuals from the extremes of the market when a socio-economic situation for a group of individuals becomes terrible. The clear majority of CSRs aim to commodify or partially commodify individuals and the labour market, with the aim to make labour more and more competitive so that it behaves like any other commodity such as goods and services produced on the market for sale. One important recent shift can be observed in 2018 as there has been a small decline in the number of CSRs that are coded as commodifying or partially commodifying. This is achieved, not by an increase in the number of CSRs that are decommodifying or partially decommodifying, but by an increase in policy issues that are a mid-point and contain elements of both decommodification and commodification. It is important not to read too much into this shift in the sense that the EU has a long history of such policies in areas such as women, the disabled and people from a migrant background. While these policies are concerned with the integration of such groups and a reduction of social exclusion, this is achieved by securing participation in the labour market. A problem here is that the latter may, or may not, lead to emancipation and/or social inclusion. The nudge within the CSRs is therefore just that.

While the analysis within this chapter provides for a rich and detailed critical evaluation of the CSRs, it is important to understand how all of this can be accounted for. How have social actors engaged in the European Semester and what strategies have they employed to further their objectives? These issues will be analysed in the next chapter.

5 Explaining outcomes of the European Semester

Introduction

The purpose of this chapter is to analyse and account for the outcomes of the European Semester regarding the European social dimension. From the previous chapter, we can observe that between 2011 and 2018, the vast majority of the CSRs are either commodifying or partially commodifying. EU activity within the European social dimension therefore tends towards the aim of deepening market forces for labour and to extend the political economy model of neoliberal economic integration to European welfare states. However, there are some CSRs that are either decommodifying or partially decommodifying, but they remain small in comparison to the overall thrust of the European Semester. Meanwhile, for the small number of CSRs in the latter group, their concern is with marginalised groups in EU Member States, such as the Roma, children or the elderly. While the social situation of these groups is important, it should be noted that the CSRs focus on a small group of individuals in very specific situations in a few Member States; they are not aimed at the majority EU citizens and nor do they aim to fundamentally reform welfare states away from processes of commodification. Along with this trend, there has also been a significant increase in political activity relating the European social dimension within the European Semester with the launch of several strategies that aim to feed into the Semester and to guide the CSRs. The challenge is to able to account for such developments in the context of the structural and agential factors that interact within the process of European integration and specifically, the European Semester – in other words, how social actors navigate and negotiate the hierarchy of the European Semester to achieve their outcomes, the strategies they pursue, and the compromises they make along the way.

The analysis within this chapter reveals that as a consequence of the political agency of both the Barroso and Juncker Commissions, the European social dimension has experienced increased political activity and attention within the European Semester, but it has been unable to fundamentally challenge the prevailing political hierarchy, as established during the forging of Europe 2020 and the European Semester and arguably, the process of European integration at large. Meanwhile, the increased political activity and attention this agency affords are synthesised with the market-driven logic of DG ECFIN, the Economic and Financial Affairs Council and national financial ministries. Political contestation within the European Semester is focussed on the status of the European social dimension within the Semester, not the politics of welfare policy and the possibility of alternative policy solutions. Contestation between the EU's financial actors and the majority of employment and social actors is about rebalancing the European Semester to give equal consideration to economic and welfare policy, this rebalancing is underpinned by a centre-left vision of a European social dimension that embraces neoliberalism. Within this political struggle, there remain some issues for which employment and social actors are marginalised and have struggled to get their voices heard – most notably pension and wage reforms. While in the policy areas of employment, education and training, and poverty and social exclusion, political outcomes are achieved by bolstering analytical capacity within the Commission to demonstrate the need for EU action in the field, continuously launching policy initiatives without legal substance to maintain political pressure, and by adopting the language and thinking of market-led integration.

This chapter is divided into three substantive sections. The first section focusses on the policy areas of pension reform and wages and how they were captured by the EU's financial actors within the European Semester. The second section analyses the political strategies of the Barroso Commission, while the third section analyses the political strategies of the Juncker Commission. The conclusion serves to highlight the significance of the findings in the context of the political struggles surrounding European integration.

Employment and social problems as neoliberal macroeconomic policy

During the early years of the European Semester, the governance structures and the political climate were not particularly conducive for the advancing of a European social dimension. While the Europe 2020 guidelines appeared to signify a prioritisation of the social dimension, as explained in Chapter 3, this progress was conditional upon the 'soundness' of the public financial situation within the Member States. Actors within the Employment Committee and the Social Protection Committee (the two bodies of national civil servants which guide and review social and employment policy-related developments at EU level) were marginalised and this corresponded with divisions in the Council between the Economic and Financial Affairs Council and the Employment, Social Policy, Health and Consumer Affairs Council. At the time, the main priority within the European Commission and the European Council was to demonstrate to financial markets that the EU could get its government spending and debt under control; and to ensure that a future similar crisis did not occur (Copeland and Daly 2014, 2015). The dependency of the Eurozone on financial markets for government borrowing in a single currency with no transfer union or the sharing of debt-risk meant that speculation surrounding the potential ability to repay could result in a vicious circle – perceived unsustainable levels of government borrowing and debt would increase the cost of borrowing, which in turn would increase unstainable levels of debt. This power asymmetry between elected governments and financial markets meant that the only perceived solution to the situation was to impose significant cuts to government spending and where possible, tax increases – also known as austerity. In such a political environment, a certain paranoia emerged in the Barroso Commission and the Economic and Financial Affairs Council: that EU institutions needed to send clear and consistent messages to financial markets that Member States needed to reduce spending, rather than the EU to be encouraging spending commitments. During the early years of the crisis, this approach precluded any genuine commitment to a set of ambitious employment and social policy objectives within the European Semester. The 2013 Annual Growth Survey overwhelming emphasises the need for the Member States to reduce their borrowing and debt. In the European social dimension, the AGS focussed on the need to make labour markets more flexible 'reducing the excessive rigidities of permanent contracts and providing protection and easier access to those left outside the labour market', as well as the further introduction of ALMPs designed to get people back into work (European Commission 2012c: 11). Lip-service was also given to poverty and social exclusion, albeit it is a non-committal discussion of the issue couched in terms of the need to secure employment as a route out of poverty. Two further issues relating to the European social dimension were also included – pensions and wage-setting. Each of these merits a further examination.

Pension reform within the European Semester

Pension reform features prominently within the 2012 AGS with the emphasis being placed on the need to ensure financial sustainability and adequacy by aligning the retirement age with increasing life expectancy, restricting access to early retirement schemes, supporting longer working lives and to further develop private savings to enhance retirement income. Despite pension systems across the EU demonstrating considerable diversity, during the early years of the crisis they were all experiencing similar problems – Europe's ageing population, combined with the economic slowdown and rise of unemployment exerted a detrimental effect on the financial flows required to keep pension systems sustainable in the long-term

(Natali and Stamati 2013: 13). The result of this situation was an increase to pension fund liabilities, and in the context of public pension pillars, such liabilities could put pressure on government finances and fiscal sustainability. This problem directly corresponded with the MIP concerning public sector debt not to exceed 60 per cent of GDP. A further advantage was gained in that Guideline 1 of the Europe 2020 BEPG explicitly mentions the need to increase retirement age (unlike during the Lisbon decade). The revised guideline also gives greater emphasis to budgetary consolidation and sustainable public finances, thereby reinforcing the need for reform. These legal foundations and the heightened sense of uncertainty surrounding the crisis enabled financial actors to capture the issue. Such actors came from the Economic and Financial Affairs Council, particularly those from Northern European Members, and DG ECFIN. This coalition was bolstered by the support of Commission President Barroso and the EU's Secretariat General, Oil Rehn – the then Commissioner for Economic and Monetary Affairs and the Euro, and Herman Van Rompuy – the President of the European Council. Actors in the Employment and Social Affairs Council, as well as DG EMPL and its two sub-committees, were frozen out of the pension reform process. This stood in contrast to the relationship between the two sides that developed during the Lisbon Strategy in which pension reform was organised around triple rubric of adequacy, sustainability and modernisation with neither the economic nor social 'side was deemed a priori senior' (Tinios 2012: 119), although towards the end of the Lisbon decade there was a growing emphasis on the financial sustainability of pension systems.

With the door closed to the EU's social actors, financial actors dominated the reform agenda for pensions within the European Semester, but for social actors, the narrow focus on increasing the age of retirement as *the* solution to pension reform was an oversimplification of the policy problem (Interviews 3, 4, 5, 10, 14). Social actors argued that increasing the statutory retirement age alone would not necessarily improve the sustainability of pension systems, as the situation is more complex – the joint reports issued by Economic Policy Committee and the Social Protection Committee during the Lisbon decade are evidence of the EU's consensus on the matter (Tinios 2012: 121), but this historic position was subsequently disregarded during the power struggles of the crisis. The problems with the reductionist approach adopted to pension reform during the early years of the crisis can be explained by four points. First, the employment rate of older workers (55–64) in the EU Member States falls below national employment rates, with an average in 2010 of 49.3 per cent. Within this, there are some significant differences with the highest employment rates recorded in Slovenia (81.25), Sweden (70.5) and Germany (57.7), and the lowest in Malta (30.2), Poland (34) and Slovakia (40.5). Social actors argued that if employment rates for older workers matched that of the 24–55 cohort, tax receipts would increase and there would be no need to extend working lives (Interviews 3, 6). Second, age discrimination remains an issue across the EU and this has a detrimental effect on the employment rates of older workers. Simply increasing the retirement age of workers may therefore have very little impact on the overall sustainability of pension systems, as the major challenge is to increase employment levels for older workers. Third, there are real concerns that increasing the retirement age for all workers may be impossible, particularly those who have had physically demanding jobs. Fourth, the extension of working life may require a rather complicated policy mix. For example, both high- and low-income earners are more likely to leave the labour market before the statutory retirement age. For high-income earners, this is normally a choice, given that such individuals are likely to have accrued a sufficient income for their retirement. For low-paid workers an early exit from the labour market may not necessarily be a choice; rather, it can reflect poor or outdated skills and a lack of training or retraining. A further complication for policymakers is the significant differences between male and female labour market participation in older workers, with women often exiting the labour market early to fulfil caring roles.

In short, the evidence suggests that simply increasing the age of retirement may not even be a necessary condition to create sustainable (public) pension systems, but in aiming to send clear signals to financial markets, the broader debate surrounding pension reform was closed-down through fear that it would either delay the issuing of 'urgent' CSRs or water-down the perceived solution to the problem (Interviews 1, 32). The AGS, particularly in the early years of the Semester, explicitly stated the need to urgently reform pension systems to make them more sustainable. If they had not already done so, they call on the Member States to increase the retirement age and link it to life expectancy, reduce early retirement schemes, and to encourage and develop complementary private savings schemes to enhance retirement income (European Commission 2010d: 6). These issues were repeated in subsequent AGSs until 2015 when it was acknowledged that 'a majority of Member States have reformed their public pension systems in recent years so as to put them on a sounder footing as European society ages' (European Commission 2015a: 12). However, it also argues that further reform in the area is required and rather than simply increasing the retirement age, Member States should explicitly link life expectancy to the statutory retirement age, thereby creating a more dynamic balance between life spent working and that spent in retirement. The 2015 AGS represents the first explicit mentioning of the importance of ensuring the adequacy of pension provision so that a decent level of income after retirement can be achieved. This is something that social actors had continued to push for throughout the early years of the crisis but had failed to get recognised until the political pressure from financial markets reduced.

Linking wages to productivity

A second policy area in which the EU's macroeconomic actors dominated both the agenda and policy outcomes, and intentionally excluded the EU's social actors, is that of wages. The EU has long been obsessed with linking wages to productivity, as it seeks to improve the competitiveness of the European economy. The relationship between wages and labour productivity had been one of the BEPG during the Lisbon Strategy, but during the boom years of the Lisbon decade, it had seldom taken centre stage. Furthermore, despite the neoliberal underpinnings of Lisbon II, the relationship between wages and productivity was more nuanced than that which emerged during Europe 2020. Throughout the Lisbon Strategy, the EU's Member States were encouraged to link wage developments to productivity over the medium term, whilst considering the differences in skills and local labour market conditions. In neoclassical economics, the causality between the two assumes that restraining wage increases below the rate of productivity growth will increase company profits. The subsequent increase in profit is then reinvested into the economy in terms of capital investment, which generates further economic growth and employment. Note that the relationship between wages and productivity assumes that 'rational' actors reinvest profits and as a result, the economy can expand and prosper, but there is nothing automatic regarding the reinvestment of profits into capital investment. Some equally plausible scenarios would be the saving of profits with zero intention of reinvesting them, or in the current global economy of hyper capital mobility and shareholders, their reinvestment in a completely different economic sector halfway around the world with the latter having close to zero impact on the location where the profits originated from.

Within the European Semester, 1 of the 11 indicators in the MIP monitors the link between unit labour costs and productivity. The sense of urgency created by the Eurozone crisis now meant that the medium-term priority of the EU objective, as established during the Lisbon decade, was now a matter of urgency and an EU priority to create investor confidence. The inclusion of the indicator within the MIP stems from the EU's concern regarding the causes of the macroeconomic imbalances that emerged during the Lisbon decade within the Eurozone – notably the current account surpluses of Northern Members and the current account deficits of Southern Members, the latter having been fuelled by a cheap credit boom which had mainly been funded by loans from the North. According to DG ECFIN and the Northern Members of the Eurozone, the credit boom had enabled the growth of wages in the South far beyond their means and they were now uncompetitive – unit labour costs were simply too high relative to the amount produced per worker per hour. The concern, then, was on the long-term sustainability of this asymmetry and how Southern Eurozone

Members could regain their competitiveness in the Eurozone vis-à-vis the Northern Members. Note that such concerns predominantly focus on the 'Southern sinners', as Dyson and Quaglia (2012) refer to them; relatively little concern is given to Northern Members of the Eurozone (particularly Germany) who, it can be argued, suppressed wage growth significantly below productivity, thereby further worsening the declining competitiveness of the Southern states in the Eurozone. Why did the EU go down this road? To answer this question, we need to delve deeper into the governance of the Eurozone.

Johnston and Regan (2016: 219) argue that the Eurozone is a single currency union of two distinct growth regimes: (1) high inflation-prone, domestic demand-led models, which predominate in the 'mixed market' economies of the Southern Europe and (2) low inflation-prone, export-led models, which dominate Northern coordinated market economies. A problem for Southern Members is that the cobbling together of these two different growth regimes into an economic and monetary union has removed the automatic macroeconomic corrector of a currency depreciation that can be used to correct the current account deficits of their demand-led models of political economy. In a global economy with floating exchange rates, countries with persistent and unsustainable current account deficits would see a currency depreciation. For international investors, signals of a persistent current account deficit would suggest that a currency was too risky and they would switch to alternatives. The sale of the currency would result in an increased supply of the currency on the currency markets, and this would lower the price of the currency and its exchange rate vis-à-vis the major global currencies. The depreciation of the currency would create inflationary pressures and make imports more expensive, relative to previous prices, but exports would become cheaper for foreign currency holders to buy, suggesting that a currency depreciation may not necessarily be all bad news, as it can boost the long-term competitiveness of a country by boosting exports. A further point to note is that this corrective process, while not perfect by any means, would happen over the medium term and is therefore potentially less dramatic compared to the EU's response to the Eurozone crisis. A problem for the Eurozone and its Southern Members is that this corrective macroeconomic tool does not exist when a currency union is comprised of divergent economic models and the exchange rate of the currency is determined by the performance of the whole currency union, rather than an individual member. The current account surpluses of the economically weaker Eurozone members were therefore not automatically corrected by shifts in the exchange rate of the Euro, rather the problem of persistent current account deficits was simply allowed to continue and to get worse. During the Lisbon decade, the Eurozone was sleepwalking into an economic crisis that could only be corrected by either a radical overhaul of its governance or a continuation of the governance arrangements, albeit with some minor modifications. The former would require a level of solidarity and unity beyond the current inclinations of the process of European integration, with a possible fiscal transfer union, while the latter would require that EU Member States follow the existing rules of the SGP and proceed with an internal devaluation to restore competitiveness. An internal devaluation requires governments to reduce public sector borrowing with resultant cuts to welfare spending and the public sector, as well as significant decreases to wages (both public and private) to restore international competitiveness. As explained in Chapter 3, the Barroso Commission as well as DG ECFIN and the Northern Members of the Eurozone opted for internal devaluations. The link between wages, productivity and competitiveness featured as 1 of the 11 indicators for the MIP, and the declining situation in Southern Europe was identified as one of the root causes of the crisis. Throughout the early years of the European Semester, the call for Member States to act on the matter extended beyond 'Southern sinners' and included the likes of Belgium, Finland and Luxembourg.

This agenda was consistently pushed and prioritised in the power grab and heightened sense of panic during the crisis, while dissenting voices or those that offered a slightly more nuanced understanding of the situation were sidelined. During the negotiations for the Six-Pack, which included the MIP, the EU's social actors were too busy defending their own historical corners of employment policy and poverty and social exclusion rather than concerning themselves with issues that the EU had previously given little priority to – such as wages and pensions (Interviews 22, 27). As a result, in the areas of wages and pensions, DG EMPL, as well as the Employment and Social Affairs Council, were excluded from the negotiations of policy reforms. This is inspite of the relationship between incomes (wages) and numerous social issues, such as poverty and social exclusion. The EU's financial actors were able to exploit their privileged position and to proceed with establishing a hard link between wages and productivity, without the need to consider the social need and situation of workers. This policy agenda also has a clear advantage over any alternative policy solutions – it is simple to understand. As a policy idea, it resonates well with financial markets that the EU is responding to its problems, as well as communicating this message to certain sections of the EU's electorate, particularly at a time when the discourse around the crisis had dichotomised into 'responsible' Northern Member States and Southern 'sinners'. Constructing a clear and easily understood counterargument against this narrative proved too difficult for the EU's social actors within the EU's institutions, added to which they were not even in the room to negotiate an alternative. Telling the electorate and financial markets why wages should be linked to productivity, regardless of the accuracy of the claim, is much easier than explaining how and why Southern

Member States of the Eurozone got into their financial difficulties, and how their economies should be reformed *whilst* minimising negative social impacts.

In the European Semester, the EU's social actors have never been in a position to challenge the dominant policy of internal devaluation and the associated downward pressures on wages (Interviews 6, 35). EU financial actors remain in charge of wage policy with the Economic and Financial Affairs Council issuing the CSRs without the consultation of the Employment and Social Affairs Council, despite the policy area being of equal concern to both. However, it is worth highlighting the limits, and even naivety, of the EU's neoliberal policy of linking wages to productivity, the first being that in the context of Southern Members of the Eurozone, they are not centrally planned economies, nor do they feature high levels of collective or sectoral bargaining that negotiate pay. Enforcing the link between wages and productivity is unlikely to be successful, as there is little a government can do in a market economy to force down wages in the private sector. Governments can, of course, enact wage cuts in the public sector, as has been done in almost all EU countries and most notably in Latvia, Greece, Ireland and Spain. However, there is scant empirical evidence that public sector wage trends have an economically significant impact on wage developments in the private sector (Gros 2012: 8). A second limitation is that in any given sector, wage levels may not be indicative of labour productivity. To explain this we can, ironically, use the basic laws of supply and demand to highlight how wages can be determined. Say, for example, there is a shortage of skilled workers in an economy, such as computer engineers or construction engineers. This shortage would manifest itself in higher wages and given the training and investment required to enter these highly skilled professions, wages will be higher than the long-term average for the profession and would probably outpace productivity levels. However, if businesses in the sector hold wages to productivity, this would block the economic signal that there is a shortage of labour in the professions and as a result, the labour shortage would persist. Linking wages to productivity may create more problems than it solves and interferes with the operation of the market! This is a simple, albeit accurate, example of how wages cannot always be linked to productivity and how various other factors can intervene to determine the wages.

There are also other reasons to the sceptical of the indicator within the MIP. While Southern Members have experienced wage growth above productivity prior to the crisis, it may not have been the root cause of their loss of competitiveness. Gros (2012) argues that if Southern Members had experienced a loss of competitiveness, this would have manifest itself in declining exports, but the evidence suggests that as a percentage of EU exports, Southern exports remained constant throughout the decade (with the exception of Italy, where they fell). The current account deficits of Southern Members were therefore by the expansion of cheap credit, rather than a genuine loss of competitiveness. This point is supported by Baccaro and Pontusson (2016: 21–22), who suggest that while trade deficits can be caused by wage increases, they can also be caused by expansions in household credit, the latter being a problem in Southern Europe. To focus on wage costs is misleading, especially given that the European Central Bank (2003: 68) claimed that competition between advanced economies is largely determined by non-price components, such as branding, quality and reliability of service. Chen *et al.* (2013) provide a different account regarding the loss of competitiveness and argue that the focus on Northern and Southern wage costs is too simple. The authors find that current account imbalances within the Eurozone were driven by the rise of China which displaced Southern European exports in global markets and the integration of Central and Eastern Europe into the production chain of Germany and other exporters, making the latter more cost-competitive.

The side-lining of social actors in the areas of pensions and wages illustrates who is in the driving seat of the EU's political economy and its welfare states. The central concern of the EU on these issues has been on the stability of the European economy, or more specifically, the Eurozone, but it is a stability that is dependent on the judgements of the Eurozone by rating agencies and the international bond markets of the economic soundness of the situation. Note that the EU institutions have also played a part in this evaluation by designing the rules of the SGP, as well as the MIP. The unprecedented influence given to financial markets within the European political economy is a political choice and it is a choice taken by the EU. With this in mind, the social concerns of these two policy areas are side-lined and are dependent on the functioning of the market. If EU citizens wish to improve their social conditions, policies need to improve the functioning of the market and people need to conform to market conditions.

The attempted repositioning of the European social dimension during the Barroso Commission

While the EU was pushing forward with its reform agenda for pensions and wages, the EU's social actors were beginning a fightback and exercise agency to get the European social dimension more prominence in the European Semester, although there were some stumbling blocks to this. Unlike actors from the EMCO, those in the Social Protection Committee felt doubly marginalised during the early years of the European Semester. At the launch of Europe 2020 and the European Semester, the social OMC that had been established to feed into the Lisbon Strategy and concerned the areas of poverty and social exclusion, pensions and health was suspended. Its absence meant that there was no specific governance process for social policy and no provision made for social reporting within the European Semester; the Social Protection Committee was also not given a formal role within the Semester (Copeland and Daly 2015: 146). DG ECFIN, the Secretariat General and the Economic and Financial Affairs Council initially refused to acknowledge the Social Protection Committee's formal involvement in Europe 2020 and thereby during the penning of the CSRs. The EU's financial actors used Treaty provisions to justify their position. Article 121 provides the basis for the EU's BEPG which are used to monitor and govern the macroeconomic policies of the Member States. Meanwhile, Article 146 provides for the European Employment Strategy and thereby the Employment Guidelines. Importantly, Article 146 states that the achievement of EU employment policy should be consistent with Article 121, thereby creating a symbiosis between the two and a justification for the Employment Committee to be included in the European Semester. Meanwhile, Article 160, which concerns the area of social protection and thereby poverty and social exclusion, does not refer of the need to do so in accordance with Article 121 and for the financial actors, served to justify the exclusion of the Social Protection Committee from the European Semester. A further point made was that this could be further justified because the MIP does not include any references to poverty and social exclusion (Interviews 11, 25).

Within the European Council, the push to rebalance the European Semester began almost as soon as negotiations surrounding Europe 2020 ended. The European Commission tabled the Six-Pack for negotiations in September 2010 and this corresponded with the Belgium Presidency of the Council of the European Union. The latter was alarmed by the EU's overwhelming focus on budgetary discipline within both Europe 2020 and the proposed Six-Pack and the Presidency aimed to push for an EU agenda in which the social consequences of macroeconomic policy decisions were also given an equal footing (Interview 16). The Belgium Presidency used its strategic position, particularly in the Employment and Social Affairs Council, to launch the Joint Assessment Framework. The Joint Assessment Framework is designed as an analytical tool for evidence-based monitoring of the Europe 2020 Employment Guidelines. In other words, it was to provide social actors in the Employment Committee, the Social Protection Committee, DG Employment and the Council's Employment and Social Protection Committee, with robust empirical information regarding the employment situation within the Member States towards the Europe 2020 targets. To this end, the Joint Assessment Framework is drawn from a set of commonly agreed indicators showing good and poor performance towards the main Europe 2020 targets. The Employment Performance Monitor is a joint Commission-Employment Committee report that is adopted twice a year by the Council. It summarises the main findings and developments of the Joint Assessment Framework so that they can be more easily understood and comparisons between the Member States more easily made. As of 2017, the Employment Performance Monitor and Joint Assessment Framework include 10 headline indicators, each with their own sub-sections, meaning that in total there are 39 indicators ranging from labour market participation to the linking of wages to productivity. While Member States can compare their performance across the set of indicators with other EU Member States, the aim of the Employment Performance Monitor is to identify key employment challenges that are common to several of the Member States so that they can be taken forward in the context of the European Semester. While this may appear to be good news for the pursuit of a social dimension within the European Semester, the Employment Performance Monitor produces certain oddities. For example, in 2017, the transition of workers from temporary to permanent employment contracts is regarded as being a problem in only two Member States: France and the Netherlands. Yet a year earlier, the European Commission reported that it had become a problem, albeit to varying levels, across half of the EU Member States (European Commission 2016). Meanwhile, the European Performance Monitor also reported that only one EU Member State (Poland) experienced inadequate employment protection legislation, thereby implying that liberal regimes such as Ireland and the UK provide workers with sufficient employment protection. The move towards a stronger evidence base for social actors to bolster their position has not always produced the desired outcome. It can be used by social actors to bolster their pursuit of a European social dimension, but it can easily be used by financial actors to argue against a European social dimension. The inclusion of the link between productivity and wages within the Employment Performance Monitor is also indicative of the power dynamics that favour financial actors within the European Semester.

As discussed above, during the early years of the European Semester, the relationship between the Employment Committee and the Social Protection Committee was not harmonious. Concerned by the employment focus of the Employment Performance Monitor, the Social Protection Committee launched the Social Protection Performance Monitor. The aim of the Social Protection Performance Monitor was identical to that of the Employment Performance Monitor: to provide social actors across the EU's institutions with robust empirical evidence to fight their corner, propose CSRs, suggest amendments to the proposed CSRs, and to engage in the monitoring of the implementation of the Recommendations in the Member States (known as Multilateral Surveillance). The Social Protection Performance Monitor is currently comprised of 13 indicators organised around three themes: social inclusion, pensions and health and long-term care. The scoreboard organises a performance in the Member States around a traffic-light system; an improvement or satisfactory situation for an indicator is represented by green, while a deterioration in the situation is presented by red. The scoreboard table provides an accessible overview of the positive and negative trends across the Member States and thereby highlights matters of common concern. Both the Employment Performance Monitor and the Social Protection Performance Monitor can also be used by social actors outside of the EU institutions to lobby the institutions into action on an employment or social issue.

While the ability of EU social actors to advance their cause and fight their corner was strengthened by the progress made with the formation for the Employment Protection Monitor and the Social Protection Performance Monitor, divisions remained within the Council regarding the overall direction and process of European integration. The Northern Member States continued to insist that bailout countries needed to get their finances in order before priority could be given to the broader political economy issues of the European social dimension (Interviews 6, 7, 22). The latter viewed the employment and social indicators as contextual background information, rather than a fundamental shift within the politics of the European Semester. They were also mindful that clear signals needed to be sent to financial markets regarding the ability of the Eurozone to reduce borrowing and debt. Such feedback signals would help to keep interest rates on government bonds low and thereby stabilise the economic situation. The Eastern Member States followed a similar logic by arguing that bailout countries needed to get their finances in order, as they had been forced to do so during their transition from state-socialism to capitalism during the 1990s. With this frame of thinking dominating the EU, employment and social policy reforms stemming from the Semester were to favour liberalisation and deregulation and the intensified commodification of individuals, as evidenced by the data in the previous chapter.

Inside the then-Barroso Commission, tensions remained between DG EMPL on the one hand and DG ECFIN and the Secretariat General on the other hand. Within the broader set of EU institutions, it had become clear to actors that the European Semester was the 'only game in town' and that policy agendas, especially those relating to the European social dimension, could only be pursed from within the Semester. The then-Commissioner for Employment, Social Affairs and Inclusion, Laszlo Andor, was a strong proponent of a greater role for the European social dimension within the European Semester. During the penning of the MIP, for example, it was he who had pushed for the inclusion of the unemployment indicator (Interviews 10, 11). Commissioner Andor had also been instrumental during the Belgian Presidency and the move towards social actors having a more robust evidence base from which to fight their corner. In the early years of the Semester, his team continued to argue for the EU to tackle social issues, emphasising the need for a more radical approach to the poverty and social exclusion target and for the EU to move forward with the establishment of social rights and the creation of a European social insurance scheme (Andor 2014). The pressure was also being exerted by the broader set of social actors. The social NGOs – especially the European Anti-Poverty

Network – and the ETUC were pushing for a stronger EU role in the area poverty and social exclusion (with some support also from the European Parliament) (Interviews 3, 5, 21, 26).

In June 2011 the Employment, Social Policy, Health and Consumer Protection Council agreed to reintroduce the social OMC that had operated during Lisbon II. It was decided that Member States would produce National Social Reports outlining progress made in the areas of social inclusion, pensions and health/social care. These reports were to be in addition to NRPs and were to feed into the annual report on the social situation by the Social Protection Committee. They were also intended to provide information on the progress made by the Member States towards the Europe 2020 targets including Multilateral Surveillance. Initially, there was a lacklustre response from the Member States – National Social Reports were prepared in 2012, but only eight Member States contributed by the deadline set. As a result, it was agreed to shift to biennial reports (EAPN 2013: 5). This move has ultimately failed to foster further support from the Member States for the Social OMC, as at the time of writing, the submission of National Social Reports remains patchy. While most Member States submit National Social Reports, they are submitted at different times and not by the agreed deadlines. As with all such reports, they vary in quality and purpose – some simply state any changes to national policy, while others are used for detailed analysis and reflection. The revival of the Social-OMC has also enabled the Social Protection Committee to conduct thematic reviews on areas of common concern (Interviews 2, 21). Such reviews involve analysis of the current situation on a specified topic, such as in-work poverty or access to healthcare, and possible options to improve the situation. Interviewees who had participated in the thematic reviews highlighted their importance in gaining a greater insight into policy problems and potential solutions. The extent to which the thematic reviews and the National Social Reports directly contribute towards policy outputs of the European Semester was difficult for interviewees to pinpoint, but as a minimum, they are context setting. Some interviewees noted that there was 'too much' happening in the field without little concrete output and ironically, claimed that the Social-OMC was a clear example of the EU doing too much reporting, too much talking, and not enough to address the social and employment situations of its citizens (Interviews 13, 14, 17, 19).

The pressure exerted by Commissioner Andor and his team also began to pay off in other ways. A growing pattern of working between the Social Protection Committee and the Employment Committee developed, and, as time went on with the Economic Policy Committee and the Economic and Finance Committee (Interviews 5, 18, 23). In effect, the Social Protection Committee was brought back into the governance mainstream of the European Semester in 2013 and was also given the opportunity to participate in the review of both the NRPs and the CSRs, as well as inclusion into the drafting process of the CSRs. The projection of CSRs by the social actors within the Commission benefited from the progress made by the Employment Protection Monitor and the Social Protection Performance Monitor. Actors could now draw on a mutually agreed evidence base from which to highlight employment and social policy weaknesses within the Member States. Furthermore, such policy weaknesses could not be easily dismissed as being based on insufficient evidence. Despite this progress, there remained a further barrier to the achievement of employment and social policy CSRs. The drafting of the CSRs is led by the Secretariat General with input from the Country Teams. The latter steered by the Secretariat General and comprised of representatives from the various Directorate Generals involved in the governance of the European Semester. In recognition of its privileged position in the Semester, the CSRs and the accompanying recitals related to the compliance with the SGP are drafted by DG ECFIN.

By 2012, the European Commission was becoming increasingly concerned by the negative backlash caused by EU-driven austerity and the impact on the EU's reputational image. In his 2012 State of Union Speech, Barroso acknowledged that in some parts of Europe there was a real 'social emergency' with rising poverty and massive levels of unemployment (Barroso 2012). The Commission's launching of both the Youth Guarantee and the Social Investment Package signify its attempt to address the social emergency. The Youth Guarantee was launched in 2013, but while the problem of youth unemployment predates the financial crisis, it increased significantly from 2008 onwards. During the first quarter of 2008, the EU youth unemployment rate – defined as the percentage number of individuals between the age of 15 and 24 who are unemployed – stood at 15.1 per cent but increased to a peak of 23.9 per cent in the first quarter of 2013. Within this increase, there was a North/South divide with youth unemployment rates in 2013 the highest in the South (Greece 58.3 and Spain 55.5 per cent) and the lowest in the North (Germany 7.8 and Austria 9.7 per cent) (Eurostat 2019). While the North/South divide reflected the differentiated impact of the EU recession and the Eurozone crisis, it also reflects pre-crisis structural asymmetries within the Eurozone. The EU's Youth Guarantee involved the ring-fencing of €6.4 billion of the European Social Fund (ESF). Under the Youth Guarantee, individuals below the age of 25 who have been unemployed for four months since leaving formal education should be provided with a job offer, apprenticeship, traineeship or continued education. The ESF provides partial funding for the scheme, while the remainder is to be covered by the Member States. To access the funds, by January 2014, the Member States were required to submit a plan to the European Commission detailing their implementation of the Guarantee. An important observation is that ideologically, the Guarantee focusses on improving the supply of labour and accords with a neoliberal vision of the welfare state. Arguably, the Member States that had the highest levels of youth unemployment at the time were suffering from a lack of domestic demand within their economies, the latter having suppressed by EU-driven austerity. Given the role played by domestic demand in their political economies for economic growth and jobs, the Youth Guarantee is arguably the wrong medicine for the patient. Job creation, stemming from government spending, is ruled out for the South and besides, direct job-creation in the form of nationalised industries or wage-subsidies would contravene EU competition law by creating anti-competitive practices. Within this political and economic context, placing the unemployed (regardless of their age) into education, training or an apprenticeship is unlikely to reduce unemployment. There will still be insufficient employment opportunities once such programmes finish with the result being that the unemployed are simply churned around a system and remain unemployed at the end of it. Rather than representing an EU success story and progress for the European social dimension, the Youth Guarantee serves to demonstrate the limits of what social and employment actors could achieve under the Barroso Commission.

The Social Investment Package, launched in 2013 by the European Commission, aimed to steer the welfare state reform in the Member States and was designed to feed into, and guide, the employment and social policy aspects of the European Semester. Social Investment is a concept at EU level that originates from the Lisbon Strategy and on a basic level is defined as investing in people. It means policies designed to strengthen people's skills and capacities and support them to participate fully in employment and social life (European Commission 2013). Social Investment is about supporting individuals and investing in future training, education, healthcare and childcare provision to ensure that current spending provides future returns on investment. A few words of caution on the matter. First, the launching of the Social Investment Package is a reinvention of the wheel rather than a genuine shift within EU policy, as those parts of social spending conventionally grouped under ALMPs can also be regarded as investments in human capital. Second, the Package is merely a rhetorical device rather than a policy action with teeth – it (loosely) guides the Semester, it does not define the Semester. Third, and even if it did define the European Semester we should have cause for concern. It regards education and training as serving an end in itself – to secure employment – rather than something that improves social well-being; in this frame of thinking, education and training are reduced to a single purpose of improving economic growth. Finally, the concept of Social Investment aims to differentiate between passive welfare spending and that which will enhance future jobs and growth. Spending on different aspects of welfare policy is not particularly clear cut. Spending on pensions and elderly care can be categorised as passive welfare spending since such individuals will not be participating in the labour market and are not productive. But spending on elderly care, for example, may relieve individuals from caring responsibilities and enable them to participate in the labour market – the effect being that such welfare spending is indirectly productive, not to mention morally correct. The Social Investment Package represents a continuation of a market-led strategy for the European social dimension and serves to justify the commodification of everyday life.

While at the end of 2014, social actors across the EU's political space had been able to increase the visibility of social and employment issues within the European Semester, increase the number of CSRs issued, and have more and better analytical tools at their disposal to fight their corner, little had changed regarding the politics of the European Semester. While the drafting of the CSRs is a bottom-up process whereby the opinions of the different DGs feed upwards to the Secretariat General, DG ECFIN, in conjunction with the Secretariat General remains in the driving seat of the whole process. Once submitted, drafts of CSRs are redrafted and a final shortlist for each Member State is drawn up. The shortlist is subsequently discussed and finalised by the 'core group' – the relevant Director-Generals of DG ECFIN, DG EMPL and DG Growth and the relevant cabinets of the various Commissioners. Interviewees from within DG EMPL noted that while they were able to upload CSRs to the Secretariat General, there was no guarantee that their suggestions would make the final cut (Interviews 23, 24, 28). Once it receives the proposed CSRs, the Secretariat General priori-tises those CSRs that relate to the MIP; those concerning employment and social policy are then tagged onto the list for each Member State. Actors from DG EMPL upload a long list of CSRs (sometimes up to 12), with the aim being to get three or four policy issues on the final list of Recommenda-tions of a Member State. Another issue is that the drafting of the CSRs by DG EMPL is often edited by DG ECFIN to become more nuanced and to support market-led integration (Interviews 4, 16, 25, 26). During the early years of the European Semester, actors from DG EMPL who were involved in the drafting of the CSRs learnt to self-censor the wording of the CSRs to make them better fit with the terminology used by DG ECFIN and in turn, the Secretariat General (Copeland and Daly 2018: 1012). While DG ECFIN does not write the CSRs for employment and social policy, it exerts struc-tural power over their content and writing, is able to edit them, and decides which ones make the final list.

Employment and social policy within the Semester need to fit with the logic of market-led integration and the deeper commodification of every-day life. One of the most significant findings from the research interviews relates to the perception of the political situation in the European Se-mester by interviewees in DG EMPL. Almost all interviewees were sup-portive of the EU's approach to the European social dimension within the European Semester. When asked of the perceived limits of the EU's strategy, some interviewees mentioned a concern with in-work poverty, while others believed that greater prominence of social and employment issues should be given in the European Semester. Interviewees were not particularly reflective on the actual politics of what was happening in the field other than to say that conforming to the ideas of DG ECFIN was a pragmatic solution to the predicament of under-representation within the Semester. Interviewees did not question the limits of market-driven policies to employment and social policy problems, suggesting that DG EMPL is more centre-left than Keynesian-left in its thinking. The battle within the European social dimension is about getting issues onto the agenda and smoothing the edges of neoliberalism, rather than an ideological battle on the fundamentals of the European political economy. Interviews outside of the European Commission, particularly those from the Permanent Representations of the EU Member States, the ETUC and civil society organisations such as the European Anti-Poverty Network were more reflective on the politics of the European social dimension and the European Semester. Some representatives claimed that employment and social policy within the Semester had been captured by financial actors and sometimes went as far as saying that including the social dimension into the Semester had been a mistake, as it had eroded the autonomy of welfare actors from all levels of governance to determine policy outcomes. As one interviewee best summed up the then-current situation:

> The European Semester presents us with a choice, to either be a big fish in a small pond but at the cost of policy autonomy for employment and social policy or to be outside of the Semester, have policy autonomy, but to be a small fish in a very big pond.
>
> (Interview 11)

The 'success' of the employment and social actors within the Semester therefore came at a cost to their autonomy to determine policy outcomes and by the need to adopt the language, policies and politics of the EU's financial actors. The number of employment and social policy CSRs increased, as well as the policy issues mentioned within each CSRs, but their overall direction remained towards the logic of commodification. Meanwhile, the mushrooming of employment and social policy CSRs resulted in claims by the Council of policy overload within the European Semester – it being impossible for governments to adequately address numerous CSRs within a 12- to 18-month period.

Business as usual and the continuous political pressure of the Juncker Commission

The political uncertainty surrounding the Juncker Commission

The 2014 European Parliamentary elections resulted in the European People's Party (EPP) being the largest political group. During the election campaign, it nominated Jean-Claude Juncker, the former Prime Minister of

Luxembourg and President of the Eurogroup, as its preferred candidate to become President of the European Commission. This change to the election of the Commission President had been introduced during the 2009 Lisbon Treaty changes and despite some contestation in the Council, notably opposition to the appointment of Juncker by the UK and Hungary, the new President was appointed in late 2014. The potential consequences of a Juncker Commission for the European Social Dimension were mixed. On the one hand, in his capacity as Prime Minister of Luxembourg, Juncker had been a strong advocate of the launching of the 1997 EES. Juncker was regarded as being a classic Christian Democrat who was sympathetic to the cause of the labour movement. Juncker also claimed that he wanted his Commission to be a political one, suggesting that in comparison to its predecessor, it would not be afraid to propose ambitious policies to further the process of European integration. While on the other hand, during his premiership not only had Luxembourg been transformed into a tax haven for multinational corporations, with corporation tax at 1 per cent, but Juncker had also continuously thwarted EU attempts to tackle tax avoidance by such companies (Guardian 2017). Meanwhile, as President of the Eurogroup, Juncker was responsible for negotiating and supervising bailout packages for Eurozone members in financial difficulty, the latter having subjected them to savaging austerity. Given that Juncker was aligned with the same political grouping as his predecessor, there was further cause to be cautious about the fate of the European social dimension. The newly formed Commission had a ten-point agenda, but in the European social dimension, there was little information regarding its future development with the exception being that future Eurozone bailout recipients would receive a social impact assessment to ensure that the conditions attached to the funding did not have an adverse effect on employment and social conditions.

One of the first achievements of the Juncker Commission was to secure agreement for the need of a social impact assessment to complement a fiscal sustainability assessment for any future financial support package for a Eurozone Member (bailout). The purpose of the social impact assessment was to respond to criticism that the various bailout packages for the Eurozone had been accompanied by austerity and dramatic consequences for employment and social conditions. A Social Impact Assessment would demonstrate to the electorate that such issues were considered by the EU when coming to the aid of Eurozone members in financial difficulty. For EU employment and social actors, the hope was that a social impact assessment would rebalance any future bailout packages away from the narrow confines of austerity to one in which EU-driven macroeconomic reform was less detrimental to employment and social cohesion. Unfortunately, this hope was short-lived when Greece received a new three-year bailout package from the European Stability Mechanism in the summer of 2015. The bailout package was accompanied by the promised social impact assessment, but it fell considerably short of the expectations of the employment and social actors. Not only was the report written by DG ECFIN, demonstrating who remained in the driving seat within the Commission, but the assessment also appeared to merely justify the EU's approach to its current and previous bailout packages. The report claims that for Greece: 'the steps to be taken to secure better fiscal sustainability are in effect structural reforms aimed to deliver more and better jobs and sustainable and inclusive growth, as well as more effective public spending' (European Commission 2015b: 20). At no point does the assessment suggest an alternative to EU-driven austerity, rather in the eyes of Brussels the social consequences of structural reforms are unavoidable if Greece is to prosper in the long term. It should go without saying that there are numerous alternatives to austerity: macroeconomic reform can be achieved without such draconian social consequences. In this context, it is easy to see why in late 2015, interviewees were sceptical of the Juncker Commission (Interviews 9, 12, 29).

The failed relaunch of Europe 2020

In various speeches, Juncker had said that he wanted to be a President of the EU social dialogue and proposed relaunching it. But confusion remained regarding the status of Europe 2020 and the European Semester. The Italian Presidency of the Council (July–December 2014) corresponded with the Juncker Commission taking office. Given that Italian public finances were under strict observation from the European Commission, the Presidency had said that it wanted EU budgetary rules to be more flexible. In response to this, on 15 January 2015, the Commission announced that it would be more flexible on EU fiscal rules for countries that demonstrated they were serious about structural reforms (European Commission 2015c). But in Europe 2020, the Italian Presidency was less successful. On October 27 2014, the Presidency organised a Europe 2020 conference in Rome, which was aimed as a stock-taking exercise of the progress achieved on the various targets and to galvanise support for a relaunched Europe 2020 that placed a greater emphasis on the environment, employment and social protection. The final days of the Barroso Commission had launched a public consultation on a possible relaunch of Europe 2020 and the conference in Rome was timed to correspond with the closing of the consultation. The idea of a relaunch of Europe 2020 had strong echoes with the relaunching of the Lisbon Strategy in 2005. While the Presidency gained broad support in the various Council configurations for its aim, divisions remained regarding the best way forward. Some Northern and Eastern Members were sceptical that a relaunched Europe 2020 would improve the ability of governments to proceed with the necessary structural reforms (Interviews 8, 15, 20). They were also resistant to the idea that Europe 2020 required a broadening of policy areas through fear that it may lack direction and purpose and weaken its focus. There was also the belief that the energy and effort put into relaunching Europe 2020 could be better spent on the domestic reform agenda. Following the conference in Rome, the Italian Presidency produced a report summarising opinion, but the Juncker Commission was less keen on moving forward on the matter. Interviewees differed in their explanations on why this was the case: some claimed that Juncker wished to distance himself from a strategy that is associated with his predecessor (Interviews 1, 3, 24); that the new Commission had little idea on how to reform Europe 2020 and did not consider it a priority (Interviews 6, 7); and, some thought that the majority of the EU's Northern and Eastern Member States in the Council did not want to open up any opportunity to jeopardise the EU's approach to economic reform (Interviews 20, 21).

For the EU's employment and social actors, the failed attempt to relaunch Europe 2020 was met with deep disappointment and a sense that they had missed an opportunity to steer the European Semester in their favour, but the differences between such actors, as evident during the Barroso Commission, did not help the situation. Southern Members of the Council, including Italy, as well as the social civil society organisations, were pushing for an ideological change within the Semester more akin to traditional Keynesianism. While the centre-left of DG Employment, Social Affairs and Consumer Protection and a small number of Eastern Members of the Council – Slovenia, Romania and Bulgaria, were pushing for a continuation, albeit with more prominence, of the current approach to employment and social issues within the European Semester.

In March 2015, the European Commission released its draft of the Integrated Guidelines for Europe 2020, which draws on the broad guidelines for the economic policies of the Member States (Article 121) and the Employment Guidelines (Article 148). The proposed revised guidelines reduced their number from ten (2010) to eight and these were agreed by the Council in June 2015 (European Council 2015). The two 'missing' guidelines stem from a reconfiguration of the Economic Policy Guidelines from six to four. The 2015 Economic Policy Guidelines, while mentioning the need for fiscal and budgetary responsibility, place a strong emphasis on the need to promote growth-friendly investment in the economy. Guideline 1 calls for governments to increase productive investment in the economy and is aligned with the 2015 Juncker Plan or the Investment Plan for Europe. The latter aimed to mobilise private investment across the European economy, which had been weak since the beginning of the financial crisis. The plan established the European Fund for Strategic Investments with the European Commission guarantying 16 billion euros from the existing EU budget and the European Investment Bank committing five billion euros. The fund could then be used to provide a safety buffer for investment projects, thereby reducing the risk of, and encouraging, private investment.

It was estimated that a multiplier effect of 15 would generate 315 billion euros of investment across the EU. Member States could contribute to the fund and 'in the context of the assessment of public finances under the SGP, the Commission will take a favourable position towards such capital contributions to the fund' (European Commission 2015d: 2). Guideline 2 asks the Member States to reform their product, labour, social welfare and pension systems to ensure sustainable public finances, while also ensuring access to all for high-quality, affordable and sustainable social services and benefits in accordance with the employment guidelines. Guideline 3 concerns further reforms required to improve the functioning of the Single European Market, while Guideline 4 focusses on the need for sustainable public finances. The refocussing of the Economic Policy Guidelines around growth-friendly policies represents a departure from the 2010 slash and burn of austerity, but they do not represent a significant departure for the political economy of the European Semester. The revised Economic Policy Guidelines are a return to business as usual for the EU, that is neoliberalism, rather than austerity. They stop short of Keynesian-inspired government spending with the overwhelming emphasis being on the need for governments to produce the 'correct' investment decisions. It should also be noted that the move away from austerity to 'growth-friendly' economic policies, despite the latter remaining a vague and poorly defined term, is afforded by the relatively good economic conditions at the time of the Juncker Commission taking office. The European economic recovery appeared to be fully underway (except for Greece) with growth rising and unemployment falling. This had enabled the Barroso Commission to introduce some flexibility on the budgetary rules of the SGP (Schmidt 2015, 2016), which the Juncker Commission was able to take full advantage of. The continued improvement of the economy gave way to what Crespy and Schmidt (2017: 100) refer to as the 'politics of numbers' surrounding accounting calculations, where there was more political space for the Commission and the Council to debate the methods of arriving at the various indicators of the MIP. One such example has been the change to calculating the deficit in terms of a 'primary' surplus (deficit minus interest payments). This creativity enabled the Commission to allow countries that posted a primary surplus to delay rapid deficit reduction in order to propel growth, which is why France and Italy were given two-year delays to meet their targets, first in 2013 and again in 2015.

In terms of the employment guidelines, Guideline 5 – 'boosting demand for labour' – calls on the need for governments to reduce the barriers businesses face hiring people, as well as the need to support the growth of SMEs and to promote the social economy. It also calls on the Member States to ensure that wage growth is related to productivity and reflects divergences in economic performance across regions and sectors. Boosting the demand for labour is therefore focussed on ensuring that labour markets work effectively, rather than the government being directly responsible for employment. Guideline 6 – 'enhancing labour supply, skills and competences' – calls on governments to improve education and training, as well as life-long learning, active ageing, female participation in the labour market and the employment of disadvantaged groups. Guideline 7 calls on the need to balance welfare reform around the principle of Flexicurity and the need to strengthen ALMPs. The final guideline focusses on social inclusion and the combating of poverty. It calls on the need for social protection systems to promote social inclusion by encouraging people to participate in the labour market. In other words, access to poverty relief is predominantly secured by labour market participation. It also specifically mentions the need to fully implement the EU's Youth Guarantee.

Compared to 2010, some issues have been removed from the Employment Guidelines altogether, such as the need to address temporary/precarious employment. The latter is particularly interesting in the context of the steady increase of temporary or atypical employment over the last two decades. There are some further important observations. Guidelines 5 and 6 focus on the different policy approaches that can be used by governments to intervene in the labour market – demand- and supply-side policies. However, a closer inspection of Guideline 5 reveals there to be considerable rhetoric on the demand-side policies to stimulate the labour market, as such stimulation is via indirect means. Guideline 5 is a semantic attempt by the Juncker Commission to redefine how the demand for labour can be stimulated whilst government does not directly intervene in the economy. In this regard, it is a clear example of how policy cannot be taken at face value – behind policy headlines the devil is in the detail. Another point worth mentioning is that the overwhelming focus of the employment guidelines, including Guideline 8 which focusses on poverty and social exclusion, is on encouraging and maintaining the link between labour market participation and access to welfare. Disadvantaged groups are to secure social inclusion by labour market participation; meanwhile, the unemployed receive benefits on the condition that they actively seek work or engage in education and training programmes, regardless of the local employment conditions. Therefore, while there has been a modest shift in the language and tone of the Economic Policy Guidelines, the 2015 Employment Guidelines remain near identical to those from 2010. Finally, one of the most dramatic changes to the 2015 Employment Guidelines is the removal of the Europe 2020 targets, including those for employment and reducing poverty and social exclusion. Their removal confirms Juncker's desire to disassociate himself from a strategy of his predecessor and to decouple the European Semester from Europe 2020. The distinction between the two is important, as is their de-coupling. Internal documents produced by the Juncker Commission state that the European Semester aims to: ensure sound public finances, prevent excessive macroeconomic imbalances in the EU, and support structural reforms for jobs and growth, and boost investment. Meanwhile, the Semester is also the monitoring framework for the delivery of Europe 2020. Presented in this way, Europe 2020 and its various objectives are less of a priority for the Juncker Commission.

The streamlined European Semester

For the employment and social actors, a considerable amount of ambiguity remained regarding the ideological direction of the Juncker Commission. On the issue of enhancing the European social dimension, in late 2015 interviewees said they were unsure what the Commission had planned or they indicated that something was being planned around 'upward convergence', although they could not elaborate on this concept (Interviews 6, 7, 24). Some interviewees expressed the belief that within the Commission, it was business as usual in that President Juncker was continuing with the approach of its predecessor and side-lining the European social dimension – the only difference being that the rhetoric had been ramped-up to make it appear that the new Commission was doing something. Meanwhile, the Juncker Commission continued to signal its intention to move forward on the European social dimension, albeit it was becoming clearer that the Commission would be focussing more on employment *per se*, rather than a more expansive vision of the social dimension. In 2014, Juncker outlined his aim for the EU to have a 'social triple A' rating and argued that the European Semester needed to be more representative of the European social dimension (Juncker 2014). The usage of 'triple A' is a play on the scores given by the credit-rating agencies, which rate the ability of a debtor to repay their debt and thereby the ability of a default ranging from the strong likelihood of debts being repaid – triple A – through to the high vulnerability of the non-payment of debts – C/D (depending on the agency). Such ratings are used to assess government bonds, corporate bonds and so forth, and became prominent during the Eurozone crisis, as the downgrading of sovereign debt of some Eurozone members is believed to have accelerated the crisis. By using the language of the credit-rating agencies, something that the EU electorate had become familiar with, Juncker was hoping that his ambition could be easily understood, even though he did not get into the specifics of what a 'social triple A' would mean in practice. Within the Council, the historic divisions between the Member States remained. Northern and Eastern Members were cautious about any attempts to deepen the European social dimension through fear that it would undermine the SGP, while Southern Members wanted to shift the ideological direction of it and increase its prominence in the European Semester.

The Juncker Commission also introduced some significant changes to the European Semester, which came into effect for the 2015 cycle. Under the Barroso Commission, not only had the number of CSRs increased significantly, but the breadth of issues also covered within a Country Specific Recommendation also ballooned. For example, the 2014 Bulgarian Country

Specific Recommendation CSRs for employment contained no less than ten different issues that needed to be addressed, while the equivalent for Italy contained seven issues, and the two Employment Recommendations for Spain contained 12 necessary reforms. The result of such ballooning was one of policy-overload, especially in context of the requirement for Member States to make progress on the CSRs within 12 months. By 2014 the CSRs, particularly in the social dimension, were potentially undermining their intended purpose of steering reform across the Member States, as they gave the impression that everything required reform and as a matter of urgency. Within the Commission, there were concerns that the policy overload of the CSRs may be responsible for a perceived low level of engagement by the Member States. In 2015, according to Vice-President of the European Commission, Valdis Dombrovskis, it was estimated that 55 per cent of the CSRs had made 'some' progress in their implementation (Dombrovskis 2015). Although in the context of the language used by Dombrovskis, it is evident that the actual number of genuine implementations is much lower, as the 55 per cent includes situations whereby a Member State intends to introduce reforms but has yet to do so.

The streamlining of the European Semester involved the release of the Country Reports and the draft CSRs much earlier in the cycle, thereby enabling greater debate within the Council to increase the opportunity for potential amendments to CSRs. The aim of this approach was to increase ownership of the European Semester by the Member States, which, it was hoped, would improve incentives to reform national policy (Interview 24). The increased space for deliberation during the formation of the CSRs aimed to move away from the top-down and prescriptive approach that had developed since the launch of the European Semester and Europe 2020. Instructions were also given that the CSRs were to avoid being descriptive and to be written in such a way that their wording would leave scope for the Member States to discuss the means of implementation. Perhaps the most significant reform to the European Semester was to reduce the number of CSRs to an average of three per Member State, while also ensuring that they were more targeted and formulated in such a way that progress could be monitored by the EU more easily. This would enable both the Commission and the Council to prioritise national reforms and contribute to the overall improvement to the engagement by the Member States. Note that the final list of CSRs remains the responsibility of the Secretariat General and DG ECFIN. The final list is then discussed by the 'core group' of directors before being released to the Member States (Interview 30). CSRs that do not make the final list can be found in the recitals, but internal working documents produced by the Commission reveal the continued conflict and discontent surrounding the final list of CSRs, including during their prioritisation by the 'core group'. In response to this problem, the Secretariat General suggests that different DGs across the Commission do not fully understand that the CSRs are regarded as the most pressing matters.

The reconfiguration of the European Semester by the Juncker Commission is an important shift in the sense that it puts social issues much higher up the political agenda than its predecessor. The 2015 CSRs were the first to be formulated under the new streamlined European Semester and compared to 2014, the number that focussed on employment and social issues fell substantially. Using the Commission's own classification scheme, according to Zeitlin and Vanhercke (2017: 163–164), the drop was particularly evident in the fields of poverty and social exclusion (from 12 to 6 Member States), education and skills (from 25 to 13), health (from 16 to 11) and long-term care (from 7 to 2). However, considered in relative, rather than absolute terms, the proportion of social CSRs did not decline (Clauwaert 2015: 10–14) – a point further emphasised by Zeitlin and Vanhercke (2017: 164). A further observation is the more integrated character of the CSRs, particularly the linking of poverty and social exclusion to labour market participation, education and training, and to redirect taxation away from labour to other sources (ibid). In this regard, the CSRs of the Juncker Commission are more focussed around the area of employment *per se*, rather than a broader vision of a European social dimension that finds an appropriate balance between the commodification and decommodification of labour. In an EU context, this is very much business as usual.

To bolster the support for employment issues, albeit through a market-making lens, within the European Semester there were also some internal shifts within the organisation of the European Commission that were intended to bolster the capacity of DG EMPL within the European Semester. The Juncker Commission believed that DG ECFIN had grown too powerful during the crisis and aimed to reduce its headcount (Interviews 3, 4, 21, 28). One result of this decision was the moving of the Labour Market Analysis Unit from the latter to the former in 2015 – some 11 individuals in total who were to form a new team and provide a level of expertise that would improve the evidence base from which decisions within the DG could be made and justified. Interviewees from within the DG were sceptical about the long-term impact of the new unit, fearing that it would be a Trojan horse for DG ECFIN to finally take control of DG EMPL (Interviews 21, 26, 27). Members of the team were regarded as being traditional students from the economics discipline with a narrow focus on labour market issues, such as debates around minimum wages, rather than broader issues around poverty and social inclusion. Others believed that this was an exaggeration and that any cultural differences between the DG and the transferred unit could be appropriately managed. DG EMPL also had a new Director, Michel Servoz, who many regarded as a safe pair of hands to steer the DG towards the mantra of Juncker's 'do fewer things and do them well' – a phrase that numerous interviewees believed was at the heart of the Commission's approach.

All the indications were that the Juncker Commission was pushing for a stronger emphasis on employment as it was perceived to be the most pressing issue across the EU.

The new Commission also reformed the MIP by adding additional employment indicators to the scoreboard. Recall that one of the original 11 indicators measures the three-year average unemployment rate, but unlike the other ten indicators, the unemployment indicator serves as guidance only and cannot trigger an in-depth review of the situation in a Member State and the potential for corrective or preventative action. Behind the 11 indicators are some 28 auxiliary indicators that serve to inform the main indicators, including, for the unemployment indicator, the activity rate, the rate of long-term unemployment and the rate of youth unemployment. The Commission proposed the inclusion of the three unemployment auxiliary indicators, increasing the main indicators to 14, although the status of the employment indicators was to remain unchanged, i.e., a breach of an employment indicator could not trigger an in-depth review. Interviewees also believed that the reform of the MIP would offer the European Parliament something in return for the appointment of the Juncker Commission. The proposal raised eyebrows in both sets of EU actors. The DG ECFIN, as well as most Northern and Eastern Members were concerned that the additional indicators may dilute the economic priorities of the MIP, while Southern Members believed that the inclusion of the new indicators would result in 'handing the keys to ECFIN and thereby control of the issue' (Interview 6).

Several other interviewees also confirmed this point (Interviews 7, 19, 22, 30). The debate on furthering the European social dimension took an important turn in 2015, as Southern Members who are ordinarily in favour of deepening integration in the field, started to resist attempts to do so. This new political position had been formed because of what interviewees described as issue capture. That is, historically, in their attempt to gain an equal footing within the EU's governance hierarchy, employment and social actors have had to settle for compromises on the margins of the integration process with subsequent policy developments often being 'add-ons' to the process of economic integration. In the context of the power struggles of the European Semester, a problem with such add-ons (e.g. the Europe 2020 poverty target) is that employment and social policy actors have tended to lose the argument for a more progressive policy response. A result is that policy outcomes for the European social dimension are often framed through the lens of economic reductionism. Interviewees pointed to the large number of CSRs that concerned employment and social policy but were issued under the MIP, not the Employment Guidelines, as one example (pensions and wages) (Interviews 36, 37, 38). CSRs issued under the MIP become the responsibility of the Economic Policy Committee under Multilateral Surveillance, not the EMCO or the Social Protection Committee. The Southern Member States therefore began to retreat from their historic position of advancing their cause in the European Semester and the agenda (Interviews 6, 7, 20, 22, 39).

The European Pillar of Social Rights

While the Juncker Commission was exercising its political agency to increase the prominence and visibility the of the European social dimension within the European Semester, the age-old problem of divisions between the Member States and the structural power of DG ECFIN and the Economic and Financial Affairs Council served to check this agenda. While the European social dimension has received more prominence during the Juncker Commission, the hierarchy of the European Semester remains fundamentally the same as in 2011. Meanwhile, the increased prominence of the European social dimension within the Semester came at a cost of the modus operandi of the European social dimension needing to accord with the logic of commodification and market-led integration, as demonstrated by the 2015–2018 analysis of the CSRs. Given the political tendencies of the Juncker Commission, this was not so much of a cost for Juncker and his cabinet, but for those outside of the Commission and on the Keynesian left, the true intentions of integration within the European social dimension are all too clear and nowhere is this more evident than in the Commission's latest attempt to increase its prominence: the European Pillar of Social Rights.

Before delving into the details of the European Pillar of Social Rights it is important to highlight the shifting conditions of the European economy from 2015 onwards which further enabled the Commission to exercise its agency within the European Semester. In 2015, the European Central Bank began its programme of quantitative easing for the Eurozone. The programme, which came to an end in 2018, involved the European Central Bank purchasing Euro-Area bonds from governments to reduce their yield rates and to encourage investment that would have ordinarily purchased such bonds into other sectors of the economy to stimulate economic growth. Undoubtedly, the EU's programme of quantitative easing, whilst controversial, aided the economic recovery across the Eurozone and enabled the Commission to pursue its agenda within the Semester (Interviews 33, 34, 40). A second factor that aided the Commission relates to the shifting priorities of the European political space. As the European economy continued to recover, the European Semester went from being to only game in town to one of several games in town, as the 2015 migration crisis and UK membership of the EU took centre stage. With pressure to reduce government spending and debt subsiding, DG ECFIN, as well as the Economic and Financial Affairs Council were prepared to accept more prominence for the European social dimension, conditional on developments being in accordance with their frame of thinking. Meanwhile, EU leaders had shifted their attention to other crises affecting the EU and the importance of the European Semester had diminished. The launching and agreement of the European Pillar of Social Rights needs to be understood in this context (Interviews 31, 32, 35).

Launched at the Gothenburg summit on 17 November 2017, the Pillar is a declaration of social and employment rights that aims to feed into the European Semester and guide the process. Regardless of the political content of the Pillar, it should be noted that it is a declaration and not legally binding. This stands in contrast to the numerous reforms to the macroeconomic governance of the Eurozone and continues the constitutional asymmetry of European integration. The European Pillar of Social Rights contains 20 principles and rights that are grouped into three themes: (1) equal opportunities and access to the labour market; (2) fair working conditions; (3) social protection and inclusion. Notably, it does not impose any requirements on EU Member States, rather it seeks to frame future policies and to safeguard the EU's social welfare programmes. The Pillar represents an amalgamation of (1) social rights already guaranteed in the Charter of Fundamental Rights of the EU, albeit updated to reflect changes in the labour market; (2) existing social and employment policy competences and activities of the EU, particularly those governed by legally non-binding modes of governance; and (3) a few policy issues that attempt to both define and steer the future of a social Europe.

There are further reasons to be sceptical of the Pillar. A first thing to note is that the European Pillar of Social Rights contains very few rights or principles that are new and, as such, it should be regarded as a stocktaking exercise that attempts to nudge the integration process forward. This has similar echoes of the 1989 Community Charter of Fundamental Social Rights which, as discussed in chapter one, delivered relatively little for the European social dimension. Meanwhile, the means to achieve the end are weak and fail to identify means by which asymmetries in the Eurozone can be addressed (Deakin 2017: 208). Second, it is unlikely that persistent divisions within the Council can be overcome to seize the moment. The European Commission can only give direction on the matter, while most of the tools to deliver on the European Pillar of Social Rights are in the hands of the Member States. Scandinavian members have made it clear that they do not want the pillar to create any new legal rights or obligations. They also argue that labour market policy and social policy should remain a competence of the Member States and that the autonomy of the social partners should be fully respected. Meanwhile, the Central and Eastern Members are opposed to any social and employment policies that will increase the cost of labour and erode their low-cost competitive position within the EU. The chances of developing social Europe in this context seem slim and it suggests that activity on the matter may eventually reach a political stalemate. A final point to note is that the European Pillar of Social Rights has a narrow focus. Despite the Pillar-covering issues such as housing and homelessness, access to essential services, childcare and support for children, the broader set of social rights are obtained via an individual's participation in the labour market and their commodification. In this regard, such rights underpin a welfare regime in which individual personal responsibility is emphasised. Meanwhile, the state has very little responsibility for an individual's situation, regardless of how they got there, other than to support them to find work and to potentially reduce welfare benefits if they do not engage. The Pillar will do little to steer the EU away from its obsession with market-led solutions to social problems. Nor does the evidence presented in the previous chapter regarding the 2018 CSRs, the first to be guided by the Pillar, suggest that there is a radical change of departure here.

Conclusion

While employment and social actors within the EU's political space have been able to navigate and negotiate the European Semester and exercise their political agency, there are limits as what can be achieved. Not only does the European Semester still prioritise the need to discipline and police the rules of the SGP and macroeconomic reform, but promoting the European social dimension within such a political space can only be successfully achieved if employment and social policy actors pursue a strategy which accords with the EU's logic of market-led integration and a neoliberal ideology. In this regard, the battle for the European social dimension is not one of ideas or ideology, it is about how much attention and prioritisation it is given within the process of the European Semester and European integration. This development suggests that in terms of Lindblom's (1977) secondary-order issues within capitalist political economy, in the context of European integration the scope for autonomy and policy independence in the European social dimension is limited. As demonstrated by the policy areas of pension reform and wages, not only is there fierce contestation around who controls the reform process within these areas and whether they are first- or second-order policy issues, but second-order policy issues such as employment, education and training and poverty and social exclusion can only be taken forward in an EU context if policy increases commodification.

This finding and overall trend of the CSRs remains consistent overtime, regardless of the different strategies employed by the Barroso Commission and the Juncker Commission, suggesting that the long-term outlook for the European social dimension is not promising, particularly for those who believe that neoliberal-driven European integration is fundamentally flawed, let alone morally wrong. One of the most concerning aspects of these developments is the inability of actors involved in the process of European integration to step outside of the box, reflect on what is happening, and to understand the politics of it all. Actors from the conventional Keynesian social democratic mindset are in a minority position, such as the Southern

European Member States and the ETUC and at present, there is little hope of this situation changing. In the final substantive chapter of this book, we will focus on the consequences of the co-opting of social actors in the process of European integration, and as I will explain, this accounts for a considerable number of the EU's problems, not least support for the European project.

6 The European social deficit

Introduction

The final chapter analyses the consequences of the current trajectory of the European social dimension in the context of the findings of the previous chapters. The chapter argues that ideological contestation within the EU's political space post-2010 has narrowed to that between a centre-left or centre-right vision of neoliberalism. In this regard, genuine alternatives to the current political and economic trajectory of integration are on the margins of the political debate and this is problematic. As a result, the EU suffers from what I refer to as a 'social deficit' in terms of the interests it represents and the policies it pursues. After outlining the limits of current literature on EU democracy and legitimacy in the first section of the paper, the second section analyses the first dimension of the social deficit, namely the hollowing out of democracy by technocratic governance in the European Semester. The third section of the paper analyses the second dimension of the social deficit – that the EU is not producing the kind of policies its citizens want. That is, the overwhelming emphasis on commodification as a driver of European integration and the European social dimension produces political backlash and undermines support for the EU. The chapter serves to highlight the severity of the problems faced by the EU and the need for it to change the course of European integration beyond tokenistic policy reforms with catchy headlines that continue to commodify individuals.

Existing approaches to EU legitimacy and democracy

For two decades, the academic literature regarding democracy, interest representation and legitimacy in the EU has provided useful insights into how the EU performs in this field (Crombez 2003; Decker 2002; Horeth 1999; Lord 2004, 2007, 2008; Schmidt 2012). Meanwhile, the EU institutions are all too aware of the problems surrounding the EU's reputation in the area. In 2015, the official EU definition claimed:

> The democratic deficit is a concept invoked principally in the argument that the European Union and its various bodies suffer from a lack of

democracy and seem inaccessible to the ordinary citizen because their
method of operating is so complex.

(Eur-Lex 2019)

The view from Brussels and the European Capitals is that the EU's democratic deficit is a result of a lack of information about the EU, and its
decision-making process held by the European electorate, combined with
the physical and cultural barriers surrounding the 'remoteness' of Brussels.
This interpretation of the democratic deficit constructs the problem as one
in which there is ultimately nothing fundamentally incorrect or contentious with the decisions that are made at EU level nor is there anything
fundamentally problematic with the overall direction of European integration. Rather, EU citizens just need to know more about the EU and
how it benefits them. Hence, the European Commission and the European
Parliament put considerable resources into communicating to citizens the
various aspects of European integration and its benefits. This communication comes in the form of information centres, web sources with accessible information, social media content and EU offices across the Member
States that engage with both state and non-state actors with a purpose to
increase awareness of the EU and how citizens can both engage and understand it better.

When it comes to the specifics of the EU's democratic deficit, the existing academic literature divides into two camps. The first position broadly
falls in line with the official position of the EU. In his 2003 study, Crombez
analyses the extent to which the policy outputs of the EU deviate from those
emerging in other political systems. Crombez argues that the institutional
structures of the EU's decision-making process mirror those of other successful bicameral polities. Accordingly, the EU has a bicameral legislature
(Council and the Parliament) and an executive appointed by the two chambers of the legislature. EU policies are chosen by the executive, they are preferred to the status quo by the two chambers and they lie between the ideal
policies of the pivotal actors in the two chambers. In this regard, the institutional arrangements are not unusual to those found in Western democracies and are by no means undemocratic. The EU has two chambers that are
elected directly or indirectly, and EU policy ends up between what the two
chambers want. If EU policy outputs are undemocratic, it is not because of
the EU's weak institutional design. Crombez (2003) suggests that some features of the European Parliament, such as QMV, result is policy outcomes
that predominantly favour the median voter. One dimension where this can
be an issue is that sometimes members of the European Parliament can
block a proposal from moving towards the median voter. The conclusion
from this analysis is that the institutional design of the EU is not undemocratic; rather, the EU's problems stem from a lack of information about
the EU within the public realm and high levels of delegation that often hide
the EU decision-making process. The proposed solution to the former is

to open up Council meetings, while for the latter there needs to be direct elections for the role of Commission President or indirect elections from the European Parliament.

Crombez's findings have strong similarities with those put forward by Majone (2000), who argues that the EU's problems are procedural and do not require fundamental change. Majone (2000) argues that as the EU is a regulatory state and EU governments have delegated regulatory policies to the European level to isolate these policies from domestic governments, the EU does not need to be democratic in the usual manner of the term. In this manner of thinking, the EU is a regional regulatory state producing policy outcomes that are Pareto-efficient (where some benefit and no one is made worse off), rather than redistributive or value-allocative (where there are both winners and losers). Should regulatory policies succumb to electoral influence, there is a danger that they will succumb to short-term policy preferences, cease to be Pareto-efficient, and jeopardise the long-term stability and interests of the majority. In this view, an EU dominated by directly elected representatives would inevitably result in the politicisation of regulatory policy-making and undermine rather than increase legitimacy (Majone 1998). One of the most important observations regarding this perspective is the claim that regulatory policies are not political decisions because they do not involve redistributive or value-allocative processes. Not only is this position based on the assumption that some decisions are political and others can be deemed apolitical or neutral, but it also sidesteps the intense political debate surrounding EU regulation. First, all decisions, no matter how small, are political regardless of how they are categorised by academics. We should always question the intentions of individuals who claim that some issues are political while others are not. The latter is academic code to reinforce the status quo and behind this façade is a deep-seated belief that certain sections of the European elite, not all the elite, know what is best for EU citizens, regardless of their beliefs and opinions. Such a defence may be couched in academic jargon to detract from the real purpose of the argument, but ultimately the status quo serves to protect and defend the European elite that prefers a market-driven form of integration.

Second, the intense debates surrounding formation of EU regulation demonstrates that regulation is anything but apolitical. Follesdal and Hix (2006: 540) highlight the difficulty of empirically proving the claim that EU policy is Pareto-efficient with no redistributive effects. For the authors, policy outcomes can be situated on a continuum with the two extremes representing redistributive policy on the one hand and Pareto-efficient policy on the other. Importantly, very few policy outcomes can be categorised at either of the two extremes of the continuum, rather policy is likely to have elements of both. In Chapter 2, we briefly discussed the 2004 renegotiations of the Working Time Directive and the political divisions surrounding this debate, which is both divisive and deep-rooted. While the Directive – a regulation – is regarded as a health and safety matter, as excessive working hours over a long period can be detrimental to the health of workers, there are also moral issues around the debate. For Member States such as the UK, restrictions on the number of hours employees can work is perceived to be a restriction on potential earnings, thereby preventing people from economically helping themselves. Meanwhile, in Member States such as France, the argument goes that an individual should earn a sufficient income without having to work excessively long hours that will be detrimental to health. This regulatory debate is therefore one which is intensely political and depending on where one is positioned on the political spectrum will also correlate to whether the Working Time Directive is regarded as being redistributive, Pareto-efficient, or both. This example also refutes Majone's (2000) argument that regulation within the European social dimension is merely concerned with correcting for market failures. Countless other examples of political division involving EU directives further demonstrate that those surrounding the Working Time Directive are not an isolated case (cf. Copeland 2014a).

Informed by his liberal intergovernmental theory, Moravcsik (2002, 2004) claims that the EU does not suffer from a democratic deficit. As the EU is an international organisation featuring Intergovernmentalism and is not an emerging polity, national governments still largely dominate the territorial and intergovernmental structure of the EU. As national governments are directly accountable to their electorates, claims that the EU has a democratic deficit are overblown. For Moravcsik, the restructuring of the nation state has resulted in a strengthening of national executives, which remain directly elected. Meanwhile, the strengthened powers of the European Parliament, the EU's only directly elected institution, are an important development within the EU policy-making process. The ordinary legislative procedure means that a majority support is required in the Council and the European Parliament. So, if a party in government is on the losing side of a QMV in the Council, it has a chance of 'winning it back' in the Parliament (Follesdal and Hix 2006: 540). Either way, members of the Council are directly accountable to their electorates, meanwhile, Members of the European Parliament are directly elected, and the executive remains in the driving seat of European integration. Meanwhile, the EU's elaborate system of checks and balances further supports the system as an overwhelming consensus is required for any policies to be agreed. There are high thresholds for the adoption of EU policies: unanimity for the reform of treaties; then either unanimity in the Council (in areas where intergovernmental rules still apply) or a majority in the Commission plus a qualified majority in the Council plus an absolute majority in the European Parliament (where supranational rules apply); and then judicial review by national courts and the ECJ (Follesdal and Hix 2006: 540). As a result of these arrangements, EU policies are inevitably very centrist and a compromise between all interest parties.

A final perspective on EU democracy that is more nuanced than the aforementioned literature is given by Schmidt (2012) who focusses on the extent to which the EU is democratically legitimate. Schmidt argues that scholars of the EU have analysed the EU's legitimacy in terms of two normative criteria: output effectiveness for the people and input participation for the people. The distinction between input and output democratic legitimation originates from Scharpf (1970), who defined output legitimation as being judged in terms of the EU's effectiveness of policy outcomes for the people and input legitimacy judged in terms of the EU's responsiveness to citizen concerns. For Scharpf (1999: 7–21), input legitimacy refers to the participatory quality of the process leading to laws and rules as ensured by the 'majoritarian' institutions of electoral representation. Output legitimacy is instead concerned with the problem-solving quality of the laws and rules and has a range of institutional mechanisms to ensure it. For Scharpf (1999), as the EU lacks majoritarian institutions of electoral representation and has a rather thin layer of input legitimacy, one needs to focus on the problem-solving logics of institutional output. This provides for a rather pessimistic account of democratic legitimacy in the EU. Schmidt responds to this critique by focussing on the missing component of the input/output distinction with the aim of opening the 'black box' of governance and highlighting the importance of 'throughout' legitimacy. This conceptualisation is intended not only to encompass the internal processes and practices of EU governance but also what is to be understood as interest intermediation with the people (Schmidt 2012: 5). Throughput legitimacy concentrates on what goes on inside governance, in the space between the political input and the policy output, which has typically been left blank by political systems theorists. Throughput focusses on the interactions between different actors and how they engage in the EU decision-making process, how such interaction contributes towards or against throughput legitimacy, as well as the accountability and transparency of the governance processes. A problem for the EU is that while increased throughput legitimacy is unlikely to get noticed by EU citizens, negative episodes surrounding throughput legitimacy, such as corruption scandals, will undermine throughput legitimacy. Importantly, while the EU scores low on input legitimacy, the European Commission has consciously sought to remedy the situation by making throughput policy-making more inclusive and accountable to civil society (Schmidt 2012: 15). This has included providing funding and support for interest groups to counterbalance for the more powerful business interest groups. Nevertheless, such policy-making remains very distant from the kind of representative democracy EU citizens are familiar with. Furthermore, accountability, understood as being subject to scrutiny by a particular forum, is also problematic as the decision-making process of the Council, Commission or comitology suffer from a lack of accountability to the European Parliament (Bovens et al. 2010; Lord 2004, Schmidt 2012). The EU also faces further problems in that it has often tried to depoliticise EU policy formulation by presenting its initiatives in neutral or reasonable language. National capitals are also happy with this depoliticisation, as it enables them to put a political spin policy. This severs to ensure that, even as the Commission seeks to make the EU policy-making process more legitimate via accountability, transparency, inclusiveness and openness, these processes tend to disappear from the national public view, so long as negative throughput is avoided, e.g. scandals or corruption. In this respect, the EU has serious problems that will be difficult to overcome.

Indeed, the empirical evidence regarding the EU supports the broader argument made by Schmidt (2012). In 1990, 66 per cent of EU citizens considered EU membership to be a good thing, with 8 per cent considering it a bad thing, 21 neither good nor bad and 6 per cent not knowing. By 2011, the respective figures were 47 per cent in favour, 18 per cent against, 31 per cent neither good nor bad, and 4 per cent not knowing (Eurobarometer 2014). While it is easy to think that the decline in support is a result of the 2007/2008 financial crisis and the subsequent Eurozone crisis, the number of citizens who regarded EU membership as a positive thing had been hovering around 50 per cent in the run-up to the crisis. In other words, falling levels of support are not simply in response to the crisis, they have been in steady decline over the last two decades. Eurobarometer data also reveal what citizens associate with the process of European integration. In 2003, 48 per cent of citizens believed that the EU had benefited them via the free movement of people, 31 per cent peace and stability, 23 per cent thought it a waste of money, 18 per cent economic prosperity and 15 per cent unemployment. In 2012, the respective figures were 42 per cent for the free movement of people, 27 per cent as a waste of money, 26 per cent for peace and stability, 18 per cent for unemployment and 12 per cent for economic prosperity. One important observation from these data is what citizens associated with European integration does not correlate to what the EU believes is its most important achievement. In Brussels and the European capitals, the Single European Market is regarded as the epitome of successful integration. The Commission has calculated that the completion of the Single European Market has resulted in at least 2.5 million extra jobs and had increased wealth by about 600 euros per person from 1992 to 2006 (European Commission 2007). However, citizens are more likely to associate the EU with being a waste of money than with economic prosperity; the rhetoric surrounding the SEM clearly does not translate to citizens (Copeland 2015: 96).

Further grist to this mill is the results from the European Parliamentary elections. The 2014 elections witnessed a rise of populist parties from both the far left and right. These include the far-left parties of Syriza in Greece and the far-right parties of the National Front in France, the Freedom Party in Austria, the Five Star Movement in Italy, the UK

Independence Party, and countless other smaller parties from across the Member States. In total, the elections produced some 194 seats out of a total of 751 for both the far-left (47 MEPs) and far-right candidates (147 MEPs) (House of Commons Library 2014). Put differently, just under a quarter of the EU's new Parliament aims for a radical overhaul of the European project or for the complete dismantling of the EU. In both France and the UK, parties supporting the explicit withdrawal/dismantling of the EU won the single largest majority, while in Italy, the Five Star Movement came second. Therefore, the election results cannot be correlated to Member States that have received bailouts during the Eurozone crisis. The anti-EU sentiment is something that is happening across the EU in small and large, old and new, and euro and non-Eurozone members. Such support is likely to be higher than the election results suggest if we consider that the most dissatisfied of individuals often do not vote during elections. In Greece and Cyprus, where voting is compulsory in European elections, voter turnout was 59 and 44 per cent. Nor should the results be regarded as a reaction against the EU's response to the financial and Eurozone crisis. While the latter played a part in support for the far left and the far right, support for such parties has been steadily increasing, even before the crisis. In the 2009 Parliamentary elections, such parties received a total of 17 per cent of the vote (123 MEPs) and this was long before Eurozone crisis began and the electorate felt the effects of the financial crisis. Support for the far left and far right increased by 8 per cent between the 2009 and 2014 European Parliamentary elections. Viewed against this backdrop, the 25 per cent support for these parties in 2014 is not so much an anomaly nor a surprise. It is a continuation of a long-term trend that was accelerated by the social consequences of the great recession.

We should also note the general trends around voter turnout in the European Parliamentary elections. The first European Parliamentary elections received a voter turnout of 62 per cent in 1979, but by 2009 voter turnout had fallen to 43 per cent and the official EU position for the 2014 elections is that voter turnout remained at 43 per cent. The latter is slightly misleading in that voter turnout fell from 42.97 per cent in 2009 to 42.61 in 2014. Behind the average EU voter turnout lies some significant variations between the Member States. The highest voter turnout was in Belgium and Luxembourg with each achieving a turnout of 90 per cent, two Member States that also have compulsory voting and are home to most of the EU's institutions. The lowest voter turnout was in Slovakia with 13 per cent, followed by 19.5 per cent in the Czech Republic and 21 per cent in Slovenia. Judged against the lowest voter turnout of Slovakia, the EU's average of 42.61 per cent voter turnout appears impressive, but it is important to note that the voter turnout of 2014 is low and is symptomatic of some serious structural problems with EU democracy.

What's wrong with the EU? The first dimension of the social deficit

The EU has, of course, attempted to respond to the worsening situation with various initiatives, including those brought in with the Lisbon Treaty Changes. Since the Treaty of Maastricht negotiations, the European Parliament has witnessed a steady increase of its powers, including broadening the use of the co-decision procedure to more policy areas (now referred to as the ordinary legislative procedure since Lisbon). This puts the European Parliament on more equal footing with the European Council during policy negotiations. The EU's OMC is also another example of how the EU has attempted to improve its democratic credentials. As discussed in Chapter 1, the openness of the OMC was designed to include non-state actors and civil society organisations, as well as national Parliaments, in the reform of the European political economy. Ironically, during the Lisbon Strategy, the OMC actually had the opposite effect and served to enhance the power of the European Commission and the Council, while the European Parliament and civil society organisations were marginalised. This arrangement has continued under Europe 2020 and the European Semester. Nevertheless, under the Lisbon Treaty changes the European Parliament has gained the right to nominate the President of the European Commission, which it did for the first time in the 2014 elections. During an election campaign, the main political groupings within the European Parliament present their candidate for Commission President to the electorate. In 2014, the European People's Party (EPP) received the largest share of the vote with 24.3 per cent (222 seats) and nominated Jean-Claude Juncker, the former Prime Minister of Luxembourg, as the President of the European Commission. The European Council accepted this in July 2014, despite opposition from the governments of the UK and Hungary. Much was made in the EU institutions of the success of the 2014 elections, both with respect to the 'Juncker effect' and the supposed maintaining of voter turnout. Nevertheless, the ability of the European Parliament to directly appoint the President is a game changer and may even result in improved relations between the two institutions. The launch of the European Citizen's Initiative (ECI) in 2011 is also regarded as a further step in the right direction towards better citizen engagement with the EU. The Initiative enables EU citizens to petition the European Commission to propose legislation on matters where the EU has a competence to legislate. The petition is required to come from at least seven Member States, with a threshold of one million signatures, as well as minimum thresholds for each of the contributing Member States, e.g. the minimum for Germany is 72,000, Poland 32,250 and Malta 4,500. A limitation of the ECI is that it assumes prior knowledge of the Commission's legal bases for legislation in the field; this is not an easy thing to understand and is not a petition in the classic sense. It favours individuals with a very specific form of social capital.

Despite these attempts to improve EU democracy, interest representation, and links to its citizens, there is a distinct lack of ambition with the EU's ability to reform itself. Meanwhile, the EU remains severely lacking in 'input' legitimacy, as well as 'throughput'. Why is this? Is it because the EU is so diverse and the roadmap forward is hard to agree? Possibly. There are competing visions of the European project and any attempt to move forward with one vision will undeniably alienate individuals attached to another. The result is that EU decisions remain compromises and fudges that no one thinks really solves the problem, but at least it is something that has been agreed and can be sold to citizens. In this frame of thinking, Copsey (2015) argues that the EU has a deep-rooted structural crisis that has been rumbling on for at least two decades. This has resulted in a situation in which political support has been waning and a market-driven approach to integration has reached a limit. Importantly, this problem predates the Eurozone crisis, thereby reminding us that there is something seriously wrong with the EU and the decline of public support is not to be correlated with one single event. The broader field of EU studies recognises the shift of support for the EU project as part of a post-Maastricht shift across the EU from 'permissive consensus to constraining dissensus' (Hooghe and Marks 2009). Post-Maastricht, within the Member States decisions can no longer be legitimatised by executives and legislatures alone. On EU matters the public demands a say through referendums. Mair (2007) argued that the depoliticisation of EU politics drove the change. Where there is a consensus between mainstream political parties on EU policies, opposition to the EU shifts towards questioning the fundamental principles of integration. The argument can be taken further: Kriesi et al. argue that the shift in politics, parties and party systems across the EU is driven by structural competition between the winners and losers of globalisation (Kriesi et al. 2006: 921), of which the EU is a regional variant (Schmidt 2002).

For Copsey (2015: 224), the solution for the EU can be reduced to three interconnected elements: (1) a new project, narrative or vision for Europe in the 21st century on which everyone can agree; (2) the means to deliver this project effectively at the European and national level; and (3) a decision about how far this new project of European integration will extend. I could not agree more with this claim, but I would argue that the limits of European integration are directly attributed to market-driven integration that is underpinned by neoliberalism. The ideological underpinnings of market-driven integration are therefore important determinants in the EU's current predicament and Copsey's 'choice for Europe', as he refers to, would need to be achieved in the context of a move away from neoliberalism.

The shift from 'permissive consensus to constraining dissensus' is symptomatic of the breakdown of the social contract between governments and their citizens; it is more than a coincidence that public support for the EU has steadily declined during the pursuit of an integration model underpinned by neoliberalism. Neoliberalism has reached its limit, but EU leaders are hell-bent on pursuing the ideology as a roadmap for European integration, even though it is producing negative consequences. The first limitation of neoliberalism relates to the fact that it is not a democratic ideology, at least compared to the form of representative democracy found within the EU's Member States. Both Hayek (2001) and Friedman (1962), the foundering fathers of neoliberalism, rejected representative democracy because it infringed on individual freedom. The problem with representative democracy, in Hayek's view, was that it is too easily twisted to become an assault upon liberty. Under such a system of democracy, elected majorities are given the right to impose their view of the world onto the entire population. However, Hayek's (2001) criticism of direct democracy goes much further than this. Unless individuals cannot learn the essential virtues that are needed to sustain a free market culture, they cannot become independent, sovereign individuals and they cannot be entrepreneurs. A consequence of this situation is that they are likely to demand employers and the state protect their standard of living and provide security. As a result, societies tend towards the slippery slope of collectivism, which is an attack on individual liberty. However, the Hayekian view goes much further than this regarding representative democracy and the problems it causes. For Hayek, government interference in the economy, presumably caused by the pressures from representative democracy, distorts the natural functioning of the business cycle which results in more extreme peaks and troughs. As an example of this interference, Hayek argues that banks in effect create money through credit provision and this process is further encouraged by central banks which provide liquidity as a lender of last resort. This credit expansion signals to entrepreneurs that real capital costs have fallen, and so this leads to a further economic expansion because of cheap credit, with the result that economic expansion continues based on less saving and more borrowing – this is a credit bubble. At some point, the bubble bursts and the real fundamentals are restored through a slowdown and even recession and this should be allowed to take its own course (Hayek 1978: 191–231). However, governments, especially those with democratic pressures, realise that this is unpopular, and so they attempt to inflate their way out of a downturn and this is counterproductive, as government intervention will undermine the value of assets through higher inflation. The solution is to eliminate central institutions, such as central banks, and to resist pressure for governments to interfere in the economy, which will make any boom or bust worse. To resolve these problems, states need to institute a narrow form of democracy to defend liberty. Hayek argued for a government based on two chambers with a limited franchise. The first chamber is a legislative assembly of representatives 45 years or above who would serve for terms of 15 years, voted for by people of the same demographic profile. The second chamber is the government assembly, elected by all citizens except those employed by, or financially dependent on the public sector, including pensioners (Hayek 2012: 447–455).

Hayek would not recognise the EU as being neoliberal and he was often disappointed with its implementation in other places, such as the UK under Prime Minister Margaret Thatcher and the USA under President Ronald Reagan. However, the expectations–capability gap between theories of political economy and their implementation remains a continuous feature of the academic discipline and we should not read too much into the mismatch. Importantly, the process of European integration is inspired by neoliberalism. Furthermore, for those who claim that the EU is founded on ordoliberalism rather than neoliberalism, the difference between the two ideologies is subtle in the way that the colour turquoise is different to that of the colour teal. Both neoliberalism and ordoliberalism prioritise individual freedom, the dominance of the market, and hyper-commodification. The main difference between the two is that while neoliberalism proposes a minimal state with market self-regulation, ordoliberalism proposes a minimal state that regulates markets to maximise competition and to protect and defend liberty from the emergence of monopolies and. Ordoliberalism is therefore a more rules-based system of market governance than the *laissez-faire* of neoliberalism, but in terms of processes of commodification, it is no different to neoliberalism. Meanwhile, in the context of democracy, Wilkinson (2019) argues that ordoliberalism and neoliberalism, while often competing within the European political space, represent a single movement in which authoritarianism and liberalism are conflated to oppose democracy. Wilkinson (2019), while highlighting the differences and similarities of the two ideologies, not only demonstrates that their end points have much in common but also their anti-democratic tendencies. In short, a claim that the EU is ordoliberal and not neoliberal is then yet another red herring to detract from the real matter at hand.

How is all of this related to democracy, representation and legitimacy in the EU? Importantly, neoliberalism is an ideological approach that believes representative democracy is dangerous and produces unintended consequences. We should not expect the process of constructing neoliberalism across the EU to replicate the democratic systems found across the Member States, as these are undesirable and will distort the pursuit of the free market and the protection of individual freedom. According to the European political elite, the European electorate does not fully understand what it wants and how best to construct a political economy in which the market reigns supreme. This is not to say that all of the European political elite agrees with this ideological position, but rather that the dominant driving forces of European integration subscribe to this ideological position. From this ideological position, the European electorate needs to be enlightened during the path towards neoliberalism and the process of European integration is the means through which this end can be achieved. Implementing neoliberalism is also a process of social engineering. The installing of technocratic governments in Greece and Italy is part of this logic and while it may be undemocratic in the conventional sense, in the eyes of the proponents of neoliberalism the greater good merits such an intervention. In 2011 and at the height of the Eurozone crisis, the elected Socialist (PASOK) Prime Minister of Greece, George Papandreou, was facing domestic economic and political turmoil. In the Greek Parliament, PASOK MPs were split over the deal imposed by the Troika – the EU, the European Central Bank and the IMF. For Papandreou, the solution to the impasse was to hold a vote of confidence on him and his government in the Greek Parliament and a national referendum on the second bailout package. Papandreou survived his vote of no confidence, but the Troika would not accept a referendum on the bailout. Brussels, Frankfurt and Berlin argued that the bailout and its terms and conditions were the only way that Greece could remain within the Eurozone. As Greeks overwhelming wanted to remain within the Euro, the referendum would be a pointless exercise. Papandreou was forced to resign and a cross-party government of national unity was formed by Lucas Papademos, the former head of the Bank of Greece. Papademos had never been elected to office, but it was believed that a technocratic government could steer Greece onto the correct economic trajectory. The steamrolling of democracy followed a slightly different course in Italy and pressure from the Troika was subtler and galvanised by the pressure of financial markets. Following the Greek crisis, financial markets were spooked and the public finances of both Euro and non-Eurozone Member States were under increased pressure. Under pressure from the EU and the IMF, the government of Prime Minister Silvio Berlusconi passed an austerity package in the summer of 2011 to reduce public debt, which was one of the largest in the Eurozone. However, for the EU, the IMF and financial bond markets, the austerity package did not go far enough and furthermore, they lacked faith in Berlusconi to deliver it. Combined with political turmoil at home, Berlusconi resigned as Prime Minister in November 2011. He was replaced by Mario Monti, a former EU Commissioner who had never been elected to office, who formed a technocratic government (2011–2013) to implement and deepen the austerity measures.

The role that the financial bond markets played in this crisis is clear to see, but as Blyth (2013) has eloquently argued, with the exception of Greece, prior to the crisis there is very little evidence that governments had been on spending splurges. Portuguese net debt to GDP in 2000 was 52 per cent and in 2007 it was 66 per cent. What concerned financial markets regarding both Italy and Portugal during the height of the crisis that economic projections regarding an ageing population suggested that at some point in the future, these countries would be unable to repay their debt. According to Blyth (2013: 71), the crisis altered the perception of risk, but there was no orgy of government spending behind all of this. This argument is even more evident if we consider the case studies of Ireland and Spain, where government debt was falling in the years preceding the crisis. Government debt in these two countries spiked because of the bursting of property bubbles and the associated banking bailouts. They were private sector debt crises in which the public sector had to intervene. Lumping these countries together into a problem of 'out-of-control' government spending, only for the problem to be resolved by austerity, was a political decision taken by elected and non-elected individuals grappling with an incomplete system of governance for a single currency and this is where the European Semester comes into play.

Despite the economic and political situation, the European Semester requires Member States to follow the rules and implement the required policies. In terms of the macroeconomic rules, as the examples of Ireland and Spain demonstrate, these need to be followed regardless of the origin or causes of perceived excessive spending. It could be argued that by allowing their property markets to form a bubble that burst spectacularly, Ireland and Spain are culpable of economic mismanagement, but this is terribly unfair. Prior to the crisis, the EU did not concern itself too much with property markets within the Member States. Meanwhile, unlike many other Eurozone Members, Spain and Ireland followed the rules of the SGP. The built-in short-termism of the EU's macroeconomic rules and the lack of European solidarity ultimately constrain the ability of governments to engage in long-term ambitious spending strategies that may reap economic and social dividends but require a considerable financial investment. Meanwhile, in the European social dimension, Member States are required to reform their employment and social policies in accordance with EU guidelines, although the obligation to do so in poverty and social exclusion is questionable, given the absence of legal provision for CSRs. The European Semester is just as much governance by technocracy as the technocratic governments that were installed in Greece and Italy. Again, in EU circles, there is nothing inherently flawed in this approach to EU integration. It is worth pausing for one moment and thinking through the consequences of this. Democratically elected governments within the Member States come to power, but their political agenda is partially dictated by the rules of the European Semester. In this regard, democracy is being slowly hollowed out and the process of European integration, in its current version, plays a very large part in this.

The counterargument to the democratic hollowing-out caused by the process of European integration would aim to highlight several aspects of the European Semester that point to political deliberation and input by the Member States within the governance processes. First, the argument can be made that the evidence base from which the economies of the Member States are monitored has improved, particularly in the field of employment and social policy where there has been a fine-tuning of indicators and the introduction on new ones. It can be said that CSRs are formulated on solid and robust evidence, but that does not mean that the process has become more democratic – this is illogical. Having better evidence has not improved the democratic processes of the European Semester, rather it just means that in the power struggles and hierarchy of the governance architecture, actors are better able to fight their corner. A second argument is that there is much deliberation during the formation of CSRs between the Council and the European Commission and the European Semester is becoming more democratic. To support this claim, research will point to examples whereby Member States in the Council were able to challenge drafts of the CSRs and get them changed. However, scant evidence is often given for this claim in the form of one or two examples and this was confirmed by the interviewees for this research. To put this into perspective, the genuine examples are given to prove this point exist in a pool of over 1,000 CSRs. This is hardly a demonstration of democracy in action, and besides the Semester is not designed to be a truly deliberative, rather the Member States are required to follow the rules. A third case in point relates to the broad nature in which the CSRs are written, giving the Member States maximum flexibility during their implementation. However, as the analysis in Chapter 4 demonstrates, CSRs have an overall thrust, regardless of the flexibility within them. As the literature on new governance has robustly demonstrated, cognitive shifts and ideas are an important and valuable outcome of actor engagement in governance processes. Unfortunately, the politics of this claim is never contextualised, but the analyses in Chapter 5 is a clear demonstration of the overall direction of cognitive shifts and ideas emanating both within and from the European Semester. Meanwhile, policy learning is also learning about an ideological position of employment and social policy. It is not about the learning of possible alternatives to market-making welfare policy. A final consideration is that of the implementation rates of CSRs. As the governance of the European Semester has evolved, Member State responses to the CSRs have steadily increased to around 50 per cent of the CSRs demonstrating some evidence of domestic reform (European Parliament 2018). An important consideration here is that during the Lisbon Strategy, Copeland and ter Harr (2013) estimated Member State responses to the Recommendations to be at around 57 per cent. Importantly, the formation of the CSRs during the Lisbon Strategy was more predictable than that which has developed under the Semester. During Lisbon, the Member States had considerable control over the content of the CSRs, as they were negotiated between the Commission and the Council. Meanwhile, their implementation was not monitored (ibid). The compliance with the CSRs under the Semester, combined with the limited input of the Member States during their formation serves to highlight the continuous drift towards EU technocratic governance. While the CSRs during Lisbon were more democratic, under the European Semester they are less democratic; rather than suggesting that there should be a trade-off between the two (democracy versus compliance), these developments suggest that such a system of governance has reached its limit.

**What's wrong with the EU? The second dimension
of the social deficit**

While the technocratic nature of the European Semester services to highlight its undemocratic system of governance, there is a second dimension to
the social deficit that is equally important – that of the continuous market-
making logic of European integration that serves to extend and deepen the
process of the commodification of everyday life. The analysis in Chapter 4
reveals that the dominant thrust of the CSRs within the European Semester
is to commodify individuals. Essentially, the solution to the EU's economic
and social problems is to heighten and intensify the role of the market and
the process of commodification for EU employment and social policies. In
this regard, the European Semester represents an advancing of the European
social dimension, but it is an advancing that continuously aims to reconfigure the final vestiges of the Keynesian welfare state towards the supply-
side policies of neoliberalism. Such policies include several different policy
thrusts. First, the linking welfare benefits to labour market participation or
the need for welfare recipients to find employment; importantly, poverty reduction is to be achieved by individuals participating in the labour market.
Second, wages are to be linked to productivity whilst also decentralising
decades-long national collective bargaining to ensure genuine local competition within national labour markets. Third, various existing employment
rights that the EU deems excessive are argued to be creating labour market
rigidities and are liberalised and weakened. Fourth, retirement ages are increased, regardless of the health of individuals or the role played by older
generations in providing care that would otherwise be provided at cost by the
state – such as care for sick or elderly relatives or day-care for grandchildren.
Fifth, education and training are purely fixated on supporting labour market
participation, labour productivity, and improving competitiveness, rather
than on a broader cultural conception of the field. Finally, there is a need
to control and even police healthcare spending in the context of Europe's
ageing population. Given the sensitivity of healthcare systems to domestic
electorates, the CSRs merely point to the need for spending to remain under
control, while also improving healthcare spending efficiencies. All-in-all, the
solution to the EU's problems is for EU citizens to behave more and more
like what Polanyi referred to as 'true commodities'. That is, human beings
are evermore treated as items that are produced for sale on the market to find
their natural price. In short, your life chances are predominantly determined
by the market and the government will only support you if you engage with
the market mechanism and behave in the appropriate manner.

The European Semester is a technocratic governance process that serves
to continuously restructure and reconfigure the welfare state of EU members. The European social dimension is slowly inching forward, but 'progress' and the progressive socialisation of the European Semester is a specific
form of progress. The progressive socialising of the European Semester may

be packaged with buzzwords such as active-ageing, the Employment Package, triple A social rating or the Pillar of Social Rights, but as the analyses within this research demonstrate, the EU's intentions are all too obvious to see. Individuals who claim that things have improved for employment and social policy within the Semester are only telling us half of the story, as 'progress' is conditional and contingent upon a market-making logic. Given the close connection of such individuals to the EU institutions, they have a clear incentive to do this. Arguments that the EU is committed to the European social dimension are therefore correct, but the real devil is in the detail. Any claim that there is no alternative to this policy paradigm is rubbish. There are always alternatives and sometimes, they can be better than the current situation; they may not always be better but often they can be. Furthermore, historically while there may be a political consensus that individuals should work as they often lead more fulfilling lives, under neoliberal employment regimes this assumption does not hold. If the employment situation is precarious, if wages are low, if employment conditions are poor, and if workers are unable to accrue sufficient welfare rights such as pension contributions, then working under such conditions is not going to lead to a more fulfilling life compared to being out-of-work.

However misleading the claims by some regarding what the EU is doing within the European social dimension, there is a fairly obvious limitation to the EU's pursuit of a market-making form of integration. While the argument of the previous section regarding the undemocratic nature of the European Semester can be considered as input and throughput aspects of legitimacy, we also need to consider output legitimacy. Importantly, when it comes to policy outputs, the European Semester is not producing the kind of policies EU citizens want. The declining public support for the EU integration project stems, not from Brussels being too remote and distant from most EU citizens, nor does it stem from a lack of knowledge about EU policy-making, rather it stems from the ideological direction in which the process of European integration has been traveling and the inability of the EU electorate to be able to change it. Over the last three decades, the increased commodification of everyday life is not what the EU electorate wants, as the consequence of this approach is to produce vulnerabilities and insecurity. Often political leaders and the electorate will find scapegoats for everyday vulnerabilities and insecurities, such as migrants and/or Brussels bureaucrats, but these are distractions from the truth of what is really happening.

To further understand this point we need to draw from Polanyi's (2001) argument regarding the dangers of commodification. Polanyi argues that commodifying human beings is problematic on two fronts: first, the concept of perfect or pure markets, i.e. where supply = demand and the price mechanism finds its equilibrium, is a fallacy and can never be achieved; and second, if we subject the everyday lives of human beings and their fate to the market mechanism, we will only produce alienation and resistance, and this will ultimately result in the failure of liberal capitalism. In other words, we cannot, and should not, treat human beings as if they are a physical good or service void of feelings and emotions. Human beings are emotionally intelligent people who have a variety of psychological needs and subjecting their life chances to the fate of the market will fail. For those who are sceptical of this claim, it is worth highlighting the groundbreaking research conducted by Michael Marmot (2006) on UK civil servants, which highlights several important traits of the human character. Marmot's study of the UK civil service investigated the causes of stress in the workplace. In the late 1960s and early 1970s, Whitehall bureaucrats were divided into 19 separate layers. Marmot asked a simple question: who was more likely to have a stress-related heart attack, the boss at the top or someone below? The results of this study were surprising – the lower an employee ranked in the hierarchy, the higher their stress levels and the likelihood of having a heart attack. The real question is: why? The answer to this question reveals some of the cornerstones of human psychology that are relevant to understanding why subjecting the fate of human beings to the market mechanism is problematic. Marmot's study revealed that if individuals have no control over their work, they are more likely to become stressed and depressed. It turns out that human beings need to feel that they belong, they need to feel valued, they need to feel that they are good at something, and they need to see that their future is secure. If a person expends effort on behalf of others, there is a reasonable expectation of reward. In the workplace, an imbalance between effort and reward is associated with increased health risks. However, the argument goes much deeper than this, with evidence that a lack of control and low social participation have a powerful influence on disease and mental illness. Subjecting individuals to the fate of the market mechanism will therefore only ever fail. Viewed from this perspective, no wonder EU approval ratings and voter turnout for the European Parliamentary elections have been on a steady decline.

There is a disjuncture between the European project, as perceived by the European elite on the one hand, and the EU electorate on the other. 'Club Europe' – the European political elite that has directly benefited from the process of European integration – is a group of individuals whose lifestyle is fundamentally different to the other 80 per cent of EU citizens. While Club Europe is more open and accessible to new members than political elites found in authoritarian regimes, this highly skilled group of individuals, with high levels of social capital, often with permanent employment contracts, healthy remuneration, and an ability to move easily around the EU for employment opportunities, has wielded itself to a process of integration that prioritises competitiveness at all levels, ever greater commodification, increased risk and uncertainty, and a lack of control over daily life for the other 80 per cent of EU citizens. But note that these conditions do not apply to Club Europe and when they do, they can protect themselves from the swings of market forces. One of the most ironic events at the height of the Greek crisis were officials in Brussels, many of which were on six-figure salaries with jobs for life, extensive holiday entitlements, subsidised private education for their children, single-figure levels of income tax, free child-care, and one of the most generous pension systems on the Continent, telling ordinary Greek citizens that none of this should apply to them; in fact, their long-term security could only be guaranteed if they moved further away from this form of employment regime. Meanwhile, EU-driven austerity was to project, and sometimes force, these policy ideas upon the EU's Member States post-2010.

We can further elaborate on the limits of neoliberalism and the European integration project. Collignon (2016: 5) argues that the neoliberal over-emphasis on negative liberty has distorted the project of modern liberty because it has stifled positive freedom. The concept of negative freedom was coined by the political philosopher Isaiah Berlin and views freedom as being derived from the freedom of interference by other people; such a definition regards liberty as a private, individual space. The Stanford Encyclopaedia of Philosophy (2016) defines negative freedom as including freedom of movement, freedom of religion and freedom of speech, as well as arguments against paternalist or moralist state intervention. The EU's four founding freedoms – the free movement of goods, services, capital and people – can be regarded as forming part of this concept. Negative freedom can be contrasted with positive freedom, which Berlin defines as the ability of an individual to act upon one's free will. The scope of individual freedom within the positive sense is thereby dependent upon the ability of individuals to exercise self-determination. In an EU context, positive integration, whereby policies are focussed on the re-regulation of sectors or individuals and correcting for market failures, aligns much more with positive freedom (however, we always need to remember that not all positive integration is market-correcting – some of it can be market-making, so this categorisation is with caution). While negative freedom is usually attributed to individual agents, positive liberty is often attributed to collectives or to individuals considered primarily as members of given collectives.

For neoliberalism, the ultimate freedom of individuals can only be achieved when the state retreats and freedom of non-interference are guaranteed. Neoliberalism, therefore, combines and conflates the philosophical concept of negative freedom with liberal economic principles that are supposed to produce the ultimate freedom for individuals, as well as the efficient distribution and allocation of scarce resources in a market society. This is where the process of European integration has gone wrong – not only has the EU attached itself to negative freedom and negative integration, but it also views the relationship between positive and negative freedom as being zero-sum when they coexist. As Collignon (2016: 5) reminds us, Berlin took care to explain that negative and positive freedom overlap (2002 [1957]: 169) or 'cannot be kept wholly distinct' (2002 [1969]: 36) and he was perfectly clear that his two concepts of liberty should co-exist and cannot substitute for each other. The EU therefore intentionally produces a specific form of negative integration based on negative freedom, and this dogmatic approach is inherently flawed. A consequence of this situation is growing discontent and the rise of policy problems which governments are seemingly incapable of resolving, as they are hamstrung by the ideological parameters of neoliberalism and its emphasis on negative freedom.

Why has the EU gone down this road as a policy solution to its problems? There are a mixture of practical and ideological reasons behind this decision. First, the lack of a fiscal transfer union for the Euro and the inability of states to devalue their currency – a macroeconomic tool that is sometimes used by governments when in financial difficulty – means that internal devaluation (reducing labour costs, both direct and indirect) becomes a logical solution to restore competitiveness and achieve low interest rates for government bonds. A problem with this solution is that it increases commodification of labour and is unpopular. Second, as discussed in other parts of this book, the political and economic differences between the Member States are regarded as a contributory factor for policy outcomes being of lowest common denominator. Within the EU decision-making process, it is much easier to agree on policies of negative integration that aim to remove barriers to trade and liberalise the economy, than it is to agree policies of positive integration, which can be either market-making or market-correcting. Market-correcting policies, such as sufficient labour market regulation to protect employees, but also policies that would see the state take more of an active role in the economy, are difficult for the EU to agree upon. However, while the institutional design of the Eurozone and the political differences of the Member States are practical obstacles that limit market-correcting policies, we also need to acknowledge that negative integration is also a political and ideological decision. Negative integration is not just an unintended consequence of regional integration, it is actively chosen by both the centre-left and the centre-right as a political economy model for the EU. Decisions regarding European integration involve political agency as much as they involve structural factors. Once we accept that much of what the EU does is intentional, we can think more critically about the process of European integration, including the limits of the EU's approach to policy problems and solutions, namely neoliberal commodification.

Importantly, the warning signs that the process of European integration, in its current version, is not working are all too obvious to see. European integration initially began as a peace-building project for the European Continent to eliminate conflict and another world war emanating from Europe. By the mid-1980s, the ethos of European integration changed to one in which the process was to both enable and manage the new global order of neoliberalism. Given the historical market-making logic of European integration, this step-change was a relatively straightforward process, as it did not alter the fundamentals of regional integration. The EU's current dilemma is that the *raison d'etre* it has pursued over the last three decades has not only reached its limit, but is now actively undermining European unity, European solidarity, peace and stability on the Continent. Neoliberal-driven European integration is undermining the EU as a peace-building project, as evidenced by the falling levels of public support for the European project and the rise of populism and nationalism across the European Continent.

Conclusion

The aim of this chapter has been to analyse the consequences of the EU's obsession with neoliberal market-led integration, as epitomised by developments within the European social dimension since the launching of Europe 2020 and the European Semester. Both Europe 2020 and its governance process, the European Semester, aim to increase the commodification of labour which extends to increasing processes of commodification for everyday life. That is, the EU's economic and social problems are resolved by deepening and extending the use of the market mechanism. What this means is that the solution to problems such as unemployment is not for elected governments to intervene to create employment opportunities, whether it be through job creation in the public sector or capital investment to create employment opportunities in the private sector. Rather, the solution to the economic and social problems affecting the EU is for individuals to continuously dehumanise themselves and behave as if they were a true commodity that achieves its natural price by the laws of supply and demand. The EU and its Member States will support individuals during this process, and those who do not engage will be forced to engage through strategies such as reducing benefit entitlements. Supply-side policies provide the illusion that a government or the state is supporting individuals through empowerment and maximising human potential, but this support is Janus-faced, as it plays on and exacerbates the vulnerabilities of individuals in situations of which they often have very little control. This situation has emerged as a result of the narrow set of interests genuinely represented within the EU and the resultant policies of commodification this produces. In my opinion, the social deficit accounts for the rising tide of public opinion against the EU, and no amount of tinkering with this trajectory will improve the situation. The EU needs to move beyond its obsession with the market and limit processes of commodification, not extend them.

Conclusion

This research has analysed developments within the European social dimension between 2010 and 2018. Central to this analysis has been understanding the politics of what has been happening within the European social dimension in the context of the broader process of the political economy of European integration. First and foremost, European integration concerns itself with pursuing and defending the four founding freedoms of goods, capital, services and workers. Since the mid-1980s, the implementation and upholding of these four freedoms have been achieved by the EU and its Member States subscribing to neoliberalism. As Crespy and Menz (2015: 85) argue, 'when reconnecting social policy to broader framework of political economy and the historical unfolding of European integration, what cannot be ignored is the many ways in which the embrace of neoliberalism has precluded the coming age of Social Europe'. Any analysis of the European social dimension needs to acknowledge the EU's *raison d'être* and the significant role it has played, and continues to play, in underpinning developments in EU policies in the fields of employment, education and training, social policy, pensions, wages and healthcare.

While the aim of a comprehensive European social dimension as a counterweight to the Single European Market emerged as the rationale for integration in the field during the late 1980s, throughout the 1990s and 2000s, this pursuit was undermined by the splitting of the European left. Those on the centre-left reconfigured to embrace neoliberalism; in reality, this meant that the EU's centre-left accepted the logic of market-led solutions to policy problems but would support individuals during their participation in the market. Meanwhile, individuals or organisations that would not engage with the market and market principles were to be forced to do so by the state. This position is radically different to post-war Keynesian social democracy, in which the role of the state was perceived as one which limits the reach of the market, rather than extending it, and protects individuals from the peaks and troughs of the economic growth cycle. Remnants of post-war social democracy have remained on the European left and can be found within the EU social actors, such as the European Anti-Poverty Network and the ETUC. Within the European Council, they can be found within

Southern Member States. A consequence of this political division was that on the eve of the Eurozone crisis, the centre-left had more in common with the centre-right that it did with post-war Keynesian social democracy.

The Eurozone crisis and the EU's response to it were to solidify the political division between the centre-left and the centre-right. Meanwhile, post-war Keynesian social democracy, as an alternative to neoliberalism, was to be further relegated to the margins of the EU's political space. The post-2010 European political space was one in which the centre-left, with its commitment to neoliberalism, was pitted against the centre-right. Political contestation surrounding the process of European integration focussed on whether or not the EU should involve itself in the European social dimension, rather than over the actual policy content of the European social dimension. While this political division has been evident since the mid-1990s, these divisions have crystallised within the European political space since 2010. Europe 2020 and the European Semester are purposefully designed not only to monitor compliance with macroeconomic guidelines from the SGP and the BEPG, but they are also intended to connect thinking between the latter policy domains and those in other areas. This includes the policy areas of the European social dimension. These governance arrangements also prioritise macroeconomic policy in the context of a stronger legal framework vis-à-vis the European social dimension.

The overall result is twofold. First, the necessary budgetary discipline of the SGP, with its post-2010 enhanced budgetary surveillance and sanctions, essentially means that governments are unlikely to engage in long-term spending commitments on policy areas within the European social dimension that may pay future dividends, but put short-term pressures on public finances. Second, these parameters, along with EU rules around state aid and competition policy, prevent governments from directly creating employment opportunities. The solution to creating employment is to increase competition between individuals within the labour market, with competitive pressures enabling the market to find its equilibrium and ultimately the economy will create jobs. This form of governance by markets creates a Darwinist struggle whereby only the fittest survive during the competitive race that is daily life.

Policy outputs in the form of CSRs from the European Semester favour the increased commodification of individuals as a solution to policy problems. The political struggles surrounding the CSRs for the European social dimension relate to their number and visibility, not the politics of such policy. It is within this context that such political struggles attempt to depoliticise the reality of what is really happening within the European social dimension – the EU can be more active in the field, but citizens will get more of the same policy, not a different type of policy. The question then presented to the electorate is: 'do you want more neoliberalism or slightly less?' To be successful in this struggle, EU social actors, including those in DG EMPL have focussed on the bolstering of analytical capacity and the continuous launching of policy initiatives without legal substance to maintain political pressure. The DG is a defender and promoter of the European social dimension, but such action is achieved by the deepening and widening of market principles, not the vision of a European social dimension that is a genuine counterbalance to protect individuals from commodification. On the minority of occasions when the EU has proposed policy that is either partially decommodifying or fully decommodifying, it is when the social situation for a group of individuals has become so severe that it cannot be ignored. Meanwhile, such groups are identified as the elderly, children or Roma communities in a handful of post-2004 Member States. The decision to intervene in this area and propose policies that decommodify is based on the assumption that such tinkering will also not change the fundamental commodifying nature of the welfare state and the European social dimension.

In this regard, the EU's secondary order issues – that is, those policy areas that do not alter the fundamental logic of macroeconomics and private enterprise – have experienced intense political contestation and battles for control. Some secondary order issues, such as wages and pensions, have been captured by the EU's financial actors, as well as Northern and Eastern Member States who wish for the rules of the SGP to be followed. Meanwhile, social actors have been able to maintain some limited control in areas such as education and training, poverty and social exclusion, employment and healthcare, but this is conditional on policy maintaining the logic of market-driven integration. The EU's secondary order issues have long been an ideological battleground for control by different groups of actors, but within a post-2010 EU, this battle has ended and any 'progress' in the social dimension needs to be understood from this logic.

Following the appointment of the Juncker Commission, President Juncker and his team were able to exercise their agency to increase the prominence of the European social dimension within the European Semester. While this was successful in the sense that employment and social issues as policy problems were taken more seriously within the European Semester and the EU, very little changed ideologically. Meanwhile, the impact of this political agency needs to be contextualised in the sense that pressure from financial bond markets had eased as a result of a programme of quantitative easing introduced by the European Central Bank in 2015. At the time when the Juncker Commission was pushing for greater prominence for the European social dimension, the EU's attention was shifting elsewhere as the political and economic conditions afforded and the EU was forced to deal with other crises, such as the UK's future relationship with the EU and the refugee crisis. In the grand scheme of things, post-2015, the European Semester has shifted from being the EU's most important priority to it being one of several important priorities. This shift enabled the Juncker Commission to achieve more prominence for the European social dimension, but the Commission was aided by other events.

Wither the European social dimension and the European integration project?

For those who take the view that the solution to the EU's economic and social problems lies in a greater reliance on the market mechanism to solve problems and, thereby, the increased commodification of individuals and everyday life, the findings of this book are not a cause for concern. Indeed, they may even provide relief that the EU has finally taken control of its welfare states and is pushing them in the right direction. However, in my opinion, this belief and position are fundamentally flawed – the solution to the EU's economic and social problems is not to increase commodification and intensify market forces. I have explained why I believe this to be the case in the previous chapter, but within these final concluding remarks, I would like to reemphasise my argument, as well as further justify the position I take on the matter.

Being influenced by the writings of Karl Polanyi, I firmly believe that the increased commodification of everyday life, in the sense that the life chances of individuals are determined by the fate of the market mechanisms and not much else, is not only immoral but will ultimately fail. Human beings are not rational robots void of emotions to the world around them; they are intelligent people who value security, stability and opportunity in the world in which they live. Pursuing our 'obsolete market mentality' in an attempt to improve the lives and well-being of society does not produce circumstances which individuals ultimately feel safe and secure, rather it produces the complete opposite of that situation. Once thrown at the market to survive, people find that their material wellbeing and physiological state is only partially self-determined. The market, through which no one seems to have any control over, determines the rest. In order to survive, individuals are required to be resilient, even under the harshest of conditions.

A perfect example of such a situation would be the EU's Youth Guarantee Programme, which provides funding and support for individuals to search for work or engage in training. However, individuals only get support from the state if they actively engage in searching for work, even when unemployment is rising. Changes in government from the centre-left to the centre-right or vice versa do very little to change this situation; the electorate gets either slightly more or slightly less of the same, not something radically different. Why bother electing governments when daily life only gets worse, not better? Meanwhile, should governments threaten to intervene in the economy, financial and business interests essentially bully them into being unable to do this, either through increases to the cost of government bonds or the threat of moving production or offices to another EU Member State, thereby negatively impacting on growth and jobs in the current host state. Intense competition between Member States, which plays out in the context of a downward pressure on levels of corporation tax, income tax, labour standards and social security cannot be won nor resolved through more competition. This is exactly what the EU has pursued over the last

30 years, and since 2010, it has deepened and extended this logic to the European welfare state.

The battle for a different kind of European social dimension that moves beyond the current logic, therefore, lies outside of the European welfare state. Current progress within the European social dimension will only lead to more of the same – greater commodification, intensified competition and increasing uncertainty and insecurity in life. Academics and politicians will continue to pretend that the EU is genuinely doing something and that there is no alternative, but the web of self-interest and deceit surrounding such individuals needs to be seen for exactly that. The shift away from this ideological *raison d'etre* will first need to challenge the EU's ideological belief of neoliberal-driven market integration. The idea that the market solves all problems needs to be abandoned and should be combined with a belief in the role of the state intervening, taking control and taking responsibility for citizens in a more constructive and proactive way (cf. De Grauwe and Ji 2017). Given the political hierarchy of European integration, this shift in thinking would need to take place, first and foremost, around the EU's macroeconomic legal framework and macroeconomic policies. It would need to break the EU's dependence on financial markets and stop them being able to pick off individual Member States and punish them when things do not go as they expect.

There is something bitter sweet about the bailout of financial institutions across Europe during the 2007/2008 crisis. Financial institutions lend on the assumption that all lending involves risk, but when investments turn sour, such institutions cut their losses and move on. They rarely offer financial lifelines to ailing organisations through fear that the investment is rotten and will never be repaid. Yet European governments did precisely this for financial institutions when they faced bankruptcy. This may have been done in the interest of all in society through fear that a failed bank would result in catastrophic consequences for the economy, but within this decision, the broader needs of society were also included. Yet despite this situation, financial institutions only ever serve themselves in the form of their investors and shareholders, they seldom serve the interests of society, despite having been rescued. For this reason, EU Member States need to curtail the power of financial institutions and restore sovereignty into the hands of people who are elected. This would require a level of solidarity never before seen on the European Continent, but it is possible. The EU created the rules of the SGP, and now financial markets beat Member States of the Eurozone with them when they are not followed. Rather than accepting this fate, why not change the rules or the governance arrangements that puts control back in the hands of elected politicians? The EU made the rules once before – why not do it again?

The 27/28 Member States would need to demonstrate solidarity in areas of taxation, employment policy and the welfare state; they would also need to reform the Treaties to enable governments to be more interventionist in the economy. This would require a radical departure from the current premise that the state is a bad thing, that it should retreat, and ultimate freedom can be guaranteed only when the state is retrenched. It would also need to move beyond the reductionist argument that human beings are self-interested and motivated by this trait alone. As Chang (2011: 41) notes: 'if the world were full of self-seeking individuals found in economic textbooks, it would grind to a halt because we would be spending most of our time cheating, trying to catch cheaters, and punishing the caught'. The EU needs to design an economic system in which certainty is guaranteed and the range of human personality traits is rewarded. As argued by Watson (2005), even Adam Smith would not recognise the contemporary interpretation of his theory, as he believed that humans were motivated by self-interest, but this trait would be checked by moral sympathy for others. In short, if we treat human beings as though they are solely self-interested, they will start to behave more and more as if they are. Some human beings are self-interested, but others are not, and it really does depend on the person. To build an economic system on the premise that human beings are self-interested is insanity and social engineering at its most coercive. This is not to say that markets should be abandoned completely; sometimes they are needed and can be useful, but we need to accept that they do not provide the solution to every problem. We need to also recognise that, at present, the market has the upper hand in politics, and this is causing problems, both in terms of constraining elected governments but also producing discontent and crises.

So, within this conclusion, I offer no 'policy recommendations', another buzzword in academic writing that aims to generate 'policy impact' beyond the ivory towers. Rather, I offer a principle or ethos through which the process of European integration should be reorganised: limit commodification, limit the reach of the market and stop exploiting peoples' vulnerabilities as the solution to all of our problems. But for those who remain sceptical that this is causing all manner of problems within the EU, I would like to finish with one final thought. As I was writing this book, the UK's decision to leave the EU became a reality, which has been a heart breaking and truly frustrating experience. While I have always been critical of the EU, I firmly believe that policy problems and their solutions can best be resolved when Europe works together. I am therefore not a Brexiteer, nor have I ever been, but to Polanyians, it is obvious why Brexit is happening – take one of the EU's most neoliberal Member States, combine it with Euroscepticism and a political elite that lies and misleads the public, and you get Brexit. This event should serve as a genuine wakeup call for the EU. However, I suspect Europe's political elite will conclude that Brexit resulted from the UK's perpetual status as the most Eurosceptic Member State, as well as the lies made by the political elite. This interpretation would leave out the role played by neoliberalism, and this would be the biggest tragedy of them all.

References

Acharya, V. and Richardson, M. (2009) 'Causes of the financial crisis', *Critical Review: A Journal of Politics and Society*, 21 (2): 195–210.

Andor, L. (2014) 'Basic European Unemployment Insurance: Countering Divergences within the Economic and Monetary Union'. Speech given at Vienna University of Economics and Business 29/09/2014). Available at: http://europa.eu/rapid/press-release_SPEECH-14-635_en.htm

Armstrong, K. (2012) 'The Lisbon Strategy and Europe 2020: From the governance of coordination to the coordination of governance', in P. Copeland and D. Papadimitriou (eds.) *Evaluating the EU's Lisbon Strategy*. Basingstoke: Palgrave Macmillan, pp. 208–228.

Armstrong, K.A. (2010) *Governing Social Inclusion: Europeanization through Policy Coordination*. Oxford: Oxford University Press.

Armstrong, K.A. and Bulmer, S.J. (1998) *The Governance of the Single European Market*. Manchester: Manchester University Press.

Ashiagbor, Diamond (2005) *The European Employment Strategy: Labour Market Regulation and New Governance*. Oxford: Oxford University Press.

Baccaro, L. and Pontusson, J. (2016) 'Rethinking comparative political economy: The growth model perspective', *Politics and Society*, 44 (2): 175–207.

Barcevičius, E., Weishaupt, T.J. and Zeitlin, J. (2014) 'Institutional design and national influence of EU social policy coordination: Advancing a contradictory debate', in E. Barcevičius, T.J. Weishaupt and J. Zeitlin (eds.) *Assessing the Open Method of Coordination: Institutional Design and National Influence of EU Social Policy Coordination*. Basingstoke: Palgrave Macmillan, pp. 1–15.

Barnard, C. (1997) 'The United Kingdom, the "Social Chapter" and the Amsterdam Treaty', *Industrial Law Journal*, 26 (3): 275–282.

Barnard, C. and Deakin, D. (2002) '"Negative" and "positive" harmonisation of labour law in the European Union', *Columbia Journal of European Law*, (8): 389–413.

Barroso, J. (2012) 'State of the Union 2010 Address'. Speech given on 12/09/2012 in the European Parliament Strasbourg. Available at: http://europa.eu/rapid/press-release_SPEECH-12-596_en.htm

Bauer, M. and Becker, S. (2014) 'The unexpected winner of the crisis: The European Commission's strengthened role in economic governance', *Journal of European Integration*, 36 (3): 213–229.

Bekker, S. (2015) 'European Socioeconomic Governance in Action: Coordinating Social Policies in the Third European Semester' (Brussels: OSE Paper Series, No 19, Jan 2015).

Bekker, S. and Klosse, S. (2013) 'EU governance of economic and social policies: Chances and challenges for social Europe', *European Journal of Social Law*, June 2013 (2): 103–120.

Begg, I. (2007) *Lisbon II, two years on: An assessment of the partnership for growth and jobs.* Centre for European Policy Studies Special Report. The Centre for European Policy Studies (CEPS), Brussels, Belgium.

Begg, I. (2008) 'Is there a convincing rationale for the Lisbon Strategy', *Journal of Common Market Studies*, 46 (2): 427–435.

Begg, I. (2010) 'Economic and social governance in the making: EU governance in flux', *Journal of European Integration*, 32 (1): 1–16.

Begg, I and Berghman, J. (2002) 'Introduction: EU social (exclusion) policy revisited?' *Journal of European Social Policy*, 12 (3): 179–194.

Bellamy, J. and Magdoff, F. (2009) *The Great Financial Crisis: Causes and Consequences.* New York: Monthly Review Press.

Bickerton, C., Hodson, D. and Puetter, U. (2015) 'The new intergovernmentalism: European integration in the post-Maastricht era', *Journal of Common Market Studies*, 53 (4): 703–722.

Bieler, A. (2005a) 'Class struggle over the EU model of capitalism: Neo-Gramscian perspectives and the analysis of European integration', *Critical Review of International Social and Political Philosophy*, 8 (4): 513–526.

Bieler, A. (2005b) 'European integration and the transnational restructuring of social relations: The emergence of labour as a regional actor?' *Journal of Common Market Studies*, 43 (3): 461–484.

Bieler, A. (2008) 'Labour and the struggle over the future European model of capitalism: British and Swedish trade unions and their positions on EMU and European co-operation', *British Journal of Politics and International Relations*, 10 (1): 85–105.

Bieler, A. and Morton, A. (2001) 'Introduction: Neo-Gramscian perspectives in international political economy and the relevance to European integration', in A. Bieler and A. Morton (eds.) *Social Forces in the Making of the New Europe: The Restructuring of European Social Relations in the Global Political Economy.* Basingstoke: Palgrave Macmillan, pp. 3–24.

Blyth, M. (2013) *Austerity: The History of a Dangerous Idea.* Oxford: Oxford University Press.

Bohle, D. and Greskovits, B. (2007) 'Neoliberalism, embedded neoliberalism and neocorporatism: Towards transnational capitalism in Central-Eastern Europe', *West European Politics*, 30 (3): 443–466.

Borrás, S. and Radaelli, C. (2011) 'The politics of governance architectures: Creation, change and effects of the EU Lisbon Strategy', *Journal of European Public Policy*, 18 (4): 463–484.

Börzel, T. (2002) 'Pace-setting, foot-dragging, and fence-sitting. Member state responses to Europeanization', *Journal of Common Market Studies*, 40 (2), 193–214.

Bovens, M., Curtin, D. and 't Hart, P. (eds.) (2010) *The Real World of EU Accountability: What Deficit?* Oxford: Oxford University Press.

Brady D. (2003) 'The poverty of liberal economics', *Socio-Economic Review*, 1 (3): 369–409.

Büchs, M. (2007) *New Governance in European Social Policy: The Open Method of Coordination.* Basingstoke: Palgrave Macmillan.

Bulmer, S. and Jonathan, J. (2016) 'European integration in crisis? Of supranational integration, hegemonic projects and domestic politics', *European Journal of International Relations*, 22 (4): 725–748.

Bulmer, S. and Lequesne, C. (2013) 'The European Union and its member states: An overview', in S. Bulmer and C. Lequesne (eds.) *The Member States of the European Union.* Oxford: Oxford University Press, pp. 1–30.

Busemeyer, M.R., de la Porte, C. Garritzmann, J.L. and Pavolini, E. (2018) 'The future of the social investment state: Politics, policies, and outcomes', *Journal of European Public Policy,* 25 (6): 801–809.

Callaghan, H. (2008) How multilevel governance affects the clash of capitalisms. MPiFG Discussion Paper 08/5. Cologne: Max Planck Institute for the Study of Societies.

Callaghan, H. and Höpner, M. (2005) 'European integration and the clash of capitalisms: Political cleavages over the Takeover liberalization', *Comparative European Politics,* 3 (4): 307–332.

Caporaso, J. (1996) 'The European Union and forms of state: Westphalian, regulatory or post-modern?' *Journal of Common Market Studies,* 34 (1): 29–52.

Carmassi, J., Gros, D. and Micossi, S. (2009) 'The global financial crisis: Causes and cures', *Journal of Common Market Studies,* 47 (5): 977–996.

Castles, F. and Mitchell, D. (1993) 'Worlds of welfare and families of nations', in F. Castles (ed.) *Families of Nations: Patterns of Public Policy in Western Democracies.* Brookfield, VT: Dartmouth, pp. 93–128.

Caune, H. Jacquot, S. and Palier, B. (2011) 'Social Europe in action: The evolution of EU policies and resources', in P. Graziano, S. Jacquot and B. Palier (eds.) *The EU and the Domestic Politics of Welfare State Reform.* Basingstoke: Palgrave Macmillan, pp. 19–47.

Cerny, P. (1994) 'The dynamics of financial globalization: Technology, market structure, and policy response', *Policy Sciences,* 27: 319–342.

Cerny, P. (1996) 'International finance and the erosion of state policy capacity', in P Gummett, (eds.) *Globalization and Public Policy.* Cheltenham: Edward Elgar, pp. 83–104.

Cerny, P. (1997a) 'Paradoxes of the competition state: The dynamics of political globalisation', *Government and Opposition,* 34 (2): 251–274.

Cerny, P. (1997b) 'International finance and the erosion of capitalist diversity', in C. Crouch and W. Streeck (eds.), *Political Economy of Modern Capitalism.* London: Sage, pp. 173–181.

Chang, H. (2011) *23 Things They Don't Tell You About Capitalism.* St Ives: Penguin.

Chang, M. (2009) *Economic and Monetary Union.* Basingstoke: Palgrave Macmillan.

Chen, R. Milesi-Ferretti, G.M. and Tressesl, T. (2013) 'External imbalances in the Eurozone', *Economic Policy,* 28 (73): 1010–1042.

Cini, M. (2016) 'Intergovernmentalism', in M. Cini and N. Borragán (eds.) *European Union Politics.* Oxford: Oxford University Press, pp. 66–78.

Clauwaert, S. (2014) *The Country Specific Recommendations (CSRs) in the Social Field: An Overview and Comparison – Update including the CSRs 2014–2015.* Background Analysis, 2014.01. Brussels: European Trade Union Institute.

Clauwaert, S. (2015) *The Country Specific Recommendations (CSRs) in the Social Field: An Overview and Comparison - Update including the CSRs 2015–2016.* Brussels: European Trade Union Institute Background Analysis.

Clift, B. (2009) 'The second time as farce? The EU Takeover Directive, the clash of capitalisms and the hamstrung harmonization of European (and French) corporate governance', *Journal of Common Market Studies,* 47 (1): 55–79.

Collignon, S. (2008) 'The Lisbon Strategy, macroeconomic stability and the dilemma of governance with governments; or why Europe is not becoming the world's most dynamic economy', *International Journal of Public Policy,* 3 (1): 72–99.

Collignon, S. (2016) Negative and Positive Liberty and the Freedom to Choose. Unpublished paper. Available at: www.stefancollignon.de/PDF/The-Freedom-to-Choose%20Negative-and-Positive-Liberty.pdf

Copeland, P. (2012a) 'Conclusion: The Lisbon Strategy – Evaluating success and understanding failure', in P. Copeland and D. Papadimitriou (eds.) *Evaluating the EU's Lisbon Strategy*. Basingstoke: Palgrave Macmillan, pp. 229–238.

Copeland, P. (2012b) 'EU enlargement, the clash of capitalisms, and the European social model', *Comparative European Politics*, 10 (4): 476–504.

Copeland, P. (2014a) *EU Enlargement: The Clash of Capitalisms and the European Social Dimension*. Manchester: Manchester University Press.

Copeland, P. (2014b) 'Central and Eastern Europe: Negotiating influence in an enlarged European Union', *Europe-Asia Studies*, 66 (3): 467–487.

Copeland, P. (2015) 'The European Union and the Social Deficit', *Representation*, 51 (1): 93–106.

Copeland, P. (2016) 'Europeanization and de-Europeanization in UK employment policy: Changing governments and shifting agendas', *Public Administration*, 94 (4): 1124–1139.

Copeland, P. and Daly, M. (2012) 'Varieties of poverty reduction: Inserting the poverty and social exclusion target into Europe 2020', *Journal of European Social Policy*, 22 (3): 273–287.

Copeland, P. and Daly, M. (2014) 'Poverty and social policy in Europe 2020: Ungovernable and ungoverned', *Policy and Politics*, 42 (3): 351–366.

Copeland, P. and Daly, M. (2015) 'Social Europe: From "add-on" to "dependence-upon" economic integration', in A. Crespy and G. Menz (eds.) *Social Policy and the Eurocrisis: Quo Vadis Social Europe*. Basingstoke: Palgrave Macmillan, pp. 140–160.

Copeland, P. and Daly, M. (2018) 'EU social policy and the European Semester', *Journal of Common Market Studies*, 56 (5): 1001–1018.

Copeland, P. and James, S. (2014) 'Policy windows, ambiguity and commission entrepreneurship: Explaining the re-launch of the European Union's economic reform agenda', *Journal of European Public Policy*, 16 (3): 272–291.

Copeland, P. and Papadimitriou, D. (eds.) (2012) *Evaluating the EU's Lisbon Strategy: Evaluating Success, Understanding Failure*. Basingstoke: Palgrave Macmillan.

Copeland, P. and ter Haar, B. (2013) 'A toothless bite: The effectiveness of the European Employment Strategy as a governance tool', *Journal of European Social Policy*, 23 (1): 21–36.

Copsey, N. (2015) *Rethinking the European Union*. Basingstoke: Palgrave Macmillan.

Costamagna, F. (2013) The European semester in action: Strengthening economic policy coordination while weakening the social dimension? LPF-WEL Working Paper No. 5. Laboratorio di Politica Comparata e Filosofia Pubblica, Torino, Italy.

Council of the European Union (1989) 'Community Charter of Fundamental Social Rights of Workers'.

Council of the European Union (2000a) Presidency Conclusions, 7–8 December 2000.

Council of the European Union (2000b) Lisbon European Council Presidency Conclusions, 23–24 March 2000.

Council of the European Union (2000c) Presidency Conclusions, Barcelona European Council, 15–16 March 2002.

Council of the European Union (2002) Presidency Conclusions, Barcelona European Council, 15–16 March 2002.

Council of the European Union (2005) Presidency Conclusions, European Council Brussels, 22–23 March 2005.

Cox, R. (1981) 'Social forces, states and world orders: Beyond international relations theory', *Millennium: Journal of International Studies*, 10 (2): 126–155.

Crespy, A. and Menz, G. (2015) 'Commission entrepreneurship and the debasing of social Europe before and after the eurocrisis', *Journal of Common Market Studies*, 53 (4): 753–768.

Crespy, A. and Schmidt, V.A. (2017) 'The EU's economic governance in 2016: Beyond austerity?' in D. Natali and B. Vanhercke (eds.), *Social Developments in the EU 2016*. Brussels: European Social Observatory (OSE) and European Trade Union Institute (ETUI), pp. 99–114.

Crespy, A. and Vanheuverzwijn, P. (2019) 'What "Brussels" means by structural reforms: Empty signifier or constructive ambiguity?' *Comparative European Politics*, 17 (1): 92–111.

Crombez, C. (2003) 'The democratic deficit in the European Union: Much ado about nothing?' *European Union Politics*, 4 (1): 101–120.

Crotty, James. (2009) 'Structural causes of the global financial crisis: A critical assessment of the new financial architecture', *Cambridge Journal of Economics*, 33: 563–580.

Daly, M. (2006) 'EU social policy after Lisbon', *Journal of Common Market Studies*, 44 (3): 461–81.

Deakin, S. (2017) 'From social pillar to new deal', in F. Vandenbroucke, C. Barnard and G. De Baere (eds.) *A European Social Union after the Crisis*. Cambridge: Cambridge University Press, pp. 192–210.

Decker, F. (2002) 'Governance beyond the nation-state. Reflection on the democratic deficit of the European Union', *Journal of European Public Policy*, 9 (2): 256–272.

De Grauwe, P. (2008, November) 'The Banking Crisis: Causes, Consequences and Remedies', University of Leuven and CESifo. Available at: www.ceps.eu/publications/banking-crisis-causes-consequences-and-remedies.

De Grauwe, P. and Ji, Y. (2017) 'Booms, busts and the Governance of the Eurozone', in F. Vandenbroucke, C. Barnard and G. De Baere (eds.) *A European Social Union after the Crisis*. Cambridge: Cambridge University Press, pp. 160–191.

Degryse, C. (2012) The new European economic governance. Working Paper 2012.14. European Trade Union Institute, Brussels.

De la Porte, C. (2011) 'Principal-agent theory and the open method of coordination: The case of the European Employment Strategy', *Journal of European Public Policy*, 18 (4): 485–503.

De la Porte, C and Pochet, P. (2003) 'Introduction', in C. De La Porte and P. Pochet (eds.) *Building Social Europe through the Open Method of Coordination*. Frankfurt am Main: Peter Lang, pp. 11–26.

Department of Work and Pensions (2012) *The Work Programme*. London: Department of Work and Pensions.

Dessler, D. (1989) 'What's at stake in the structure-agency debate?' *International Organization*, 43 (3): 441–473.

Devine, F. (2002) 'Qualitative methods', in D. Marsh and G. Stoker (eds.) *Theory and Methods in Political Science*. Basingstoke: Palgrave Macmillan, pp. 197–215.

Dinan, D. (2011) 'Institutions and governance: Implementing the Lisbon Treaty in the shadow of the euro crisis', *Journal of Common Market Studies*, 49 (S1): 103–121.

Dombrovskis, V. (2015) Country Specific Recommendations 2015 – Speaking Points of Vice-President Dombrovskis. Available at: http://europa.eu/rapid/press-release_STATEMENT-15-4980_en.htm – accessed January 2019.

Dunne, T. and Schmidt, B.C. (2011) 'Realism', in J. Baylis and S. Smith (eds.), *The Globalization of World Politics,* 2nd Edition. Oxford: Oxford University Press, pp. 162–183.

Dyson, K. (2000) *The Politics of the Eurozone.* Oxford: Oxford University Press.

Dyson, K. and Quaglia, L. (2012) 'Economic and Monetary Union and the Lisbon Strategy', in P. Copeland and D. Papadimitriou (eds.) *Evaluating the EU's Lisbon Strategy.* Basingstoke: Palgrave Macmillan, pp. 189–207.

Ebbinghaus, B. (1999) 'Does a European social model exist and can it survive', in G. Huemer, M. Mesch and F. Traxler (eds.) *The Role of Employer Associations and Labour Unions in the EU.* Aldershot: Ashgate, pp. 1–28.

Ebbinghaus, B. and Manow, P. (eds.) (2006) *Comparing Welfare Capitalism Social Policy and Political Economy in Europe, Japan and the USA.* London: Routledge.

Edler, J. (2012) 'Research and innovation and the Lisbon Strategy', in P. Copeland and D. Papadimitriou (eds.) *Evaluating the EU's Lisbon Strategy.* Basingstoke: Palgrave Macmillan, pp. 168–188.

Eising, R. (2015) 'Multi-level governance in Europe', in J.M. Magone (ed.) *Routledge Handbook on European Politics.* London: Routledge, pp. 165–183.

Esping-Andersen, G. (1987) 'Citizenship and socialism: De-commodification and solidarity in the welfare state', in M. Rein, G. Esping-Andersen and L. Rainwater (eds.) *Stagnation and Renewal in Social Policy: The Rise and Fall of Policy Regimes.* New York: M.E. Sharpe, pp. 78–101.

Esping-Andersen, G. (1990) *The Three Worlds of Welfare Capitalism.* Princeton, NJ: Princeton University Press.

EurActiv (2008) EU Lisbon Agenda Gets Social Makeover, 18 March. Available at: www.euractiv.com/innovation-enterprise/eu-lisbon-agenda-gets-social-mak-news-219576

EurActiv (2010) Brussels Unveils Economic 2020 Roadmap for Europe, 3 March. Available at: www.euractiv.com/priorities/brussels-unveils-2020-economic-rnews-302202

Eur-Lex (2019) Democratic Deficit. Available at: https://eur lex.europa.eu/summary/glossary/democratic_deficit.html

Eurobarometer (2014) Eurobarometer Interactive Search System. Available at: http://ec.europa.eu/public_opinion/cf/index_en.cfm

European Anti-Poverty Network (2013) EAPN Toolkit on Engaging in the National Reform Programmes and National Social Reports 2013. Available at: www.eapn. eu/en/news-and-publications/news/eapn-news/new-eapn-toolkit-on-engaging-in-the-national-reform-programmes-and-national-social-reports-2013

European Central Bank (2003) Developments in the euro area's international cost and price competitiveness. Economic Bulletin, Issue 8. Available at: www.ecb. europa.eu/pub/pdf/other/pp67_74_mb200308en.pdf?22348d883471eb96c46a65c5 e341ac96 – accessed June 2019.

European Commission (1995) European Economy: Broad Economic Policy Guidelines. Available at: http://ec.europa.eu/economy_finance/publications/publication7973_en.pdf

European Commission (2000) 'The Lisbon European Council – An Economic and Social Renewal for Europe', Contribution of the European Commission to the Special European Council in Lisbon, DOC/00/07, Brussels: European Commission.

European Commission (2002) The state of the Internal Market for services. Com (2002) 441 final, Brussels, 7 August 2002.

European Commission (2004) Extended impact assessment of proposal for a Directive on services in the Internal Market, COM (2004) 2 final, 13 January, Brussels.

European Commission (2007) *A Single Market for Services.* Available at: http://ec.europa.eu/internal_market/top_layer/index_19_en.htm

European Commission (2008) *Communication from the Commission to the European Council: A European Economic Recovery Plan.* Luxembourg: European Communities. COMM (2008) 800 final.

European Commission (2009) *Economic Crisis in Europe: Causes, Consequences and Responses.* Luxembourg: European Communities.

European Commission (2010a) 'Europe 2020: A strategy for smart, sustainable and inclusive growth', Commission Communication, COM (2010) 2020 final, 3 March 2010.

European Commission (2010b) 'Study to support an impact assessment of further action at European level regarding Directive 2003/88/EC and the evolution of working time organisation. Diegem: Deloitte Centre for Strategy and Evaluation Services.

European Commission (2010c) *Communication from the Commission: Europe 2020. A Strategy for Smart, Sustainable and Inclusive Growth. COM (2010) 2020 final.* Brussels: European Commission.

European Commission (2010d) List of key initiatives accompanying document to Communication from the Commission, The European Platform against Poverty and Social Exclusion. A European framework for social and territorial cohesion, Commission Staff Working Paper, SEC (2010) 1564 final.

European Commission (2010e) Annual Growth Survey: Advancing the EU's comprehensive response to the crisis. COM (2011) 11 final.

European Commission (2012a) Treaty on Stability, Coordination and Governance in the Economic and Monetary Union. Press Release 01/02/2012. Available at: http://europa.eu/rapid/press-release_DOC-12-2_fr.htm – accessed October 2017.

European Commission (2012b) Communication from the Commission to the European Parliament, The Council, The European Economic and Social Committee and the Committee of the Regions: Towards a job-rich recovery, Strasbourg: COM (2012) 173 final.

European Commission (2012c) Communication from the Commission: Annual Growth Survey 2013. Com (2012) 750 final.

European Commission (2013) *Towards Social Investment for Growth and Cohesion: Including Implementing the European Social Fund 2014–2020,* Communication from the Commission to the European Parliament, the Council, the European Economic and Social Committee and the Committee of the Regions, Brussels: COM(2013) 83 final.

European Commission (2015a) Annual Growth Survey. COM (2014) 902 final.

European Commission (2015b) Commission Staff Working Document: Assessment of the Social Impact of the new Stability Support Programme for Greece. SWD (2015) 162 final

European Commission (2015c) Stability and Growth Pact: Commission Issues Guidance to Encourage Structural Reforms and Investment. Available at: http://europa.eu/rapid/press-release_IP-15-3220_en.htm

European Commission (2015d) Factsheet: Where Does the Money Come From? Available at: https://ec.europa.eu/commission/sites/beta-political/files/factsheet2-where-from_en.pdf

European Commission (2016) Temporary Employment in the EU: Springboards or Career Dead Ends? Available at: https://ec.europa.eu/social/main.jsp?langId=en&catId=89&newsId=2581&furtherNews=yes

European Commission (2017a) The European Semester Timeline. Available at: https://ec.europa.eu/info/business-economy-euro/economic-and-fiscal-policy-coordination/eu-economic-governance-monitoring-prevention-correction/european-semester/european-semester-timeline_en

European Commission (2017b) The European Plus Pact. Available at: https://ec.europa.eu/epsc/publications/strategic-notes/euro-plus-pact_en

European Council (2008) Brussels European Council conclusions, 13/14 March 2008.

European Council (2013) Council Recommendation of 22 April 2013 on establishing a Youth Guarantee (2013/c 120/01).

European Council (2014) Council Recommendation on Lithuania's 2014 National Reform Programme and delivering a Council Opinion on Lithuania's 2014 Convergence Programme. COM (2014) 416 final.

European Council (2015) Council Recommendation on the broad guidelines for the economic policies of EU countries and of the EU as a whole. 2015/1184.

European Parliament (2017a) Factsheets on the European Union: The Principle of Subsidiarity. Available at: www.europarl.europa.eu/factsheets/en/sheet/7/the-principle-of-subsidiarity

European Parliament (2017b) Factsheets on the European Union: Social Dialogue. Available at: www.europarl.europa.eu/factsheets/en/sheet/58/social-dialogue

European Parliament (2018) Implementation of the 2017 Country-Specific Recommendations. Available at: www.europarl.europa.eu/RegData/etudes/ATAG/2018/614500/IPOL_ATA(2018)614500_EN.pdf

European Stability Mechanism (2017) History. Available at: www.esm.europa.eu/about-us/history

European Trade Union Confederation (2005) ETUC Challenges Commission Proposal for Liberalisation of Services. Available at: www.etuc.org/a/436

European Trade Union Confederation (2012) Economic and Employment Policies – Europe 2020. Available at: www.etuc.org/r/6

Eurostat (2017) The Macroeconomic Imbalances Procedure (MIP) Introduced. Available at: http://ec.europa.eu/eurostat/statistics-explained/index.php/The_Macroeconomic_Imbalance_Procedure_(MIP)_introduced

Eurostat (2019) Youth Unemployment. Available at: https://ec.europa.eu/eurostat/data/database?node_code=tipslm80

Fabbrini, S. (2013) 'Intergovernmentalism and its limits: Assessing the European Union's answer to the euro crisis', *Comparative Political Studies*, 46 (9): 1003–1029.

Falkner, G., Hartlapp, M. and Treib, O. (2007) 'Words of compliance: Why leading approaches to European Union implementation are only "sometimes true theories"', *European Journal of Political Research*, 46 (3): 395–416.

Falkner, G. and Treib, O. (2008) 'Three worlds of welfare compliance or four? The EU-15 compared to the new member states', *Journal of Common Market Studies*, 46 (2): 293–313.

Featherstone, K. (2010) 'The JCMS annual lecture: The Greek Sovereign debt crisis and EMU: A failing state in a skewed regime', *Journal of Common Market Studies*, 49 (2): 193–217.

Follesdal, A. and Hix, S. (2006) 'Why there is a democratic deficit in the EU: A response to Majone and Moravcsik', *Journal of Common Market Studies*, 44 (3): 533–562.

Fraser, N. (2014) 'Can societies be commodities all the way down? Post-Polanyian reflections on capitalist society', *Economy and Society*, 43 (4): 541–558.

Fraser, N., Gutierrez, R. and Pena-Casas, R. (eds.) (2011) *Working Poverty in Europe*. Basingstoke: Palgrave Macmillan.

Frieden, J. and Walter, S. (2017) 'Understanding the political economy of the Eurozone crisis' *Annual Review of Political Science*, 20: 371–390.

Friedli, L. and Stearn, R. (2015) 'Positive affect as coercive strategy', *Medical Humanities*, 4 (1): 40–47.

Friedman, M. (1962) *Capitalism and Freedom*. Chicago, IL: University of Chicago Press.

Furlong, P. and Marsh, D. (2010) 'A skin and not a sweater: Ontology and epistemology in political science', in D. Marsh and G. Stoker (eds.) *Theory and Methods in Political Science*. Basingstoke: Palgrave Macmillan, pp. 184–210.

Gal, J. (2004) 'Decommodification and beyond: A comparative analysis of work-injury programmes', *Journal of European Social Policy*, 14 (1): 55–69.

Gamble, A. (2013) 'Neo-liberalism and fiscal conservativism', in V. Schmidt and M. Thatcher, (eds.) *Resilient Liberalism in Europe's Political Economy*. Oxford: Oxford University Press, pp. 53–76.

Giddens, A. (1998). *The Third Way: The Renewal of Social Democracy*. Cambridge: Cambridge University Press.

Grahl, J. and Teague, P. (1997) 'Is the European social model fragmenting', *New Political Economy*, 2 (3): 405–426.

Graziano, P. (2011) 'Europeanization and domestic employment policy change: Conceptual and methodological background', *Governance*, 24 (3): 583–605.

Graziano, P. and Vink, M. (2013) 'Europeanization: Concept, theory and methods', in S. Bulmer and C. Lequesne (eds.) *The Member States of the European Union*. Oxford: Oxford University Press, pp. 31–56.

Green Cowles, M., Caporaso, J. and Risse, T. (eds.) (2001) *Transforming Europe: Europeanization and Domestic Change*. Ithaca, NY: Cornell University Press.

Gros, D. (2012) Macroeconomic imbalances in the Euro Area: Symptom or cause of the crisis? CEPS Policy Brief, 266 April 2012.

Gwiazda, A. (2011) 'The Europeanization of flexicurity: The Lisbon Strategy's impact on employment policies in Italy and Poland', *Journal of European Public Policy*, 18 (4): 546–65.

Hall, P. (2007) 'The evolution of varieties of capitalism in Europe', in B. Hancké, M. Rhodes and M. Thatcher (eds.) *Beyond Varieties of Capitalism: Conflict, Contradictions, and Complementarities in the European Economy*. Oxford: Oxford University Press, pp. 39–88.

Hall, P. and Gingerich, D.W. (2009) 'Varieties of capitalism and institutional complementarities in political economy: An empirical analysis', in B. Hancké, (ed.) *Debating Varieties of Capitalism*. Oxford: Oxford University Press, pp. 135–179.

Hall, P. and Soskice, D. (2001) 'An introduction to varieties of capitalism', in P. Hall and D. Soskice (eds.) *Varieties of Capitalism: The Institutional Foundations of Comparative Advantage*. Oxford: Oxford University Press, pp. 1–71.

Hall, P.A. and Taylor, R.C.R. (1996) 'Political science and the three new institution-alisms', *MPIfG discussion paper*, No. 96/6.

Hamel, M.-P. and Vanhercke, B. (2009) 'The open method of coordination and do-mestic social policy making in Belgium and France: Window dressing, one-way impact, or reciprocal influence', in M. Heidenreich and J. Zeitlin (eds.) *Changing European Employment and Welfare Regimes: The Influence of the Open Method of Coordination on National Reforms*. Oxford: Routledge, pp. 84–110.

Hantrais (2007) *Social Policy and the European Union*, 3rd Edition. Basingstoke: Palgrave Macmillan.

Hass, E. (1964) *Beyond the Nation-State: Functionalism and International Organiza-tion*. Stanford, CA: Stanford University Press.

Hayek, F.A. (1978) *New Studies in Philosophy, Politics, Economics and the History of Ideas*. London: Routledge.

Hayek, F.A. (2001) *The Road to Serfdom*. London: Routledge.

Hayek, F.A. (2012) *Law, Legislation and Liberty: A New Statement of the Liberal Principles of Justice and Political Economy*. London: Routledge.

Helleiner, E. (1995) 'Explaining the globalization of financial markets: Bringing states back in', *Review of International Political Economy*, 2 (2): 315–341.

Helleiner, E. (2000) 'From Bretton Woods to global finance: A world turned upside down', in R. Stubbs and G. Underhill, (eds.) *Political Economy and the Changing Global Order*. Oxford: Oxford University Press, pp. 163–175.

Hemerijck, A. (2018) 'Social investment as a policy paradigm', *Journal of European Public Policy*, 25 (6): 810–827.

Hicks, A. and Kenworthy, L. (2003) 'Varieties of welfare capitalism', *Socioeconomic Review*, 1: 27–61.

Hodson, D. (2010) 'The Euro area in 2009', *Journal of Common Market Studies*, 48 (S1): 225–242.

Hodson, D. and Puetter, U. (2016) 'The Eurozone crisis and European integration', in M. Cini and N. Pérez-Solórzano Borragán (eds.) *European Union Politics*. Oxford: Oxford University Press, pp. 367–379.

Hodson, D. and Puetter, U. (2019) 'The European Union in disequilibrium: New intergovernmentalism, postfunctionalism and integration theory in the post-Maastricht period', *Journal of European Public Policy*. Available at: www.tandfonline.com/doi/full/10.1080/13501763.2019.1569712

Hoffmann, S. (1966) 'Obstinate or Obsolete? The fate of the Nation-State and the Case of Western Europe', *Daedalus*, 95 (3): 862–915.

Hoffmann, S. (1995) *The European Sisyphus: Essays on Europe: 1964–1994*. Boulder, CO: Westview.

Hooghe, L. (1998) 'EU cohesion policy and competing models of European capital-ism', *Journal of Common Market Studies*, 36 (4): 457–477.

Hooghe, L. and Marks, G. (1999) 'The making of a polity: The struggle over European integration', in H. Kitschelt, P. Lange, G. Marks and J. Stephens (eds.) *Continuity and Capitalism in Contemporary Capitalism*. Cambridge: Cambridge University Press, pp. 70–100.

Hooghe, L. and Marks, G. (2009) 'A postfunctionalist theory of European integra-tion: From permissive consensus to constraining dissensus', *British Journal of Po-litical Science*, 39 (1): 1–23.

Hooghe, L. and Marks, G. (2019) 'Grand theories of European integration in the twenty-first century', *Journal of European Public Policy*. Available at: www.tandfonline.com/doi/full/10.1080/13501763.2019.1569711

Höpner, M. (2013) 'Soziale Demokratie? Die polit-ökonomische Heterogenität Europas als Determinante des demokratischen und sozialen Potenzials der Europäischen Union'. *Europarecht*, Beiheft 1/2013, pp. 69–89.

Höpner, M. and Schäfer, A. (2010) 'A new phase of European integration: Organised capitalisms in post-Richardian Europe', *West European Politics*, 33 (2): 344–368.

Horeth, M. (1999) 'No way out for the beast? The unsolved legitimacy problem of European governance', *Journal of European Public Policy*, 6 (2): 249–268.

House of Commons Library (2014) European parliament elections 2014. Research Paper No. 14/32. House of Commons Library, London.

Huber, E. and Stephens, J. (2001) 'Welfare states and production regimes in the era of retrenchment', in P. Pierson (ed.) *The New Politics of the Welfare State*. Oxford: Oxford University Press, pp. 107–145.

Huo, J., Nelson, M., and Stephens, J. (2008) 'Decommodification and activation in social democratic policy: Resolving the paradox', *Journal of European Social Policy*, 18 (1): 5–20.

Idema, T. and Keleman, D.R. (2007) 'New modes of governance, the open method of co-ordination and other fashionable red herring', *Perspectives on European Politics and Society*, 7 (1): 108–123.

Ivanoa, M. (2011a) 'Money, housing and world market: The dialectic of globalised production', *Cambridge Journal of Economics*, 35: 853–871.

Ivanoa, M. (2011b) 'Housing and hegemony: The US experience', *Capital and Class*, 35 (3): 391–414.

James, S. (2012) 'The origins and evolution of the Lisbon Agenda', in P. Copeland and D. Papadimitriou (eds.) *Evaluating the EU's Lisbon Strategy*. Basingstoke: Palgrave Macmillan, pp. 8–28.

Jepsen, M. and Serrano Pasual, A. (2005) 'The European social model: An exercise in deconstruction', *Journal of European Social Policy*, 15 (3): 231–245.

Jessoula, M. (2015) 'Europe 2020 and the fight against poverty: Beyond competence clash, towards "Hybrid" governance solutions?' *Social Policy & Administration*, 49 (4): 490–511.

Jessoula, M. and Madama, I. (eds.) (2019) *Fighting Poverty and Social Exclusion in the EU*. Oxon: Routledge.

Johnson, A. (2005) *European Welfare States and Supranational Governance of Social Policy*. Basingstoke: Palgrave Macmillan.

Johnston, A. and Regan, A. (2016) 'European Monetary integration and the incompatibility of national varieties of capitalism', *Journal of Common Market Studies*, 54 (2): 318–336.

Juncker, J.-C. (2014) Time for Action – Statement in the European Parliament Plenary Session Ahead of the Vote on the College. Available at: http://europa.eu/rapid/press-release_SPEECH-14-1525_en.htm

Kauppi, N. (2011) 'EU policies', in A. Favell and V. Guiraudon (eds.) *Sociology of the European Union*. Basingstoke: Palgrave Macmillan, pp. 150–169.

Keohane, R. and Hoffman, S. (eds.) (1991) *The New European Community: Decision making and Institutional Change*. Boulder, CO: Westview.

King, L.P. (2007) 'Central European capitalism in comparative perspective', in B. Hancké, M. Rhodes and M. Thatcher (eds.) *Beyond Varieties of Capitalism*. Oxford: Oxford University Press, pp. 308–327.

King, L.P. and Sznajder, A. (2006) 'The state-led transition to liberal capitalism: Neoliberal, organizational, world systems, and social structural explanations of Poland's economic success', *The American Journal of Sociology*, 112 (3): 751–801.

Knill, C. and Liefferink, D. (2007) *European Politics in the European Union: Policy-Making, Implementation and Patterns of Multi-Level Governance*. Manchester: Manchester University Press.

Kohler-Koch, B. (1996) 'Catching up with change: The transformation of governance in the European Union', *Journal of European Public Policy*, 3 (3): 359–380.

Kohler-Koch, B. and Eising, R. (eds.) (2000) *The Transformation of Governance*. London: Routledge.

Kohler-Koch, B. and Rittberger, B. (2006) 'Review article: The "Governance Turn" in EU studies', *Journal of Common Market Studies*, 44 (Annual Review): 27–49.

Kohler-Koch, B. and Larat, F. (eds.) (2009) *European Multi-Level Governance: Contrasting Images in National Research*. Cheltenham: Edward Elgar.

Kok, W. (2004) Facing the Challenge: The Lisbon Strategy for Growth and Employment. Available at: http://ec.europa.eu/growthandjobs/pdf/kok_report_en.pdf

Kowalsky, W. (2005) The European Commission's Services Directive: Criticisms, myth and prospects. European Economic and Employment Policy Brief No. 8. Brussels: ETUI-REHS.

Kox, H., Lejour, A. and Montizaan, R. (2004) *The Free Movement of Services in the EU*. Den Haag: CPB Netherlands Bureau for Economic Policy Analysis.

Kriesi, H., Grande, E., Lachat, R., Dolezal, M., Bronschier, S. and Frey, T. (2006) 'Globalisation and the transformation of the national political space: Six European countries compared', *European Journal of Political Research*, 45 (6): 921–956.

Labour Party (1997) *New Labour: Because Britain Deserves Better*. London: Labour Party.

Ladi, S. and Tsarouhas, D. (2014) 'The politics of austerity and public policy reform in the EU', *Political Studies Review*, 12 (2): 171–180.

Lahr, J. (ed.) (2002) *The Diaries of Kenneth Tynan*. London: Bloomsbury.

Leibfried, S. (2010) 'Social policy: Left to the markets and the judges', in Wallace, H., Wallace, W. and Pollack, M. (eds.) *Policy Making in the European Union*. Oxford: Oxford University Press, pp. 253–282.

Leibfried, S. and Pierson, P. (1992) 'Prospects for social Europe', *Politics and Society*, 20 (3): 333–366.

Leschke, J., Theodoropoulou, S. and Watt, A. (2012) 'Towards "Europe 2020?" Austerity and new economic governance in the EU', in S. Lehndorff (eds.) *The Triumph of Failed Ideas in Europe*. Brussels: ETUI, pp. 242–281.

Lindberg, L. and Scheingold, S (1970) *Europe's Would-Be Polity: Patterns of Change in the European Community*. Englewood Cliffs, NJ: Prentice-Hall.

Lindblom, C. (1977) *Politics and Markets: The World's Political-Economic Systems*. New York: Basic Books.

Linsenmann, I. Meyer, C. and Wessels, W. (eds.) (2007) *Economic Government of the EU: A Balance Sheet of Modes of Policy Coordination*. Basingstoke: Palgrave Macmillan.

Lipset, S.M. and Rokkan, S. (1967) 'Cleavage structures, party systems, and voter alignments: an introduction', in S.M. Lipset and S. Rokkan (eds.) *Party Systems and Voter Alignments: Cross-national Perspectives*. New York: Free Press, pp. 1–64.

Lord, C. (2004) *A Democratic Audit of the European Union*. Basingstoke: Palgrave Macmillan.

Lord, C. (2007) 'Contested meanings, democracy assessment and the European Union', *Comparative European Politics*, 5 (1): 70–86.

Lord, C. (2008) Some indicators of the democratic performance of the European Union and how they might relate to the RECON models. RECON Online Working Paper 2008/11. Available at: www.reconproject.eu/projectweb/portalproject/RECONWorkingPapers.html

Lucarelli, B. (2012) 'Financialization and global imbalances: Preclude to crisis', *Review of Radical Political Economics*, 44 (4): 429–447.

Mailand, M. (2008) 'The uneven impact of the European employment strategy on member states' employment policies: A comparative analysis', *Journal of European Social Policy*, 18 (4): 353–365.

Mair, P. (2007) 'Political opposition and the European Union', *Government and Opposition*, 42 (1): 1–17.

Majone, G. (1996) *Regulating Europe*. London: Routledge.

Majone, G. (1998) 'Europe's "democratic deficit": The question of standards', *European Law Journal*, 4 (1): 5–28.

Majone, G. (2000) 'The credibility crisis of community regulation', *Journal of Common Market Studies*, 38 (2): 273–302.

Maricut, A. and Puetter, U. (2018) 'Deciding on the European semester: The European Council, the Council and the enduring asymmetry between economic and social policy issues', *Journal of European Public Policy*, 25 (2): 193–211.

Marks, G. (1993) 'Structural policy and multi-level governance in the EC', in A. Cafruny and G. Rosenthal (eds.) *The State of the European Community: The Maastricht Debate and Beyond*. Boulder: Westview, pp. 391–411.

Marks, G., Hooghe, L. and Blank, K. (1996) 'European integration from the 1980s: State-centric v. multi-level governance', *Journal of Common Market Studies*, 34 (3): 341–378.

Marlier, E., Atkinson, A.B., Cantillon, B. and Nolan, B. (2007) *The EU and Social Inclusion Facing the Challenges*. Bristol: Policy Press.

Marmot, M. (2006) 'Status syndrome: A challenge to medicine', *The Journal of the American Medical Association*, 295 (11): 1304–1307.

Martens, H. and Zuleeg, F. (2009) 'Where Next for the Lisbon Agenda?' EPC Policy Brief, June 2009, Brussels: European Policy Centre. Available at: www.epc.eu/documents/uploads/319978211_Lisbon%20Agenda.pdf

Martin, A. and Ross, G. (1999) 'In the line fire: The Europeanisation of labour representation', in A. Martin and G. Ross, (eds.) *The Brave New World of European Labour: European Trade Unions and the Millennium*. Oxford: Berghahn Books, pp. 312–368.

Menz, G. (2015) 'Whatever happened to social Europe? A three-pronged attack on European social policy', in A. Crespy and G. Menz (eds.) *Social Policy and the Eurocrisis: Quo Vadis Social Europe*, Basingstoke: Palgrave Macmillan, pp. 45–62.

Mishra, R. (1999) *Globalization and the Welfare State*. Cheltenham: Edward Elgar.

Moravcsik, A. (1993) 'Preferences and power in the European community. A liberal intergovernmentalist approach', *Journal of Common Market Studies*, 31 (4): 473–524.

Moravcsik, A. (1998) *The Choice for Europe: Social Purpose and State Power from Messina to Maastricht*. Ithaca, NY: Cornell University Press.

Moravcsik, A. (2002) 'In defence of the "Democratic Deficit": Reassessing the legitimacy of the European Union', *Journal of Common Market Studies*, 40 (4): 603–634.

Moravcsik, A. (2004) 'Is there a "Democratic Deficit" in world politics? A framework for analysis', *Government and Opposition*, 39 (2): 336–363.

Moravcsik, A (2018) 'Preferences, power and institutions in 21st-century Europe', *Journal of Common Market Studies,* 56 (7): 1648–1674.

Moravcsik, A. and Schimmelfennig, F. (2009) 'Liberal Intergovernmentalism', in A. Wiener and T. Diez (eds.) *European Integration Theory.* Oxford: Oxford University Press, pp. 67–90.

Morgenthau, H. (1985) *Politics among Nations: The Struggle for Power and Peace,* 6th Edition. New York: Knopf.

Natali, D. and Stamati, F. (2013) Reforming pensions in Europe: A comparative country analysis. Working Paper 2013.08. European Trade Union Institute, Brussels.

Nelson, K. (2012) 'Countering material deprivation: The role of social assistance in Europe', *Journal of European Social Policy,* 22 (2): 148–163.

Newell P. and Paterson M. (2010) *Climate Capitalism: Global Warming and the Transformation of the Global Economy.* Cambridge: Cambridge University Press.

Nolan, B. (2013) 'What use is "Social Investment?"' *Journal of European Social Policy,* 23 (5): 459–468.

Nolan, B. and Whelan, C.T. (2011) *The EU 2020 Poverty Target.* GINI Discussion Paper 19. Amsterdam: Amsterdam Institute for Advanced Labour Studies.

Notre Europe (2010) On the Europe 2020 agenda: Contributions after the Lisbon Agenda experience. Lisbon Agenda Group, Notre Europe 2010, Brussels.

Nugent, N. (1999) *The Politics and Government of the European Union,* 4th Edition. Basingstoke: Macmillan.

O'Connor, J. (1973) *The Fiscal Crisis of the State.* London: St Martin's Press.

OECD (2017) Understanding the Socio-Economic Divide in Europe. Available at: www.oecd.org/els/soc/cope-divide-europe-2017-background-report.pdf

OECD (2018) Employment Protection Indicators. Available at: www.oecd.org/els/emp/oecdindicatorsofemploymentprotection.htm

OECD (2019) GDP Per Hour Worked. Available at: https://data.oecd.org/lprdty/gdp-per-hour-worked.htm

Official Journal of the European Union (2010) Council Recommendation of 13 July 2010 on broad guidelines for the economic policies of the Member States of the Union (2010/410/EU).

Official Journal of the European Union (2011a) Regulation (EU) No. 1175/2011 of the European Parliament and of the Council of 16 November 2011 amending Council Regulation (EC) No 1466/97 on the strengthening of the surveillance of budgetary positions and the surveillance and coordination of economic policies. L306/12

Official Journal of the European Union (2011b) Council Regulation (EU) No. 1177/2011 of 8 November 2011 amending Regulation (EC) No 1467/97 on speeding up and clarifying the implementation of the excessive deficit procedure.

Official Journal of the European Union (2011c) Regulation (EU) No. 1173/2011 of the European Parliament and of the Council of 16 November 2011 on the effective enforcement of budgetary surveillance in the euro area.

Official Journal of the European Union (2011d) Council Directive 2011/85/EU of 8 November 2011 on requirements for budgetary frameworks of the Member States.

Official Journal of the European Union (2011e) Regulation (EU) No. 1176/2011 of the European Parliament and the Council of 16 November 2011: On the prevention and correction of macroeconomic imbalances.

Official Journal of the European Union (2011f) Regulation (EU) No. 1174/2011 of the European Parliament and the Council of 16 November 2011: On enforcement measures to correct excessive macroeconomic imbalances in the euro area.

Official Journal of the European Union (2013a) Regulation (EU) No. 472/2013 of the European Parliament and of the Council of 21 May 2013: On the strengthening of economic and budgetary surveillance of Member States in the euro area experiencing or threatened with serious difficulties with respect to their financial stability.

Official Journal of the European Union (2013b) Regulation (EU) No. 473/2013 of the European Parliament and of the Council of 21 May 2013: On common provisions for monitoring and assessing draft budgetary plans and ensuring the correction of excessive deficit of the Member States in the euro area.

Painter, C. (1999). 'Public service reform from Thatcher to Blair: A third way', *Parliamentary Affairs*, 52 (1): 94–112.

Papadopoulos, T. (2005) The recommodification of European labour: Theoretical and empirical explorations. Working Paper Series No. WP-05-03. The European Research Institute, Brussels.

Phinnemore, D. (2016) 'The European Union: Establishment and development', in M. Cini and N. Borragán (eds.) *European Union Politics*. Oxford: Oxford University Press, pp. 9–29.

Piattoni, S (2009) 'Multi-level governance: A historical and conceptual analysis', *European Integration*, 31 (2): 163–180.

Pierson, P. 1996. 'The path to European integration – A historical institutionalist analysis', *Comparative Political Studies*, 29 (2): 123–163.

Polanyi, K. (2001) *The Great Transformation: The Political and Economic Origins of our Time*. Boston, MA: Beacon Press.

Pollack, M.A. (2010) 'Theorizing EU policy-making', in H. Wallace, M.A. Pollack and A. Young (eds.) *Policy-Making in the European Union, 6th edition*. New York: Oxford University Press, pp. 14–43.

Pontusson, J. (1997) 'Between neoliberalism and the German model: Swedish Capitalism in Transition', in C. Crouch and W. Streeck, (eds.) *The Political Economy of Modern Capitalism: Mapping Convergence and Diversity*. London: Sage, pp. 55–70.

Quaglia, L. (2009) 'The "British Plan" as a pace-setter: The Europeanization of banking rescue plans in the EU', *Journal of Common Market Studies*, 47 (5): 1063–1083.

Quaglia, L., Eastwood, R. and Holmes, P. (2009) 'The financial turmoil and EU policy cooperation 2007–2008', *Journal of Common Market Studies*, 41 (1): 63–87.

Radaelli, C.M. (2003, March), 'The open method of coordination: A new governance architecture for the European Union?' *Swedish Institute for European Policy Studies*, 1. https://ore.exeter.ac.uk/repository/bitstream/handle/10036/22489/Radaelli%20Open%20Method.pdf?sequence=2&isAllowed=y

Rhodes, M. (2000) 'Lisbon: Europe's "Maastricht for welfare?"' *ECSA Review*, 13: 2–7.

Rhodes, M. (2005) 'Varieties of capitalism and the political economy of European welfare states', *New Political Economy*, 10 (3): 363–370.

Rochi, S. (2018) 'Which roads (if any) to social investment? The recalibration of EU welfare states at the crisis crossroads (2000–2014)', *Journal of Social Policy*, 47 (3): 459–478.

Room, G. (2000) 'Commodification and Decommodifi-cation: A developmental critique', *Policy and Politics*, 28 (3): 331–351.

Rosamond, B. (2000) *Theories of European Integration*. Basingstoke: Palgrave Macmillan.

Ruggie, J. (1982) 'International regimes, transactions, and change: Embedded liberalism in the postwar economic order', *International Organization*, 36 (2): 379–415.

Sandholtz, W. and Zysman, J. (1989) '1992: Recasting the European bargain', *World Politics*, 42 (1): 95–128.

Scharpf, F.W. (1970) *Demokratietheorie zwischen Utopie und Anpassung*. Konstanz: Universitätsverlag.

Scharpf, F.W. (1996) 'Negative and positive integration in the political economy of European welfare states', in G. Marks, F.W. Scharpf, P.C. Schmitter and W. Streeck (eds.) *Governance in the European Union*. London: Sage, pp. 15–39.

Scharpf, F.W. (1999) *Governing in Europe: Effective and Democratic?* Oxford: Oxford University Press.

Scharpf, F.W. (2002) 'The European social model: Coping with the challenges of diversity', *Journal of Common Market Studies*, 40 (4): 645–670.

Scharpf, F.W. (2006a) 'Employment and the welfare state: A Continental dilemma', in Ebbinghaus, B. and Manow, P. (eds.), *Comparing Welfare Capitalism: Social Policy and Political Economy in Europe, Japan and the USA*. Oxon: Routledge, pp. 270–286.

Scharpf, F.W. (2006b) 'The joint-decision trap revisited', *Journal of Common Market Studies*, 44 (4): 845–864.

Schmidt, V.A. (1996) *From State to Market? The Transformation of Business in France*. Cambridge: Cambridge University Press.

Schimmelfennig, F. and Winzen, T. (2019) 'Grand theories, differentiated integration', *Journal of European Public Policy*. Available at: www.tandfonline.com/doi/full/10.1080/13501763.2019.1576761

Schmidt, V.A. (2002) *The Futures of European Capitalism*. Oxford: Oxford University Press.

Schmidt, V.A. (2008) 'Discursive institutionalism: The explanatory power of ideas and discourse', *Annual Review of Political Science*, 11: 303–326.

Schmidt, V.A. (2012) 'Democracy and legitimacy in the European Union revisited: Input, output and throughput', *Political Studies*, 61 (1): 2–22.

Schmidt, V.A. (2015) 'Forgotten democratic legitimacy: "Governing by the rules" and "ruling by the numbers"', in M. Mattheijs and M. Blyth (eds.) *The Future of the Euro*. Oxford: Oxford University Press, pp. 90–116.

Schmidt, V.A. (2016) 'Reinterpreting the rules "by Stealth" in times of crisis: A discursive institutionalist analysis of the European Central Bank and the European Commission', *West European Politics*, 39 (5): 1032–1052.

Schmidt, V.A. and Thatcher, M. (2014) 'Theorizing ideational continuity: The resilience of neoliberal ideas in Europe', in V.A. Schmidt and M. Thatcher (eds.) *Resilient Liberalism in Europe's Political Economy*. Cambridge: Cambridge University Press, pp. 1–50.

Schoeller, M.G. (2018) 'The rise and fall of Merkozy: Franco-German bilateralism as a negotiation strategy in Eurozone crisis management', *Journal of Common Market Studies*, 56 (5): 1019–1035.

Scruggs, L. and Allan, J. (2006) 'Welfare-state decommodification in 18 OECD countries: A replication and revision', *Journal of European Social Policy*, 16 (1): 55–72.

Seikel, D. (2016) 'Flexible austerity and supranational autonomy. The reformed excessive deficit procedure and the asymmetry between liberalisation and social regulation in the EU', *Journal of Common Market Studies*, 54 (6): 1398–1416.

Sloman, J. (1995) *Economics*. London: Prentice Hall.

Smith, M. (2011) 'Toward a theory of EU foreign policy-making: Multi-level governance, domestic politics, and national adaptation to Europe's common foreign and security policy', *Journal of European Public Policy*, 11 (4): 740–758.

Stanford Encyclopaedia of Philosophy (2016) Positive and Negative Liberty. Available at: https://plato.stanford.edu/entries/liberty-positive-negative/

Stoker, G. (1998) 'Governance as theory: Five propositions', *International Social Science Journal*, 50 (155): 17–28.

Stone Sweet, S. and Sandholtz, W. (1997) 'European integration and supranational governance', *Journal of European Public Policy*, 4 (3): 297–317.

Stone Sweet, S. and Sandholtz, W. (1998) 'Integration, supranational governance, and the institutionalisation of the European polity', in S. Stone-Sweet and W. Sandholtz (eds.) *European Integration and Supranational Governance*. Oxford: Oxford University Press, pp. 1–30.

Stone Sweet, S. and Sandholtz, W. (1999) 'European integration and supranational governance revisited: Rejoinder to Branch and Øhrgaard', *Journal of European Public Policy*, 6 (1): 144–154.

Strange, S. (1994) 'Wake up, Krasner! The world has changed', *Review of International Political Economy*, 1 (2): 209–219.

Strange, S. (1997) *Casino Capitalism*. Manchester: Manchester University Press.

Strange, S. (1998) *Mad Money*. Manchester: University of Manchester Press.

Streeck, W. (1995) 'Neo-voluntarism: A new European social policy regime', *European Law Journal*, 1 (1): 31–59.

Strøby Jensen, C. (2016) 'Neofunctionalism', in M. Cini and N. Borragán (eds.) *European Union Politics*. Oxford: Oxford University Press, pp. 53–64.

Teague, P. (1998) 'Monetary Union and social Europe', *Journal of European Social Policy*, 8 (2): 117–137.

ter Haar, B.P. and Copeland, P. (2010) 'What are the future prospects for the European social model? An analysis of EU equal opportunities and employment policy', *European Law Journal*, 16 (3): 273–291.

Thatcher, M. (2013) 'Supranational neo-liberalization: The EU's regulatory model of economic markets', in V.A. Schmidt and M. Thatcher (eds.) *Resilient Liberalism in Europe's Political Economy*. Cambridge: Cambridge University Press, pp. 171–200.

The Guardian (2017) Jean-Claude Juncker blocked EU curbs on tax avoidance, cable shows. (01/01/2017).

Tholoniat, L. (2010) 'The career of the open method of coordination: Lessons from a "soft" EU Instrument', *West European Politics*, 33 (1): 93–117.

Tinios, P. (2012) 'Pensions and the Lisbon Strategy', in P. Copeland and D. Papadimitriou (eds.) *The EU's Lisbon Strategy: Analysing Success and Understanding Failure*. Basingstoke: Palgrave Macmillan, pp. 111–129.

Toynbee, P. and Walker, D. (2010) *The Verdict*. London: Granta.

Trubek, D.M. and Mosher, J.S. (2003) 'New governance, employment policy, and the European social model', in J. Zeitlin and D.M. Trubek (eds.) *Governing Work and Welfare in a New Economy – European and American Experiments*. Oxford: Oxford University Press, pp. 33–58.

Van Apeldoorn, B. (2002) *Transnational Capitalism and the Struggle over European Integration*. London: Routledge.

Vaughan-Whitehead, D. (2003) *EU Enlargement versus Social Europe? The Uncertain Future of the European Social Model*. New York: Edward Elgar.

Velluti, S. (2010) *New Governance and the European Employment Strategy*. London: Routledge.

Verdun, A. (1996) 'An asymmetrical Economic and Monetary Union in the EU: Perceptions of monetary authorities and social partners', *Journal of European Integration*, 20 (2): 55–72.

Wallace, H., Caporaso, J., Schampf, F. and Moravcsik, A. (1999) 'Review section symposium: The choice for Europe: Social purpose and state power from Messina to Maastricht', *Journal of European Public Policy*, 6 (1): 155–179.

Watson, M. (2005) *Foundations of Political Economy*. Basingstoke: Palgrave Macmillan.

Watt, A. (2009) A quantum of solace? An assessment of fiscal stimulus packages by EU Member States in response to the economic crisis. Working Paper 2009.5. European Trade Union Institute, Brussels.

Webber, D. (2019) 'Trends in European political (dis)integration. An analysis of postfunctionalist and other explanations', *Journal of European Public Policy*. Available at: www.tandfonline.com/doi/full/10.1080/13501763.2019.1576760

Wendt, A. (1987) 'The agent-structure problem in international relations theory', *International Organization*, 41 (3): 335–370.

Wilkinson, M. (2019) 'Authoritarian liberalism in Europe: A common critique of neoliberalism and ordoliberalism', *Critical Sociology*. In Press.

Wincott, D. (1995) 'Institutional interaction and European Integration: Towards an everyday critique of Liberal Intergovernmentalism', *Journal of Common Market Studies*, 33 (4): 597–609.

Young, A.R. (2005) 'The single market', in H. Wallace, W. Wallace and M.A. Pollack, (eds.) *Policy-Making in the European Union*. Oxford: Oxford University Press, pp. 93–112.

Zeitlin, J. (2005) 'The open method of co-ordination in action: Theoretical promise, empirical realities, reform strategy', in J. Zeitlin, P. Pochet and L. Magnusson (eds.) *The Open Method of Coordination in Action: The European Employment and Social Inclusion Strategies*. Brussels: Peter-Lang, pp. 447–503.

Zeitlin, J. (2009a) 'Changing European employment and welfare regimes: The influence of the open method of coordination on national reforms', in M. Heidenreich and J. Zeitlin (eds.) *The Influence of the Open Method of Coordination on National Reforms*. London: Routledge, pp. 214–245.

Zeitlin, J. (2009b) 'The open method of coordination and reform of national social and employment policies: Influences, mechanisms, effects', in M. Heidenreich and J. Zeitlin (eds.), *Changing European Employment and Welfare Regimes*. London: Routledge, pp. 214–245.

Zeitlin, J. Pochet, P. with Magnussen, L. (eds.) (2005) *The Open Method of Coordination in Action*. Brussels: P.I.E.-Peter Lang.

Zeitlin, J. and Vanhercke, B. (2017) 'Socializing the European semester: EU social and economic policy co-ordination in crisis and beyond', *Journal of European Public Policy*, 25 (2): 149–174.

Zuleeg, F. (2010) The European Council: Balancing short term crisis and long term strategy, Commentary, 4 March. European Policy Centre, Brussels. Available at: www.epc.eu/documents/uploads/1086_the_european_council_-_balancing_short_term_crisis_and_long_term_strategy.pdf?doc_id=1076 – accessed June 2019.

Appendix
List of Interviewees

(Interview 1) A Representative from the European Commission Secretariat General (15/10/2015)

(Interview 2) A Representative from the European Commission Directorate General for Employment, Social Affairs and Inclusion (21/10/2015)

(Interview 3) A Representative from the European Trade Union Confederation (21/10/2015)

(Interview 4) A Representative from the European Commission Directorate General for Employment, Social Affairs and Inclusion (21/10/2015)

(Interview 5) A Representative from the European Commission Directorate General for Employment, Social Affairs and Inclusion (21/10/2015)

(Interview 6) A Representative from a Permanent Representation to the European Union (22/10/2015)

(Interview 7) A Representative from a Permanent Representation to the European Union (22/10/2015)

(Interview 8) A Representative from a Permanent Representation to the European Union (23/10/2015)

(Interview 9) A Representative from a Permanent Representation to the European Union (23/10/2015)

(Interview 10) A Representative from a Permanent Representation to the European Union (27/10/2015)

(Interview 11) A Representative from a Permanent Representation to the European Union (27/10/2015)

(Interview 12) A Representative from a Permanent Representation to the European Union (28/10/2015)

(Interview 13) A Representative from a Permanent Representation to the European Union (28/10/2015)

(Interview 14) A Representative from a Permanent Representation to the European Union (28/10/2015)

(Interview 15) A Representative from a Permanent Representation to the European Union (29/10/2015)

(Interview 16) A Representative from the European Commission Directorate General for Employment, Social Affairs and Inclusion (30/10/2015)

(Interview 17) A Representative from BusinessEurope (02/11/2015)

(Interview 18) A Representative from the European Commission Directorate Economic and Financial Affairs (4/11/2015)

(Interview 19) A Representative from a Permanent Representation to the European Union (4/11/2015)

(Interview 20) A Representative from a Permanent Representation to the European Union (5/11/2015)

(Interview 21) A Representative from the European Commission Directorate General for Employment, Social Affairs and Inclusion (05/11/2015)

(Interview 22) A Representative from a Permanent Representation to the European Union (6/11/2015)

(Interview 23) A Representative from the European Commission Directorate Economic and Financial Affairs (9/11/2015)

(Interview 24) A Representative from the European Commission Secretariat General (9/11/2015)

(Interview 25) A Representative from the European Anti-Poverty Network (9/11/2015)

(Interview 26) A Representative from the European Commission Directorate General for Employment, Social Affairs and Inclusion (10/11/2015)

Interview 27) A Representative from the European Commission Directorate General for Employment, Social Affairs and Inclusion (10/11/2015)

(Interview 28) A Representative from the European Commission Directorate Economic and Financial Affairs (10/11/2015)

(Interview 29) A Member of the European Parliament (Party of European Socialists) (12/11/2015)

(Interview 30) A Representative from a Permanent Representation to the European Union (18/12/2015)

Interview 31) A Representative from the European Commission Secretariat General (30/04/2018)

(Interview 32) A Representative from the European Commission Directorate General for Employment, Social Affairs and Inclusion (02/05/2018)

(Interview 33) A Representative from a Permanent Representation to the European Union (02/05/2018)

(Interview 34) A Representative from a Permanent Representation to the European Union (02/05/2018)

(Interview 35) A Representative from the European Commission Directorate Economic and Financial Affairs (03/05/2018)

(Interview 36) A Representative from the European Parliament Research Service (03/05/2018).

(Interview 37) A Representative from the European Parliament Research Service (03/05/2018).

(Interview 38) A Representative from the European Parliament Research Service (03/05/2018).

(Interview 39) A Representative from the European Commission Directorate General for Employment, Social Affairs and Inclusion (04/05/2018)

(Interview 40) A Representative from the European Commission Directorate General for Employment, Social Affairs and Inclusion (04/05/2018)

Index

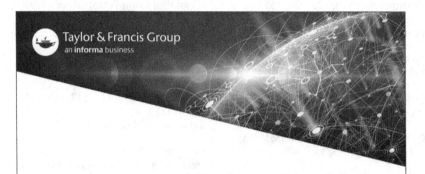

Printed in the United States
by Baker & Taylor Publisher Services